高级实用英语系列教材

Myriads of Culture 文化万象 英语视听说

Listen, Look and Learn

（基础篇）

主　编　李海燕　余志红

副主编　杨　焯　褚　颖　曾　新

中国人民大学出版社

·北京·

序 言

学子之惑

金榜题名，人生得意。然而，初识大学英语，几家欢乐几家愁：

- “我上课听不懂，怎么办？”
- “我口语很差，怎么办？”
- “老师，我想提高英语听力水平，可是我对英语不感兴趣，怎么办？”
- “老师，我想提高英语听说能力，可是我不知该怎么提高，怎么办？”
- “老师，我想找些课后学习材料，可是不知哪些材料适合我，怎么办？”

……

管中一窥

1）距离之美

世上本没有路，走的人多了便成了路。每个学习者自身的情况都不同，因此最适合自己的学习方法也各不相同，但只要用心思考和寻找，总会找到一条最接近的道路。

我们常说“距离产生美”，上述有关同学所说的兴趣问题其实也是一个学习者及其所学语言之间的距离把控问题。不可否认的是，学习始终都是在两个循环当中进行的：良性循环和恶性循环。学习的过程和结果决定了学习者在特定阶段进入哪种循环之中，英语学习同样如此。事实上，经过努力学习取得进步乃至骄人的成绩是进入良性循环的必经之路，还没有走上这条路的学习者，由于缺少成就感则很难喜欢上这种学习。

欲要前行，必须放下过去的负担。纠结于一时的喜恶毫无益处，应该立刻行动起来，拉近与英语的距离，也许你会从此爱上这门世界性语言。

2）核心词汇

多数一线英语教师大致认同这样的观点：我们掌握的语言词汇按照不同的认知程度分布在三个区域当中。依据其从内而外、从紧密到疏离的关系，依次为核心词汇区（Core Zone）→积极词汇区（Active Zone）→被动词汇区（Passive Zone）。

- **核心词汇**意味着可以在第一时间内依靠本能调动的词汇，通常出现在我们的口语会话当中。
- **积极词汇**就是那些对我们来说很熟悉，也很容易被激活的词汇。这些词汇，通常是我们在听的时候能够迅速反应出来，而且能听懂的词汇。
- **被动词汇**则指那些在说的时候无法被调动，听的时候也不能完全听明白（也许听起来觉得耳熟），但是阅读时没有理解障碍的词汇。

核心词汇、积极词汇和被动词汇其实在很大意义上等同于我们的口语词汇、听力词汇和阅读词汇。这解释了为什么有些同学整天花时间背单词，可是口语和听力还是没有丝毫进步的现象——被动词汇量大，核心词汇量和积极词汇量小。这也可以用来解释为什么有些同学口语似乎很流利，可是考试成绩总是不太理想——核心词汇量较大，积极词汇量和被动词汇量小。这三种词汇，首先构成了部分重叠关系——能说出来的词汇，一定能听懂；能听懂的词汇，自然也能看懂。在实践中，通过合理的刺激和反刺激，也存在互相转化的关系。这里所说的“刺激”听上去很玄乎，其实指的是词汇的运用：听、说、读。通过“读”，陌生区域的词汇进入被动区域；通过“听”，被动区域的词汇进入积极区域；通过“说”，积极区域的词汇最终进入核心区域。“反刺激”则指的是“不读不听不说”。不过，词汇在某个区域的停留不是恒定的。如果缺乏复习和巩固，进入某一区域的词汇会在时间的推移下逃逸到外层区域当中。这解释了语言的遗忘规律。同理，如果我们一段时间不开口说英语，口语自然就退步了。

3）第二语言习得

美国的 Jim Cummins 教授和 Virginia Collier 教授的研究发现：如果人们能够足够多地接触第二语言，达到流畅地使用这种语言进行交流大概需要 1~3 年的时间。他们把这种能力称为“BICS”（Basic Interpersonal Communicative Skills）。Jim Cummins 教授和 Virginia Collier 教授还提出 CALP（Cognitive Academic Language Proficiency）这一概念，即掌握复杂的抽象概念的学术语言，具备能够用第二语言思考并作为学习工具的能力。[1]

[1] 见Cummins, J. (1979) “Cognitive/Academic language proficiency, linguistic interdependence, the optimum age question and some other matters”. *Working Papers on Bilingualism*, No. 19, pp.121-129.

研究发现，如果学习者的母语素养（Native Language Literacy）较高，小学至高中阶段的同学需要5~7年的时间才可以掌握第二语言的CALP。不具有很高的母语素养的学习者往往需要7~10年的时间掌握并运用第二语言的CALP。据此，不难得出以下结论：我们可以流利地运用第二语言进行英语交流，前提是我们对英语的接触要达到一定的量，而且要提高自身的母语素养。

一家之言

我们认为，当代大学生需要认识到：大学不是英语学习的终点，而是求学生涯中的一个新起点。基于目前国内大部分地区的英语教学现状，中学阶段的英语学习模式和思维到了大学阶段必须尽快实现“量”和“质”两个方面的蜕变。从今以后，你可能需要着重培养的一个非常重要的能力那就是——终生的学习习惯和独立的自学能力。

作为学习英语的同道中人，作为从事听说课教学十余年，甚至几十年的老师们，我们经常被问到上述问题。其解决之道，无外乎“内因”和“外因”两个方面：学习者的努力—思考—再努力即为“内因”，适宜的环境和素材即为“外因”。因此，我们这个团队决心致力于为学习者创造一个有利于英语学习的外部环境并提供相关素材。这套“文化万象”教程志在为学习者提供基于学习者自身视角的英语视听说及英语文化学习的素材和相关体验。我们希望，在使用本教程的实践中，学习者会获得英语学习的乐趣并找到学好英语的秘诀。

我们编写本套辅助教材的初衷来自广大学生及一线大学英语听说教师的反馈。一方面，同学们喜欢大学英语听说课程，喜欢（甚至依赖）在课堂环境中在老师的指导下操练自己的听说技能，提高英语水平；另一方面，由于学校课程设置的局限性，英语听说课程课时不足（大多仅为每周两课时），远远满足不了同学们语言实践的需要。据此，我们大学英语听说教学团队在我院一些多年从事听说教学的资深教师的启发下，对他们十多年来辛勤采集和编辑的国外音频、视频资料进行了整理，从其中归纳出十五个与文化相关的主题，随后根据需要继续完善了与主题相关的材料，对其进行深度加工，并配套了循序渐进的相关练习。我们相信，这套教材有望让同学们在课余时间里参照课堂教学的训练方法，自我训练，自我提高。

“行远必自迩，登高必自卑。”——《中庸》里的这句话，说的是无论目标多么远大，都要从眼前做起。希望“文化万象”这套书，能带给我们的读者和听众点滴的启发、无尽的收获。

本教程的设计及编订凝聚着华东政法大学外语学院听说教学团队的集体努力与智慧，并得到了外语学院领导的大力支持和关注，在此表示由衷的感谢。感谢深得广大师生爱戴的余志红老师提供了大量资料和指导意见，感谢杨焯老师、褚颖老师、曾新老师前期规划中的献计献策，感谢范鹏老师在编写过程中对格式规范的全力付出，当然更要感谢张纯辉副教授、薛朝凤博士、曾新博士、李燕秋博士、王璐博士、褚颖、甘翠平博士、邓群芳、张培智、陈贤光、李超、刘雁等其他参与编写的老师们的辛勤努力和无私奉献。本书所用图文音像资料均注明了出处，若有未尽之处，或存在版权费用问题，请与我们联系。

由于编者水平有限，编写时间仓促，不足之处在所难免，敬请谅解。

余志红 & 李海燕

上海 & 纽约

使用指南

本套“文化万象”辅助教程分为上下两册,共计 **15** 个单元,涵盖的主题有: 艺术、文学、礼仪、广告、饮食、健康、节日、婚姻、旅游、影视、教育、网络、访谈、都市和中国文化 15 项专题。每个专题的架构如下:

- 第一部分为与该单元文化主题有关的名人名言或英语谚语、俗语，意在明确主题并为后面的口语练习提供素材。当然，该部分意在抛砖引玉，希望同学们在今后自学的过程中，收集名人名言。名人名言不仅语言精练，而且往往蕴含丰富的哲理。此外，在日常交流中，名人名言还可以起到沟通的桥梁作用。

- 第二部分为“背景知识”，其目的在于通过阅读让同学们有机会梳理和提取自己在某一个领域里的被动词汇库，为之后的视听练习提供知识储备和词汇积累。同学们也可以将这部分作为翻译材料和口语表达素材。

- 第三部分为视、听、写、译、说练习。通过这些练习，被动区域词汇将被逐渐激活并准备进入积极区域。在口语练习部分，通过完成书中指定的各种练习，已被激活的消极词汇有可能进入核心词汇区，变为积极词汇。每个专题包括 **10** 关（也就是 **10** 段材料），每一段材料都与该单元主题紧密相关，同学们可以自主选择相关音频或视频材料进行练习和自我测试。每个主题突出不同的训练重点：有的章节偏重翻译训练，有的章节注重细节听写练习，有的章节侧重口语表达，有的章节强调泛听练习……全方位地训练英语能力，以提高英语水平。从接受性地进行视听训练，到主动地写、译，最后达到流畅地沟通表达，这样的学习过程或许更加顺应了语言的习得规律。专题的每一关都附有相关背景介绍，为同学们熟悉相关文化知识和提高语言表达做知识铺垫，也可以潜移默化地提高同学们的母语及外语素养，为用第二语言沟通和交流打下基础。背景介绍的语言分为中文、英文，训练的重点不同。建议同学们用这部分内容更好地理解英文材料，同时也为后期的口语表达做内容储备。在熟悉中文背景基本内容的基础上，同学们可以尝试用英文表达相关信息。针对英文部分的背景介绍，建议同学们将其改写为介绍性的小短文。此外，根据材料难度的不同，每一段材料都以星级标注，同学们可以根据自己的听力基础选择适合自己水平的材料进行练习。每一个主题后面有两个自我评价表，同学们可以记录自己两周内的学习情况，同时可以比较不同时期的学习情况。

■ 第四部分为听说“秘籍”，专门就英语学习者感到困惑的相关技能进行简要介绍，辅以配套练习。请同学们不妨一试，或许会有所启发。

华东政法大学外语学院
大学英语听说教学团队

目录

Chapter 1

Festivals and Holidays

Part 1 Famous Quotes

A man may die, nations may rise and fall, but an idea lives on.

—John F. Kennedy

人有生死，国有兴亡，思想永存。

——约翰·F·肯尼迪

You have to believe in yourself. That's the secret of success.

—Charles Chaplin

人必须有自信，这是成功的秘密。

——查尔斯·卓别林

The empty vessels make the greatest sound.

—William Shakespeare

满瓶不响，半瓶咣当。

——威廉·莎士比亚

Part 2 Background Knowledge

Legend of the Chinese Spring Festival

(Extracted from: http://www.chinaculture.org/gb/en_chinaway/node_165.htm.)

Vocabulary

returnee	[rɪˌtɜːˈniː]	*n.*	返回者
porridge	[ˈpɒrɪdʒ]	*n.*	稀饭；粥
glutinous	[ˈgluːtənəs]	*adj.*	黏性的；胶状的
millet	[ˈmɪlɪt]	*n.*	小米
seeds of Job's tears	薏米；薏仁		
jujube	[ˈdʒuːdʒuːb]	*n.*	大枣
longan	[ˈlɒŋgən]	*n.*	龙眼；桂圆
gingko	[ˈgɪŋkəʊ]	*n.*	银杏
utensil	[juːˈtensl]	*n.*	器具；器皿
rejoice	[rɪˈdʒɔɪs]	*vi.*	欢庆
calligraphy	[kəˈlɪgrəfɪ]	*n.*	书法
ingot	[ˈɪŋgət]	*n.*	（常为砖形的）铸块；锭
homophone	[ˈhɒməfəʊn]	*n.*	同音异形异义词

The Spring Festival is the most important festival for the Chinese people, when all family members get together, just like Christmas in the West. All people living away from home go back. The Spring Festival has become the busiest time for transportation systems. Airports, railway stations and long-distance bus stations are crowded with home returnees.

The Spring Festival falls on the 1st day of the 1st lunar month, often one month later than the Gregorian calendar. It originated in the Shang Dynasty (c.1600 BC–c. 1100 BC) from the people's sacrifice to gods and ancestors at the end of an old year and the beginning of a new one.

Strictly speaking, the Spring Festival starts every year in the early days of the 12th lunar month and will last till the mid 1st lunar month of the next year. Of them, the most important days are the Spring Festival Eve and the first three days. The Chinese government now stipulates people have seven days off for the Chinese Lunar New Year.

Many customs accompany the Spring Festival. Some are still followed today, but others have weakened.

On the 8th day of the 12th lunar month, many families make Laba porridge, a delicious kind of porridge made with glutinous rice, millet, seeds of Job's tears, jujube berries, lotus seeds, beans, longan and gingko.

The 23rd day of the 12th lunar month is called Preliminary Eve. At this time, people offer sacrifice to the kitchen god. Now however, most families make delicious food to enjoy them.

After the Preliminary Eve, people begin preparing for the coming New Year. This is called "Seeing the New Year in."

Store owners are busy then as everybody goes out to purchase necessities for the New Year. Materials not only include edible oil, rice, flour, chicken, duck, fish and meat, but also fruit, candies and kinds of nuts. What's more, various decorations, new clothes and shoes for the children as well as gifts for the elderly, friends and relatives, are all on the list of purchasing.

Before the New Year comes, people completely clean the indoors and outdoors of their homes as well as their clothes, bedclothes and all their utensils.

Then people begin decorating their clean rooms featuring an atmosphere of rejoicing and festivity. All the door panels will be pasted with Spring Festival couplets, highlighting Chinese calligraphy with black characters on red paper. The content varies from house owners' wishes for a bright future to good luck for the New Year. Also, pictures of the god of doors and wealth will be posted on front doors to ward off evil spirits and welcome peace and abundance.

The Chinese character "*fu*" (meaning blessing or happiness) is a must. The character put on paper can be pasted normally or upside down, for in Chinese the "reversed *fu*" is homophonic with "*fu* comes", both being pronounced as "*fudao*." What's more, two big red lanterns can be raised on both sides of the front door. Red paper-cuttings can be seen on window glass and brightly colored New Year paintings with auspicious meanings may be put on the wall.

People attach great importance to Spring Festival Eve. At that time, all family members eat dinner together. The meal is more luxurious than usual. Dishes such as chicken, fish and bean curd cannot be excluded, for in Chinese, their pronunciations, respectively "*ji*", "*yu*"and "*doufu*", mean auspiciousness, abundance and richness. After the dinner, the whole family will sit together, chatting and watching TV. In recent years, the Spring Festival party broadcast on China Central Television (CCTV) is essential entertainment for the Chinese both at home and abroad. According to custom, each family will stay up to see the New Year in.

Waking up on New Year, everybody dresses up. First they extend greetings to their parents. Then each child will get money as a New Year gift, wrapped up in red paper. People in Northern China will eat *jiaozi*, or dumplings, for breakfast, as they think "*jiaozi*" in sound means "bidding farewell to the old and ushering in the new." Also, the shape of the dumpling is like gold ingot from ancient China. So people eat them and wish for money and treasure.

Southern Chinese eat *niangao* (New Year cake made of glutinous rice flour) on this occasion, because as a homophone, *niangao* means "higher and higher, one year after another." The first five days after the Spring Festival is a good time for relatives, friends, and classmates as well as colleagues to exchange greetings, gifts and chat leisurely.

Burning fireworks was once the most typical custom in the Spring Festival. People thought the spluttering sound could help drive away evil spirits. However, such an activity was completely or partially forbidden in big cities once the government took security, noise and pollution factors into consideration. As a replacement, some buy tapes with firecracker sounds to listen to, some break little balloons to get the sound too, while others buy firecracker handicrafts to hang in the living room.

The lively atmosphere not only fills every household, but permeates to streets and lanes. A series of activities such as lion dancing, dragon lantern dancing, lantern festivals and temple fairs will be held for days. The Spring Festival then comes to an end when the Lantern Festival is finished.

China has 56 ethnic groups. Minorities celebrate their Spring Festival almost the same day as the Han people, and they have different customs.

Task 1 Word Hunting

Directions: *Try your best to spot the equivalent English words and expressions of the following words and expressions while reading the article.*

1. 公历 ______________________
2. 起源于商朝 ______________________
3. 祭祀诸神及祖先 ______________________
4. 农历腊月 ______________________

5. 除夕 ____________________
6. 春节放假 7 天 ____________________
7. 祭灶神 ____________________
8. 欢乐的节日气氛 ____________________
9. 春联 ____________________
10. 驱邪 ____________________
11. 辞旧迎新 ____________________
12. 庙会 ____________________
13. 56 个民族 ____________________

Task 2 Matching Game

Directions: Match the traditional Chinese festivals with their respective symbols.

1. Chinese Lunar New Year
2. Lantern Festival
3. Dragon Boat Festival
4. Mid-autumn Festival
5. Tomb Sweeping Festival

A. dragon and lion dance performance
B. dragon boat racing
C. Spring Festival couplets and firecrackers
D. moon cakes
E. going hiking and flying kites

Task 3 Matching Game

Directions: Identify and match the following western festivals with their respective symbols. Write your answers in the brackets.

1. Easter ( )

2. Mother's Day ( )

3. Halloween (   )

4. Christmas Day (   )

5. Thanksgiving Day (   )

A. Easter egg and bunny
B. Trick or treat costumes
C. Santa Claus
D. Roast turkey and pumpkin pie
E. Carnation

Part 3 Listening and Speaking Practice

Pass 1 American Thanksgiving Day

(Difficulty: ★★★)

背景知识

美国的感恩节是美国人合家欢聚的节日。1620 年，著名的“五月花”号船满载 100 多名清教徒到达美洲，在当地印第安人的帮助下，他们终于度过寒冬并在第二年秋天喜获丰收。在欢庆丰收的日子，清教徒移民们感谢上帝，并为感谢印第安人的帮助而邀请他们一同庆祝。1621 年 11 月下旬的一个星期四是美国历史上的第一个感恩节，它的许多庆祝方式一直流传后代。

感恩节晚宴 (Thanksgiving Dinner) 是美国人一年中很重要的一餐。在美国，像中国的春节一样，感恩节当天，成千上万的人们不管多忙，都尽量和自己的家人团聚，大家一起享受一顿丰盛的节日晚餐。火鸡是感恩节餐桌上的传统主菜，此外，感恩节的传统食品中还有南瓜饼等。餐后，大多数家庭都会进行一些传统的感恩节游戏。

（资料来源：http://www.wutongzi.com/a/153003.html。）

Vocabulary

cranberry	['krænbərɪ] *n.* 小红莓；蔓越莓
smoker	['sməʊkə(r)] *n.* 吸烟者；薰制工
federation	[ˌfedə'reɪʃn] *n.* 同盟，联合会
pilgrim	['pɪlgrɪm] *n* 朝圣者；清教徒
feast	[fiːst] *n.* 盛会；宴会；宗教节日
colony	['kɒlənɪ] *n.* 殖民地
settler	['setlə(r)] *n.* 定居者
colonist	['kɒlənɪst] *n.* 殖民者
the Great Depression	美国经济大萧条
bald eagle	美国白头海雕（美国国徽正面图案的主要形象）
the Civil War	美国内战

Task 1 General Understanding

Directions: Listen to the passage once and try to grasp its main idea, getting ready to introduce the American Thanksgiving Day. You may do this either in Chinese or English.

Task 2 Q&A

Directions: Listen and answer the following questions.

1. When is Thanksgiving Day celebrated in the United States of America?

____

____

2. What does the typical Thanksgiving Day meal include?

____

____

3. What is the origin of the American Thanksgiving Day?

____

____

Task 3 Blank Filling

Directions: Listen again and fill in the following blanks.

The Pilgrims' (1) ________ in (2) ________ is often considered the nation's first Thanksgiving. The Pilgrims were early (3) ________ of Plymouth Colony in what is now Massachusetts. They (4) ________ a (5) ________ to celebrate a (6) ________. However, other European (7) ________ in North America also held (8) ________ of thanks. These included British (9) ________ in Virginia in (10) ________.

In (11) ________, during the Civil War, President Abraham Lincoln (12) ________ the last Thursday of November as a national day of Thanksgiving. In (13) ________, as the Great Depression was ending, President Franklin Roosevelt (14) ________ the holiday on the fourth Thursday. He did not want to (15) ________ the Christmas holiday shopping season in years when November has a (16) ________ Thursday. The season (17) ________ begins with a busy shopping day on the Friday after Thanksgiving, although some stores are now opening on the holiday itself.

Task 4 Shadow Speaking Practice

Directions: Listen to the above two paragraphs again and repeat after the speaker. Pay attention to your speed, pronunciation and intonation.

Pass 2 Oktoberfest 1

(Difficulty: ★★★)

背景知识

Oktoberfest (The Munich Oktoberfest) 即德国慕尼黑啤酒节。Oktoberfest 的本名是"十月节"，这个节日虽然叫十月节，但并不完全在十月举行。它是从九月的最后一个星期开始到十月的第一个星期日结束。这个节日期间主要的饮料是啤酒，所以人们习惯性地称其为啤酒节。慕尼黑啤酒节起源于 1810 年 10 月 12 日，至今已有 200 多年的历史，是慕尼黑一年中最盛大的活动。自 1946 年起，慕尼黑啤酒节规模越来越大，发展成为一个盛大的民间节日，至 20 世纪末已经逐渐发展成为一个世界知名的民俗节日，每年吸引约 600 万人参与其中。

1914—1918 年，慕尼黑啤酒节因第一次世界大战被迫中断 5 年，1939—1945 年因第二次世界大战停办 7 年。1950 年，慕尼黑市长托马斯·维门尔用木槌敲开第一罐新酿啤酒桶，宣布啤酒节开幕，从此这种特别的开幕方式成为了慕尼黑啤酒节的传统。除了这一传统、盛大的开幕式，慕尼黑啤酒节开幕当天还会举行游行活动。很多游客都穿上传统的皮裤和紧身连衣裙等节日盛装加入到游行队伍。

（资料来源：http://mt.sohu.com/20150922/n421808430.shtml。）

Vocabulary

Munich	['mjuːnɪk]	*n.*	慕尼黑
Oktoberfest	[ɒk'təʊbəfest]	*n.*	慕尼黑啤酒节；十月啤酒节
mayor	[meə(r)]	*n.*	市长
tap	[tæp]	*n.*	水龙头；龙头，阀门
barrel	['bærəl]	*n.*	桶；酒桶
hammer	['hæmə(r)]	*n.*	锤子，榔头
mug	[mʌg]	*n.*	马克杯，杯子
Bavarian	[bə'veərɪən]	*adj.*	巴伐利亚州的
governor	['gʌvənə(r)]	*n.*	州长
oxen	['ɒksn]	*n.*	公牛（ox的复数形式）
reveler	['revlə]	*n.*	狂欢者；饮酒狂欢者
spree	[spriː]	*n.*	狂欢；狂饮
descend on	突然造访		

Task 1 Word Matching

Directions: Match the words of Column A to their explanations in Column B.

A	B
Oktoberfest	engaging without restraint in an activity and indulging
spree	an autumn festival that involves merrymaking and beer drinking
mug	a person in charge of the political administration of a region
governor	a large deep cup with straight sides and a handle
descend on	to pay a sudden visit to

Task 2 General Understanding

Directions: Watch the report three times and try to grasp its main idea. Summarize orally the main idea in English.

Task 3 True or False

Directions: Watch the clip and then decide whether the following statements are true or false (T/F).

1. ( ) Large numbers of beer drinkers are visiting Munich.
2. ( ) Munich's mayor starts the folk festival Oktoberfest.
3. ( ) About 50,000 roast chickens and 19 roast oxen will be served to the visitors from around the world.
4. ( ) The folk festival is expected to last for 19 days and will attract 600,000 visitors.

Task 4 Blank Filling

Directions: Listen and fill in the blanks. Pay attention to the accuracy of the numbers.

Well, beer drinkers by the (1) ________ are (2) ________ Munich for the world's biggest (3) ________, Germany's famous Oktoberfest. Munich's (4) ________ opened the festival by driving a tap into the first barrel lay there. There were 3 blows from a wooden hammer and passing a mug of beer to Bavarian (5) ________ Edmund Stoiber. Some (6) ________ roast chickens and (7) ________ roast oxen will be (8) ________ to travelers from around the world. The (9) ________ drinking spree is expected to draw (10) ________ visitors.

Pass 3 Oktoberfest 2

(Difficulty: ★★★)

Vocabulary

lederhosen	['leɪdəˌhəʊzən] *n.*	皮短裤；皮裤
brusque	[bruːsk] *adj.*	粗鲁的，莽撞的
liter	['liːtə(r)] *n.*	公升（容量单位）
under way		正在进行中
in full swing		活跃；蓬勃高涨；如火如荼
wash down		冲洗；（用水）送服

Task 1 Word Matching

Directions: Match the words/phrases of Column A to their explanations in Column B.

A	B
in full swing	in motion; set in motion
wash down	leather shorts often worn with suspenders; worn especially by men and boys in Bavaria
under way	at the highest level of activity; proceeding with full vigor
lederhosen	to eat food accompanied by lots of liquid; also used metaphorically

Task 2 Word Hunting

Directions: Please watch the report carefully and then find out the equivalent English expressions for the following.

1. 世界上规模最大的啤酒节

____

2. 慕尼黑

____

3. 如火如荼地开展

____

4. 将如此多的啤酒递送给这么多顾客

____

5. 50 万只用来下酒的烤鸡

____

Task 3 Self-dictation

Directions: Listen again and note down all the exact numbers and figures and get ready to tell what each of them refers to.

____

____

____

____

____

____

____

____

Task 4 True or False

Directions: Listen again and decide whether the following statements are true or false (T/F).

1. ( ) Munich's Oktoberfest this year is expected to attract 60 million visitors.
2. ( ) Munich's mayor is proud to spend a Saturday serving drinks.
3. ( ) Munich's Oktoberfest has only ever been canceled through war.
4. ( ) With 1,800 waitress, it is not a difficult job to deliver liters of beer to the visitors.
5. ( ) The visitors to Oktoberfest beer festival will be able to enjoy the drinking, roast chickens and the music.

Pass 4 Valentine's Day

(Difficulty: ★★★★)

背景知识

每年的2月14日是西方的传统节日"情人节"，也被称作"圣瓦伦丁节"（St. Valentine's Day）。关于该节日来源的说法甚多，但广为接受的观点是，这一节日是为了纪念公元3世纪时，为了正义和纯洁的爱情而在2月14日被处死的罗马圣教徒瓦伦丁。

情人节与玫瑰、浪漫、巧克力和贺卡紧密相连。在希腊神话中，玫瑰是美神的化身，是用来表达爱情的，不同颜色和不同朵数的玫瑰往往有着不同的寓意。情人节的巧克力也是必不可少的。巧克力自它诞生以来，就与情爱有着密切的联系。相爱的人们用香甜的巧克力来表达对爱人的浓浓情意。

中国的传统节日"七夕"也称作"中国情人节"。

（资料来源：http://tieba.baidu.com/p/2162759768。）

Vocabulary

Valentine	['væləntaɪn] *n.* 瓦伦丁（姓氏）；情人；情人节
flock	[flɒk] *vi.* 群集，成群结队而行；蜂拥
retailer	['riːteɪlə(r)] *n.* 零售商；零售店
cater	['keɪtə(r)] *vi.* 满足需要，适合；投合，迎合
cash-strapped	[kæʃ stræpt] *adj.* 囊中羞涩的；缺钱的
hit	[hɪt] *n.* 成功而轰动一时的事物

personality	[ˌpɜːsə'nælətɪ]	*n.* 人物；名人
guru	['gʊruː]	*n.* 专家；权威
downbeat	['daʊnbiːt]	*adj.* 消沉的；悲观的；低迷的
shoestring	['ʃuːstrɪŋ]	*n.* （非正式用语）极少的钱
cuddle	['kʌdl]	*v.* 拥抱；依偎
proactive	[prəʊ'æktɪv]	*adj.* 主动的；主动出击的
flock to	蜂拥而至	
cater to	迎合	
Valentine's Day	情人节	

Task 1 General Understanding

Directions: Watch the report for three times and try to grasp its main idea. You may do this either in Chinese or English.

Task 2 Word Hunting

Directions: Please listen and find out the equivalent English expressions for the following.

1. 省钱妙招

____

2. 浪漫之都巴黎

____

3. 迎合囊中羞涩的消费者的需求

____

4. 爱情无价

____

5. 在当地电台为他 / 她点播一首歌曲

____

Task 3 Back Translation

Directions: Please listen to the passage attentively and then translate the following Chinese sentences into English.

1. 全世界许许多多的人们都将以他们独特的方式庆祝情人节。

____

____

2. 日本零售商很有创意地迎合囊中羞涩的消费者的需求。

____

____

3. 她的节目涵盖很多主题，其中包括爱情和浪漫情调。

____

____

4. 丈夫刚刚失业，她非常绝望。

____

____

Task 4 Listening Comprehension

Directions: Listen to the passage again and choose the best answer from the four choices marked A), B), C) and D).

1. Which of the following is NOT true according to the passage?
   A) Despite the cold and rain, many couples have flocked to Paris, an obvious romantic destination for this Valentine's Day.
   B) Chinese retailers are affected greatly as shoppers are cutting back in these tough economic times.
   C) Valentine's Day, though a western holiday, is getting quite popular, especially among young people.
   D) Japanese retailers try hard to meet the needs of cash-strapped consumers.

2. Which of the following is NOT true about the HK radio talk show and its host?
   A) Today's show is encouraging listeners to call in with some tips on how to express love to their honeys but not actually spend a lot of money.
   B) One listener is going to make a strawberry milkshake for her husband because strawberries look heart-shaped.
   C) Others say that they will write love letters or cards, or cook a big dinner to celebrate.
   D) A lady who called not long ago is still depressed because her husband is staying at home without a job.

Task 5 Shadow Speaking Practice

Directions: Listen to the passage a couple of times and repeat the words that you've just heard sentence by sentence. Retell the passage first on your own then check your work with your friends. Finally report the passage to your classmates.

Pass 5 Celebrating St. Lucia's Day

(Difficulty: ★★★★)

背景知识

圣露西亚节 (St. Lucia's Day) 在每年的 12 月 13 日举行，是瑞典的传统节日。"Lucia"

源自拉丁语“Lux”，是“光”的意思。“Lucia”被誉为“光明女神”，在北欧最黑暗的冬日给人们带来光明。

一般在St. Lucia's节这一天，瑞典的家庭里，由家里长女扮成“光明女神”（St. Lucia/Luciabrud, brud在瑞典语中是“新娘”的意思），穿着白色长袍，束着红色腰带，头上戴着越橘叶做成的花冠，花冠上插着点燃的白色蜡烛。早晨起来给父母送上一盘藏红花小圆面包和咖啡，弟弟妹妹跟随其后，女孩子点着蜡烛，男孩子戴着尖尖的帽子，叫做“星童”。如今，不仅在家庭，在工厂、学校、教堂这一天都会举办扮演St. Lucia的节日庆祝活动。在瑞典的一些大城市，还会举行选美比赛，冠军则被选为“圣女露西亚”(Saint Lucia)。

（资料来源：http://www.linlinhouse.com/714.html。）

Vocabulary

reenact	[ˌrəˈnækt]	*v.*	再次展现，再现，重现
procession	[prəˈseʃən]	***n.***	队列；游行
martyr	[ˈmɑːtə(r)]	***n.***	烈士；殉道者
fast	[fɑːst]	***n. vt.***	禁食，（尤指）斋戒
sash	[sæʃ]	***n.***	腰带
symbolize	[ˈsɪmbəlaɪz]	*v.*	象征；代表
Scandinavia	[ˌskændɪˈneɪvɪə]	***n.***	斯堪的纳维亚（半岛）

Task 1 General Understanding

Directions: Watch the report three times and try to grasp its main idea. You may do this orally either in Chinese or English.

Task 2 Word Matching

Directions: Listen and identify the following words in the passage and then match them with their respective paraphrases. Write down your choices in the corresponding brackets.

words:

1. fast (　　)　2. procession (　　)　3. martyr (　　)　4. symbolize (　　)

paraphrases:

A. the group action of a collection of people or animals or vehicles moving ahead in more or less regular formation

B. to abstain from certain foods, as for religious or medical reasons

C. to express indirectly by an image, form, or model

D. someone who is killed or made to suffer greatly because of their religious or political beliefs, and is admired and respected by people who share those beliefs

Task 3 Q&A

Directions: Listen and answer the following questions.

1. In Sweden, who is at the center of the St. Lucia's Day celebration?

____

2. How is St. Lucia's Day celebrated in Sweden?

____

3. What is one of the origins of St. Lucia's Day according to the passage?

____

4. What does St. Lucia symbolize?

____

5. What is the connection between St. Lucia's Day and Christmas, and how important is it for the Swedish?

____

Task 4 Blank Filling

Directions: Listen again and fill in the following blanks.

Each year, the Lucia tradition is (1) ________ in homes and public places throughout (2) ________ . It is celebrated widely with (3) ________________________.

The (4) ________ of St. Lucia's Day is many, and one of them is the (5) ________ Saint Lucia who died in the year (6) ________ as a (7) ________ and her day of death was celebrated on the (8) ________. And in Sweden, this day was very important because the Christmas (9) ________ began on this day and it was the (10) ________ of the year.

(11) ________ the (12) ________ daughter in the family (13) ________ Lucia. She is dressed in a (14) ________ gown with a (15) ________ sash, with a crown full of (16) ________ and wakes the household singing the traditional Lucia song.

Task 5 Shadow Speaking Practice

Directions: Listen to the above three paragraphs again and repeat after the speaker. Pay attention to your speed, pronunciation and intonation.

Pass 6 The Claus Wars

(Difficulty: ★★★★)

背景知识

圣诞节是西方的传统节日，是每年的12月25日。圣诞节是一个宗教节日，因为人们把它当做耶稣的诞辰来庆祝，故名“耶诞”。圣诞节也是西方世界以及其他很多地区的公共假日。

关于圣诞老人的故事，在欧洲民间流传的版本很多，但被世界大多数人认可的还是来自北欧芬兰的圣·尼古拉斯（Saint Nicholas）的故事。传说在公元3世纪，有一位生活在芬兰北部名叫尼古拉斯的老人，他拥有无穷无尽的财富而又乐善好施。他喜欢乘坐鹿拉雪橇漫游各地，遇到穷困人家，总会慷慨地伸出援助之手，帮助他们渡过难关。

圣诞老人是圣诞节最重要的象征。每年圣诞节前夕，也就是12月24日平安夜，圣诞老人会驾着鹿拉的雪橇从北方而来，由烟囱进入各家，把圣诞礼物装在袜子里，然后挂在孩子们的床头上或火炉前。

圣诞老人的英文名称有 Santa Claus, Father Christmas, Saint Nicholas 以及 Santa 等。

（资料来源：http://www.smhaida.com/2016/shengdanjie_0225/319483.html。）

Vocabulary

championship	['tʃæmpɪənʃɪp] *n.* 锦标赛；优胜，冠军称号
jolly	['dʒɒlɪ] *adj.* 快活的；兴高采烈的
shatter	['ʃætə(r)] *vt.* 使破碎，使碎裂；*vi.* 粉碎，损坏
affectionately	[ə'fekʃənətlɪ] *adv.* 挚爱地，亲切地
festive	['festɪv] *adj.* 节日的；喜庆的
parade	[pə'reɪd] *n.* 游行；巡游
sleigh	[sleɪ] *n.* 雪橇
Himalayan	[ˌhɪmə'leɪən] *adj.* 喜马拉雅的
ostrich	['ɒstrɪtʃ] *n.* 鸵鸟
contestant	[kən'testənt] *n.* 参赛者；选手
Estonia	[e'stəʊnɪə] *n.* 爱沙尼亚
Switzerland	['swɪtsələnd] *n.* 瑞士
world championships	世界锦标赛
be shattered by	打碎；打破
Bob sleigh	雪橇，雪橇车
a sack of	一袋；一麻袋
Father Christmas	圣诞老人（美国英语中用"Santa Claus"）
Santa (Claus)	*n.* 圣诞老人

Task 1 Word Hunting

Directions: Please watch the news report and find out the equivalent English expressions of the following words and phrases.

1. 圣诞老人 ______________________________

2. 圣诞庆祝活动 ____________________

3. 开始真正的竞赛 ____________________

4. 雪橇 ____________________

5. 大约 100 位参赛选手 ____________________

6. 活动主办方 ____________________

Task 2 Q&A

Directions: Listen and answer the following questions.

1. Which country holds the Santa Claus World Championships according to the passage?

____

____

2. How many contestants take part in the Santa Claus World Championships?

____

____

3. What is the Santa Claus World Championships known as?

____

____

Task 3 Blank Filling

Directions: Listen and fill in the blanks.

Now the race has begun to find the world's greatest (1) ________. (2) ________ men and women from all over the world are taking part in the Santa Claus World Championships in Switzerland. It's the season to be jolly as the silence of the (3) ________ mountain village of Samnaun was (4) ________ the beginning of the Santa Claus World Championships. (5) ________ known as "The Claus Wars", it's one of several festive events celebrating Christmas. It (6) ________ through the village before the Santas get down to serious competition. And what could be a greater competition than Santas in a Bob sleigh? There's (7) ________ gingerbread decorating and that well-known favorite, (8) ________ . And then of course they're with the more obvious Santa skills, like (9) ________ loaded with (10) ________ presents. As they're keen to point out, it's not easy being a Santa.

Task 4 Shadow Speaking Practice

Directions: Listen to the above paragraph again and repeat after the speaker. Pay attention to your speed, pronunciation and intonation.

Task 5 Back Translation

Directions: Please translate the following Chinese sentences into English based on your listening.

1. 来自世界各地的约 100 名女士和先生前来参加在瑞士举行的“圣诞老人世锦赛”。

____

____

2. “圣诞老人世锦赛”开赛，打破了瑞士小山村的宁静。

____

____

3. 庆祝活动一开始是在村子里列队游行，然后“圣诞老人”们正式比赛。

____

____

4. 约有 100 名参赛选手远道而来，他们中有的来自俄罗斯、爱沙尼亚、西班牙、法国以及瑞典。

____

____

Pass 7 The London Carnival

(Difficulty: ★★★★)

背景知识

英国诺丁山狂欢节 (Notting Hill Carnival) 是欧洲规模最大的街头文化艺术节，仅次于巴西的里约热内卢狂欢节 (Rio Carnival)。诺丁山狂欢节创立的初衷之一就是弘扬文化多元性。早在 1959 年，加勒比移民聚居的诺丁山区出现针对黑人的种族暴力事件 (riots)，为弘扬加勒比文化并倡导种族融合与团结，英国第一届室内加勒比狂欢节于当年 8 月应运而生，后于 1964 年演变成街头狂欢，即诺丁山狂欢节。该节日于每年 8 月底的最后一个周末在英国伦敦西区诺丁山地区举行，从周日到周一（周一是 Bank Holiday，即英国的公共假期），共历时两天，以非洲和加勒比地区文化为主题，是英国多元文化的象征之一。诺丁山地区的移民文化孕育了诺丁山狂欢节，几十年后，该节日发展成为规模盛大的多元文化节日，也是伦敦最炙手可热的旅游项目之一。诺丁山狂欢节每年吸引大批来自世界各地的游客。

（资料来源：http://baike.baidu.com。）

Vocabulary

carnival	['kɑːnɪvl] *n.* 狂欢节；嘉年华
riot	['raɪət] *n.* 骚乱，暴动，暴乱，骚动
stab	[stæb] *vt.* 刺；将……刺入；对……做出刺或戳的动作
heal	[hiːl] *vt.* 治愈，愈合，痊愈
the Notting Hill Carnival	诺丁山狂欢节

in full swing	如火如荼地（举行）；全面开展
in the wake of	尾随，紧跟；随着，在……之后
trouble free	没有事故发生的；无忧无虑的
cast a shadow over	蒙上一层阴影
at its best	处于最佳状态

Task 1 General Understanding

Directions: Watch the news report three times and try to grasp its main idea. You may do this either in Chinese or English.

Task 2 Word Hunting

Directions: Please listen and find out the equivalent English expressions of the following words and phrases.

1. 警力 / 警力介入 ______________________________
2. 在暴乱发生之后 ______________________________
3. 一个弥合暴乱导致的伤口的机会 ______________________________
4. 欧洲规模最大的街头狂欢 ______________________________

Task 3 Listening Comprehension

Directions: Listen to the report again and choose the best answer from the four choices marked A), B), C) and D).

1. How many police officers are on duty at this week's Notting Hill Carnival?
   A) There are 6,200 police officers on duty.
   B) There are 6,000 police officers on duty.
   C) There are 6,500 police officers on duty.
   D) There are 5,000 police officers on duty.
2. Which of the following statements about the Notting Hill Carnival is NOT true according to the passage?
   A) On Monday over a million people were on the streets.
   B) There was no trouble involved in this week's carnival because there is a larger police presence.
   C) Children are dancing on the streets, and there are children on their dad-shoulders.

D) People do not mind police presence while they are participating in the street carnival party.

Task 4 Blank Filling

Directions: Listen and fill in the blanks.

This week started with the Notting Hill Carnival (1) ________________. There was a larger (2) ________________ than usual (3) ________________ in England with (4) ________________ officers on duty. On Monday more than (5) ________________ people were on the streets. The event was (6) ________________. One man though was stabbed. There were 88 arrests. Graham Satchell reports.

The riots in London (7) ________________ threatened to (8) ________________ over this year's carnival. But family day was pretty much business-as-usual. Children dancing on the streets, children on their dad-shoulders. These are the pictures the mayor of London Boris Johnson would have been hoping for when he said the (9) ________________ was a chance to heal the wounds of the (10) ________________.

Task 5 Shadow Speaking Practice

Directions: Listen to the above paragraph again and repeat after the speaker. Pay attention to your speed, pronunciation and intonation.

Pass 8 July 4th: Exploding the Myths

(Difficulty: ★★★★)

背景知识

美国国庆日也称“独立日”（Independence Day，又称 Fourth of July, 4th of July 或 July Fourth），是美国的主要法定节日之一，日期为每年的 7 月 4 日，以纪念 1776 年 7 月 4 日大陆会议在费城正式通过《独立宣言》，美国摆脱英国的殖民统治。《独立宣言》开宗明义地阐明，“所有人生而平等，具有追求幸福与自由的天赋权利”。

这一天，美国举国欢腾，万家同乐，民众悬挂国旗，举行节日游行，观看焰火表演，举办烧烤聚会。

（资料来源：http://www.history.com/topics/holidays/july-4th。）

Vocabulary

bash	[bæʃ] *n.* 盛大的聚会；（俚语）闹宴，舞会
pageantry	['pædʒəntrɪ] *n.* 盛况，盛典；正规庆典的传统特征
colonial	[kə'ləʊnɪəl] *adj.* 殖民地的；殖民的
proclaim	[prə'kleɪm] *vt.* 宣告，声明，公布
icon	['aɪkɒn] *n.* 图标，记号
pyrotechnic	[ˌpaɪrə'teknɪk] *adj.* 烟火的
explosive	[ɪk'spləʊsɪv] *n.* 炸药
kaleidoscopic	[kəˌlaɪdə'skɒpɪk] *adj.* 万花筒般的；千变万化的
dazzle	['dæzl] *vt.* 目眩；使惊异不已
celebratory	[ˌselə'breɪtərɪ] *adj.* 快乐的，庆贺的；庆祝的
centennial	[sen'tenɪəl] *n.* 一百周年（纪念）*adj.* 世纪的；百年纪念的
inauguration	[ɪˌnɔːgjə'reɪʃn] *n.* 就职；就职典礼
skew	[skjuː] *vt.& vi.* 使歪斜；歪斜
complex	['kɒmpleks] *n.* 建筑群
the Declaration of Independence	美国《独立宣言》
the Gallup Poll	盖洛普民意调查
blend with	混合；融为一体
Brookhaven	布鲁克海文（美国密西西比州西南部城镇）
Grucci	美国 Grucci 家族烟花公司
the Brooklyn Bridge	布鲁克林大桥（纽约的标志性建筑之一）

Task 1 General Understanding

Directions: Watch the report three times and try to grasp its main idea. You may do this orally either in Chinese or English.

Task 2 Word Matching

Directions: Listen and identify the following words in the passage and then match them with their respective paraphrases. Write down your choices in the corresponding brackets.

Words:

1. dazzle (   ) 2. explosive (   ) 3. centennial (   ) 4. proclaim (   )
5. inauguration (   )

Paraphrases:

A. a chemical substance that undergoes a rapid chemical change (with the production of gas) on being heated or struck

B. to declare formally; declare someone to be something

C. amaze or bewilder, as with brilliant wit or intellect or skill

D. the 100th anniversary (or the celebration of it)

E. the ceremonial induction into a position

Task 3 Word Hunting

Directions: Please listen and find out the equivalent English expressions of the following words and phrases.

1.《独立宣言》正式通过

____

2. 在大家的记忆中

____

3. 在任何一年里

4. 令人叹为观止的表演

5. 开幕式及闭幕式

6. 总统就职演说

Task 4 Q&A

Directions: Listen and answer the following questions.

1. When did people formally adopt *the Declaration of Independence*?

2. By means of the formal adoption of *the Declaration of Independence*, what was declared and proclaimed?

3. If there is one, what is the one single icon that represents the 4th of July according to the passage?

4. When and where did the Grucci fireworks family business start?

5. When did the Grucci family immigrate to the United States of America and what did they bring with them?

____

____

6. How much of the Grucci fireworks' annual business comes from producing shows for the 4th of July?

____

____

Task 5 Back Translation

Directions: Please listen and translate the following Chinese sentences into English.

1. 7 月 4 日就是用来纪念美国历史上的这一重大时刻。

____

____

2. 这一天，店铺关门，人们点燃烧烤炉，全国各地国旗飘扬。

____

____

3. 根据盖洛普民意调查显示，在任何一年，60% 以上的美国人都打算在国庆节假日观看焰火表演。

____

____

4. 他们提供的焰火出现在美国当代历史的许多重要庆典中。

____

____

Task 6: Oral Practice

Directions: Look at the following topic carefully and then choose one topic and deliver a short (1–3 minutes) presentation.

Please give an introduction of the celebratory events of the Chinese National Day.

Pass 9 Learning About the Halloween Celebration

(Difficulty: ★★★★★)

背景知识

按照基督教的习惯，每年的 11 月 1 日是万圣节，是纪念所有圣徒的日子。万圣节前夕即万圣节的前一天，也就是每年的 10 月 31 日。在中世纪的英格兰，万圣节被称作 "All Saints' Day" 或者 "All Hallows"，万圣节前夕便是 "All Hallows Eve"，万圣节前夕这一名称逐渐演变为 Halloween。

Halloween 是西方传统"鬼节"，因为这一天的活动很多都与"鬼"有关。不过这一天的气氛，却远不像它的名称那样令人"毛骨悚然"。人们举办万圣节舞会，小孩子会穿上各种千奇百怪的服饰并戴上面具，挨家挨户收集糖果。小孩子们会说："不给糖，就捣蛋 (trick or treat)。"万圣节原本是赞美秋天的节日，庆祝活动基本都是在教堂举行，时至今日，人们已经将其发展为尽情玩闹、讲鬼故事和互相吓唬的节日。

万圣节前夜起源于与邪恶幽灵相关的庆祝活动，所以骑着扫帚的女巫、幽灵、小妖精和骷髅都是万圣节的标志物。蝙蝠、猫头鹰和其他夜间活动的动物也是万圣节的普遍标志。

黑色是传统的万圣节颜色，这可能是因为万圣节前夜的各种传统活动或仪式都是在晚上举行。

南瓜也是万圣节的标志物。南瓜是橘黄色的，所以橘黄色成了传统的万圣节颜色。用南瓜雕制南瓜灯（jack o'lantern）也是一个万圣节传统，凯尔特人相信死亡之神 Samhain 在 10 月 31 日的晚上会和鬼魂一起重返人间，寻找替身。因此他们点燃火炬，焚烧动物以作为死亡之神的献礼。南瓜灯样子吓人，悬挂在树枝上或大门上，据说这样可以驱走妖魔鬼怪。

（资料来源：http:www.zybang.com。）

Vocabulary

Halloween	[ˌhæləʊ'iːn] *n.* 万圣节前夕（很多时候被误译为“万圣节”）
costume	['kɒstjuːm] *n.* （戏剧或电影的）戏装，演出服；服装
elaborate	[ɪ'læbərət] *adj.* 精心制作的；精心设计的
Gothic	['gɒθɪk] *adj.* （描写怪诞、神秘的恐怖故事）哥特式的；野蛮的
latecomer	['leɪtkʌmə(r)] *n.* 迟到者；后来者
creepy	['kriːpɪ] *adj.* 令人毛骨悚然的；令人不寒而栗的
Celtic	['keltɪk] *n.* 凯尔特人 *adj.* 凯尔特人的
myth	[mɪθ] *n.* 神话
curb	[kɜːb] *vt.* 控制；抑制
vandalism	['vændəlɪzəm] *n.* 故意破坏，破坏行为；破坏公物；恶意破坏
haunted	['hɔːntɪd] *adj.* （房屋等）有鬼魂出没的；闹鬼的
hayride	['heɪraɪd] *n.* （尤指夜间）乘坐装有干草的大车出游；夜游
forego	[fɔː'gəʊ] *vt.* 摒弃；摒绝；放弃
malicious	[mə'lɪʃəs] *adj.* 恶意的，有敌意的；恶毒的
spirit	['spɪrɪt] *n.* 鬼魂；幽灵；精灵
dressing up	角色扮演；乔装打扮
Samhain	（古凯尔特人庆祝新年的）萨温节；死神节；死亡之神
jack o'lantern	（或 jack-o'-lantern）南瓜灯
ghosts and goblins	鬼魅；妖魔鬼怪

Task 1 General Understanding

Directions: Listen to the report three times and try to grasp its main idea. You may do this either in Chinese or English.

Task 2 Word Matching

Directions: Watch the clip, identify the following words in the passage and then match them with their respective paraphrases. Write down your choices in the corresponding brackets.

words:

1. jack o'lantern ( ) 2. latecomer ( ) 3. costume ( ) 4. hayride ( )

paraphrases:

A. a pleasure ride, usually at night, in an open truck, wagon or sleigh which has been decorated with hay or straw

B. the attire worn in a play or at a fancy dress ball

C. someone who arrives after the time that they should have done, or later than others

D. a carved pumpkin, lit from within by a candle

Task 3 Word Hunting

Directions: Please listen to the report and find out the equivalent English expressions of the following words and phrases.

1. 第二最受欢迎的节日 / 除了……之外，最受欢迎的节日

____

2. 美国人最期待的节日之一

____

3. 将南瓜雕刻成吓人的南瓜灯

____

4. 有些学者对此提出异议

____

5. 凯尔特人和欧洲的各种神话、传说以及文化传统

____

Task 4 Listening Comprehension

Directions: Listen to the report again and choose the best answer from the four choices marked A), B), C) and D).

1. Which of the following statements is NOT true according to the passage?
   A) Halloween has developed to be the third most popular holiday in the nation over the years.
   B) Halloween celebrations include scary costumes, elaborate parties and events, horror film festivals and Gothic trappings.
   C) Halloween was not really popular in the US until the early 20th century.
   D) Halloween is not originally celebrated in the US.
2. How do people in the United States of America celebrate Halloween?
   A) They wear scary costumes and things that are wonderfully creepy.
   B) They make scary jack o'lanterns.
   C) Families get treats from their neighbors at night.
   D) All of the above.
3. Which of the following is NOT true about the origin and traditions of Halloween celebration?
   A) The monster and horror films of the early twentieth century are significant contributors to the look and feel of modern Halloween celebrations in the USA.
   B) Samhain is considered to be a significant influence on Halloween celebrations.
   C) Trick or treat started at the beginning of the 20th century to curb the vandalism and destruction that once characterized this holiday in the USA.
   D) Hayrides and other nighttime events are also very popular in big cities.

Task 5 Back Translation

Directions: Please listen and translate the following Chinese sentences into English.

1. 在美国，人们庆祝万圣节的方式一般包括：将南瓜雕刻成吓人的南瓜灯，尽力将自己家装点得具有令人“毛骨悚然”的气息，并且会穿上精心设计的万圣节服装。

____

____

____

2. 美国有些家庭和社会团体会精心设计和装点“鬼屋”，并邀请人们去免费参观或者参观并捐款。

____

____

____

3. 很多人，特别是年轻人，摒弃了万圣节的黑色恐怖主题。他们装扮成惊险片里的人物或者文学作品里的人物，甚至还会装扮成历史人物。

____

____

____

4. 苏格兰和爱尔兰曾经并且从某种程度上说现在仍然庆祝萨温节。这个节日更多的是用来庆祝一年中的最后一次收获，并不是与恐怖的鬼魅相关，尽管鬼怪精灵仍然在这一节日中占有一席之地。

____

____

____

Task 6 Oral Practice

Directions: Look at the following topic carefully and then deliver a short (1–3 minutes) presentation on them.

Please give a brief introduction about Halloween.

Pass 10 The Hajj: Pilgrimage to Mecca

(Difficulty: ★★★★★)

背景知识

麦加朝觐，是穆斯林朝觐沙特阿拉伯麦加省麦加·穆卡拉玛市时，必须履行的多项宗教仪式的总称，是伊斯兰教五功之一，中国穆斯林称其为朝功。朝觐是伊斯兰教的第五个基柱，是伊斯兰教为信徒所规定的必须遵守的基本制度之一，每一位有经济条件和有体力的成年穆斯林都负有朝拜麦加的宗教义务。所有穆斯林，无论是男还是女，都会尽最大努力争取一生至少前往麦加朝觐一次。

公元 627 年，从伊斯兰教教义出发，穆罕默德参照阿拉伯部落自古盛行的朝觐宗教圣地的民俗，亲自制定了穆斯林朝觐克尔白的全部宗教礼仪。1932 年沙特阿拉伯王国建立后，麦加被称为“宗教之都”，来此朝觐的人更加摩肩接踵，已经有来自 70 多个国家说着不同语言的穆斯林来到此地朝觐。每年在伊斯兰教历的第 12 个月，数以百万计的穆斯林都会聚集在沙特的麦加，参加一年一度的朝觐。朝圣期间，他们聚集在“圣城”麦加周围，一起祈祷、吃饭、学习。“麦加朝圣”是伊斯兰教每年最盛大的宗教活动。

（资料来源：http://news.ifeng.com/a/20150717/44189822_0.shtml。）

Vocabulary

hajj	[hædʒ]	*n.*	麦加朝圣
pillar	['pɪlə(r)]	*n.*	（组织、制度、信仰等的）核心
pilgrimage	['pɪlgrɪmɪdʒ]	*n.*	朝圣之旅；参拜圣地

faithful	['feɪθfl] *n.* 信徒
overwhelming	[ˌəʊvə'welmɪŋ] *adj.* 势不可挡的，压倒一切的，巨大的
pilgrim	['pɪlgrɪm] *n.* 香客，朝圣者；清教徒
ritual	['rɪtʃʊəl] *n.* （宗教等的）仪式
prophet	['prɒfɪt] *n.* 预言家，先知
sermon	['sɜːmən] *n.* 布道；讲道
follower	['fɒləʊə(r)] *n.* 追随者；信徒
sin	[sɪn] *n.* 违背宗教（道德原则）的恶行；罪恶，罪孽
purity	['pjʊərətɪ] *n.* 纯洁，纯净
cleanse	[klenz] *vt.* 净化；使……清洁
literally	['lɪtərəlɪ] *adv.* 差不多，简直（用于加强语意）
Mecca	['mekə] *n.* 麦加（在沙特阿拉伯，为伊斯兰教圣地）
mosque	[mɒsk] *n.* 清真寺，伊斯兰教寺院
circle	['sɜːkl] *v.* 环绕
Muslim	['mʊzlɪm] *n.* 穆斯林，伊斯兰教信徒
Koran	[kə'rɑːn] *n.* 《古兰经》
reenactment	[ˌriːɪ'næktmənt] *n.* 重现；重新扮演；再次展现
ihram	[iː'rɑːm] *n.* 伊斯兰教朝圣服
unstitched	[ʌn'stɪtʃt] *adj.* 未缝合的
Arafat	['ærəfæt] *n.* 阿拉法特山谷
Saudi Arabia	['saʊdɪ ə'reɪbjə] *n.* 沙特阿拉伯
Mount Mercy	慈悲山
Prophet Mohammed	先知穆罕默德
the Ka'aba	天房[1]
tawaf	绕行[2]
under way	进行中
in anticipation for	预期；期待

[1] The Ka'aba (literally "the cube" in Arabic) is an ancient stone structure that was built and re-built by prophets as a house of monotheistic worship. It is located inside the Grand Mosque in Makkah, Saudi Arabia. The Ka'aba is considered the center of the Muslim world, and is a unifying focal point for Islamic worship. 麦加朝圣共有六道程序：第一道程序是受戒，第二道程序是举行瞻礼，第三道程序是环游天房，第四道程序是站驻阿拉法特山，第五道程序是射石，第六道程序是宰牲。

[2] Tawaf，伊斯兰教朝觐功课仪式之一，亦称"环游天房"。它是阿拉伯语"塔瓦夫"的意译，即绕行天房克尔白。

Task 1 General Understanding

Directions: Watch the news report three times and try to grasp its main idea. You may do this either in Chinese or English.

Task 2 Word Hunting

Directions: Please listen and find out the equivalent English expressions of the following words and phrases.

1. 平生夙愿 / 毕生梦想 ______________________________
2. 数以百万计的信徒 ______________________________
3. 麦加朝圣之旅 ______________________________
4. 最后一次向其信徒布道 ______________________________
5. 从日出到日落 ______________________________
6. 对于穆斯林来说最神圣的地方 ______________________________
7. 人如潮涌 / 大批涌来的人们 ______________________________

Task 3 Q&A

Directions: Listen and answer the following questions.

1. What is the lifelong dream for many faithful people according to the passage?

____

____

____

2. Why is Mount Arafat so significant?

____

____

____

3. How do the pilgrims look like when they pray?

____

____

____

4. What does it symbolize when the pilgrims circle and go around 7 times the Ka'aba, the holiest site for Muslims?

____

____

____

5. What is the ihram?

____

____

____

Task 4 Back Translation

Directions: Please listen to the clip attentively and then translate the following Chinese sentences into English.

1. 一年一度的麦加朝圣之旅正在沙特阿拉伯如火如荼地举行。

____

____

2. 这对于绝大多数来此朝圣的人们而言，无疑是无与伦比的经历。

____

____

3. 对于麦加朝圣者而言，这是最为重要的一天。他们中的许多人晚上就睡在帐篷里，还有些人就直接睡在地上，期待着今天的朝圣仪式开始。

____

____

4. 所有这些仪式都跟先知穆罕默德在 1 400 年前所进行的仪式一样。

____

____

Task 5 Blank Filling

Directions: Listen to the report again and fill in the following blanks.

And this most certainly is an (1) __________ experience for most of the

(2) __________ who are here. We are in Arafat at the base of Mount Mercy. And this is the most significant day of the Hajj for pilgrims, many of them actually spending the night here (3) __________, others just sleeping on the ground (4) __________ for today's (5) __________ to begin, which actually began when the sun came up. Mount Arafat is significant because it is here (6) __________ this mount where Prophet Mohammed (7) ______________________________, asking God to forgive his followers. Today the pilgrims will be doing the same, spending all day (8) ____________________ praying that God forgive them their sins. We climbed the mountain earlier. We saw them praying, their arms outstretched. Many of them overcome with emotion, tears coming out of their eyes, holding their hands, their head in their hands as they were praying. Pilgrims who we spoke to had performed the hajj in the past were saying that (9) __________ this was the most significant moment for them. It was here at Mount Mercy where they felt closest to God, where they thought they were able to (10) __________________ with God, walking away with this experience with (11) __________ as if their souls have been cleansed and that they were (12) __________ being given a second chance at life.

Task 6 Shadow Speaking Practice

Directions: Listen to the above paragraph again and repeat after the speaker. Pay attention to your speed, pronunciation and intonation.

Part 4 英语听说秘籍之数字 (Number)

(Difficulty: ★★★★★)

数字在英语听力理解中占有相当大的比重，培养自己对英文数字的敏感度，是听力训练中必不可少的。

一、数字的读法

数字在信息传递中极为重要，无论是日常对话还是新闻听力，都会涉及数字，有时候一听而过，稍有差错就会“失之毫厘，谬以千里”。数字的形式和内容涉及年代和日期、时间、价格、股票指数、温度、门牌号、电话号码等。数字听力是英语听力训练中的一个重要方面，有时候也会是一大难点。很多学生往往很难在短时间内准确地捕捉到精准的数字信息并快速记录。

数字种类繁多，有基数词、序数词、分数、小数、百分数等。有时一个数字还有多种不同读法，要注意了解和学习一些数字的特殊读法，特别是在财经新闻中常常会遇到违反常规的读法。

基数词，要特别注意四位以上的大额数字。依照中文的习惯，数字由每四位划分一个单位，而英文则是每三位划分一个单位（thousand, million, billion, trillion）。正是这样的差异，使得四位以上的英文数字听力成为一个难点，也是平时数字训练时应该关注的一个重点。英语中没有“万”和“十万”这个表述，所以“十万”要用“one hundred thousand”表示，也没有“亿”这个表述，“一亿”要用“one hundred million”来表示。另外，美式英语中会听到用百位数来表述千位数字，例如，“1 200”我们一般会读成“one thousand and two hundred”，美国人可能直接说成“twelve hundred”。在英式英语中，一个数的最后两位（十位和个位）要用“and”连接，但美式英语中则不用。例如：美式英语中的“3,077”读作“three thousand seventy-seven”。BBC 新闻记者将“6 500”读成“6 and a half thousand”，这样特殊的读法平时应多注意积累。

分数的分子用基数词表示，分母则用序数词表示，先读分子，再读分母。若分子大于 1，则分母用复数。如“1/7”读作“one seventh”,“2/7”则读作“two sevenths”。在日常生活中，表示“1/4”时，用“one quarter”的频率可能高于“one fourth”。另外，如果分子或分母数值较大，常常会用“over”来读分数线。例如，“31/42”会读作“thirty-one over forty-two”。

小数的整数部分按照基数词的规则读，小数部分的数字一般是逐个读出，小数点“.”则读作“point”。例如，“9.57”读作“nine point five seven”，有时这个小数也会读作“nine point fifty-five”。应特别注意，如果小数点前为 0，则读作“zero”，或者不读。例如“0.85”一般会读作“zero point eight five”，但在新闻报道和日常对话中也常常读成“point eight five”或者“point eighty-five”。

百分数的读法比较简单，通常是在基数或小数后面加上百分号“%”，读作“percent”。例如：“27%”读作“twenty-seven percent”，“41.8%”读作“forty-one point 8 percent”。但应特别注意的是，有时百分号前的小数会被读作分数，例如“1.5%”读作“one and one half percent”。

英语中的倍数一般在表示两倍时用“twice”，三倍以上用“times”。但要注意其他一些表示倍数的词，它们是：double（两倍），triple（三倍），quadruple（四倍）等。倍数还可以用基数词加上后缀“-fold”表示，如“5 倍”写作 5-fold（也可以写作 five-fold）。

读具体价格时，需要注意带零头的数字。例如，“$3.35”，比较正式的读法是“three dollars thirty-five cents”，也可读作“three dollars thirty-five”，或简单地读作“three thirty-five”。“ £3.35”读作“three (pounds) thirty-five(pence)”。

温度，首先要分清两种单位：摄氏度（centigrade 或者 Celsius）和华氏度（Fahrenheit）。其次要注意零度和零下的读法。例如：“0℃ ”读作“zero degrees Centigrade”，“–5℃ ”可读作“five degrees below zero”或“negative/minus five degrees”。

年代及日期的读法：数字表示的年份通常分成两半来说。例如：公元前 2000 年（2000B. C.）读作："two thousand BC"。"1558（年）"读作"fifteen fifty-eight"，"1603"可读作"sixteen hundred and three"。"921"读作"nine twenty-one"。

英语中表示约数时常用的词语除了"about"，还有"around""some"。

数字听力往往无法依靠上下文语境来推断，需要借助短时记忆和快速反应获取信息。提高英语数字听力水平，应从掌握数字的正确英文读法开始，能流利地读出各种数字是记忆数字的前提。平时的学习中，应该进行数字读法及速记技巧训练，尽力攻克数字听力这一难关。

二、数字听力训练

Vocabulary

given	['gɪvn] *adj.* 指定的，确定的；假设的，假定的
exploitation	[ˌeksplɒɪ'teɪʃn] *n.* 利用；剥削；占……的便宜
source	[sɔːs] *n.* 根源，本源；源头
transit	['trænzɪt] *n.* 通过；中转
traffic	['træfɪk] *vi.* 交易；买卖 *vt.* 用……作交换；用……做交易
human trafficking	人口贩卖；贩卖人口
UNICEF	*abbr.* United Nations International Children's Emergency Fund 联合国儿童基金会

Task 1 Figure Training

Directions: Listen to the paragraphs and dictate all the numbers.

(1) ______________________________

____

____

(2) ______________________________

____

____

Task 2 Oral Practice

Directions: Listen to the two paragraphs three times, and summarize each of them in English. Pay attention to the preciseness of the numbers.

English Listening-and-Speaking Learning Planner

<table>
<tr><td>Monday
Practicing Hour:
______
Tape Hour:
______
Commitment:
______</td><td>Tuesday
Practicing Hour:
______
Tape Hour:
______
Commitment:
______</td><td>Wednesday
Practicing Hour:
______
Tape Hour:
______
Commitment:
______</td><td>Thursday
Practicing Hour:
______
Tape Hour:
______
Commitment:
______</td><td>Friday
Practicing Hour:
______
Tape Hour:
______
Commitment:
______</td></tr>
<tr><td>Saturday
Practicing Hour:
______
Tape Hour:
______
Commitment:
______</td><td>Sunday
Practicing Hour:
______
Tape Hour:
______
Commitment:
______</td><td colspan="3">General Performance for Week ______:
(vocabulary, long sentence, background information, etc.)

Self-rating ☆☆☆☆☆</td></tr>
<tr><td>Monday
Practicing Hour:
______
Tape Hour:
______
Commitment:
______</td><td>Tuesday
Practicing Hour:
______
Tape Hour:
______
Commitment:
______</td><td>Wednesday
Practicing Hour:
______
Tape Hour:
______
Commitment:
______</td><td>Thursday
Practicing Hour:
______
Tape Hour:
______
Commitment:
______</td><td>Friday
Practicing Hour:
______
Tape Hour:
______
Commitment:
______</td></tr>
<tr><td>Saturday
Practicing Hour:
______
Tape Hour:
______
Commitment:
______</td><td>Sunday
Practicing Hour:
______
Tape Hour:
______
Commitment:
______</td><td colspan="3">General Performance for Week ______:
(vocabulary, long sentence, background information, etc.)

Self-rating ☆☆☆☆☆</td></tr>
</table>

Appendix

一、节日介绍

1. 日本京都祇园祭（the Gion Festival）

The ancient capital of Japan, Kyoto is taken back in time during the Gion Festival by Yasaka Shrine (Gion was the old name of this shrine.) The Gion Festival is one of the biggest festivals in Japan.

This Japanese festival begins on July 1st and lasts until July 31st. At this time, there are many street vendors with games and Japanese festival food. Also, many people who go to this festival wear *yukata* and *geta*, which are traditional Japanese outfits. It is said that the summer of Kyoto begins with the Gion Matsuri. It is a traditional summer festivity.

The Gion Festival was started in 869 A.D. when a bad plague spread through Kyoto. In the first festival, young men carried numbers of wooden floats. It was a divine intervention to stop the plague. The plague soon ended, and this event became a popular festival. In the Edo Era, the current form of the decorated floats appeared in the festival.

There are many events held during this festival, but the highlights are Yoi-yama（宵山祭）on the 16th and Yamahoko-junko（山牟巡行）on the 17th. At Yoi-yama, people open the doors of their houses to show their treasured old folding screens. Yamahoko-junko is the parade of colorful floats through downtown Kyoto. The floats are pulled through the streets by teams of men dressed in traditional costumes. Each of the large floats carries musicians.

There are two kinds of floats: yama and hoko. Yama are smaller floats (weight: 1.2 ton–1.6 ton, height: about 6m) and carried by people on their shoulders. Hoko are giant floats (weight: 4.8 ton–12 ton, height: about 25m) on large wooden wheels and pulled by people. There are 32 floats in the parade: 25 yama floats and 7 hoko floats.

The floats are decorated with tapestries or fabrics from Nishijin, Kyoto. Many of them were imported from India, Belgium, Persia, Turkey and other countries in the 15th century.

(Extracted from: http://www.tingvoa.com/html/20150328/232223.html.)

2. 法国里昂玫瑰节（the Festival of Roses）

The Festival of Roses is celebrated annually in Lyon, France at the end of May. Lyon, France is blooming! The Festival of Roses is an attraction at the end of May where visitors can view three renovated rose gardens in the *Parc de la Tête d'Or*. The festival also includes a variety of activities and classes including creating floral displays, painting, gardening, a rose themed fashion show, and much more. The Festival of Roses concludes with a fireworks display that can be viewed by the riverbank.

3. 哈尔滨冰雕节（Harbin Ice and Snow Festival）

Considered to be the largest ice and snow festival in the world, Harbin's annual festival includes the world's biggest ice sculptures. The sculptures, built entirely out of snow and ice, are then decorated with lights and lasers, creating a spectacular display for visitors. While sculptures can be found around the city, there are two centralized exhibition areas: Sun City & Ice and Snow World.

Ice and Snow World is open during the night and comprised largely of life-sized buildings made from blocks of ice. Sun City is a day attraction displaying more artistic and creative snow sculptures. Both are impressive, to say the least.

Additional Harbin activities include the Ice Lantern Fair, winter swimming, sleigh rides and ice skating, skiing and snowboarding, Ice Hotels, dog sledding and Siberian tigers tours.

Pack VERY warmly as below zero Fahrenheit temperatures can be common.

4. 印度贾沙梅尔沙漠节（Desert Festival in Jaisalmer）

Held each February in the walled golden city of Jaisalmer, India, the festival lasts three days long, and is filled with lots of fun activities including parades, folk music, camel rides. There are also unusual camel attractions including a camel tug of war, camel decoration, camel polo, and camel dances.

Other attractions include the crowning of Mr. Desert, the longest mustache competition, fire dancing, puppet shows, a turban tying competition, snake charmers, and more.

To get to the Desert Festival, you can take a camel safari or ride an SUV from Jaisalmer.

5. 泰国泼水节（the Songkran Festival）

The Songkran Festival, also known as the Thailand Water Festival, is in full force mid-April each year, complete with water pistols, hoses, buckets of water and water balloons. Nothing beats the world's biggest water fight!

During April, the hottest month in Thailand, prepared to be soaked.

Considered the Thai New Year, the festival gives blessings through water for peace. There are bathing rites for different age groups as well.

The festival is celebrated all over Thailand with fervor, and includes the important ritual of bathing the Buddha.

二、关于节日主题的学习网站

1. 易呗网：http://www.yibei.com。
2. 普特网：http://www.putclub.com。
3. 名人名言网：www.allgreatquotes.com。
4. 世界文化节：http://www.artofliving.org/world-culture-festival。
5. http://www.worldfestivaldirectory.com。
6. 英国节日：http://www.ukfestivalguides.com。
7. 世界上最特别的 25 个节日：http://www.haokoo.com/else/2092575.html。

Chapter 2

Education

Part 1 Famous Quotes

The roots of education are bitter, but the fruit is sweet.

—Aristotle

教育的根是苦的，但其果实是甜的。

——亚里士多德

Education's purpose is to replace an empty mind with an open one.

—Malcolm Forbes

教育的目的是用一个开阔的心灵去替换一个空洞的心灵。

——马尔克姆·福布斯

Education is what remains after one has forgotten everything he learned in school.

—Albert Einstein

教育就是当一个人把在学校所学全部忘光之后剩下的东西。

——阿尔伯特·爱因斯坦

Part 2 Background Knowledge

(1) Higher Education: Is College Worth It?

(See: http://www.economist.com/news/united-states/21600131-too-many-degrees-are-waste-money-return-higher-education-would-be-much-better.)

Vocabulary

swell (swelled swollen)	[swel]	*vt.& vi.*	增强；肿胀，膨胀；充满（激情）
ponder	['pɒndə(r)]	*vt.*	思索，衡量
gateway	['geɪtweɪ]	*n.*	门，入口，途径
nuanced	['nju:ɑ:nst]	*adj.*	有细微差别的
impecunious	[ˌɪmpɪ'kju:nɪəs]	*adj.*	没钱的，不名一文的
lucrative	['lu:krətɪv]	*adj.*	获利多的，赚钱的
plonk	[plɒŋk]	*vt.*	随意放下，扑通地放下
		n.	劣质酒；一记重击
grumble	['grʌmbl]	*vi.*	抱怨，发牢骚，嘟囔，隆隆响
premium	['pri:mɪəm]	*n.*	额外费用，保险费，附加费
transparency	[træn'spærənsɪ]	*n.*	透明，透明性，透明的东西
luxurious	[lʌg'ʒʊərɪəs]	*adj.*	奢侈的，豪华的；辞藻华丽的

Too many degrees are a waste of money. The return on higher education would be much better if college were cheaper.

When LaTisha Styles graduated from Kennesaw State University in Georgia in 2006 she had $35,000 of student debt. This obligation would have been easy to discharge if her Spanish degree had helped her land a well-paid job. But there is no shortage of Spanish-speakers in a nation that borders Latin America. So Ms. Styles found herself working in a clothes shop and a fast-food restaurant for no more than $11 an hour.

Frustrated, she took the gutsy decision to go back to the same college and study something more pragmatic. She majored in finance, and now has a good job at an investment consulting firm. Her debt has swollen to $65,000, but she will have little trouble paying it off.

As Ms. Styles's story shows, there is no simple answer to the question "Is college worth it?" Some degrees pay for themselves; others don't. American school kids pondering whether to take on huge student loans are constantly told that college is the gateway to the middle class. The truth is more nuanced, as Barack Obama hinted when he said in January that "folks can make a lot more" by learning a trade "than they might with an art history degree." An angry art history professor forced him to apologise, but he was right.

College graduates aged 25 to 32 who are working full time earn about $17,500 more annually than their peers who have only a high school diploma, according to the

Pew Research Centre, a think-tank. But not all degrees are equally useful. And given how much they cost—a residential four-year degree can set you back as much as $60,000 a year—many students end up worse off than if they had started working at 18.

PayScale, a research firm, has gathered data on the graduates of more than 900 universities and colleges, asking them what they studied and how much they now earn. The company then factors in the cost of a degree, after financial aid (discounts for the clever or impecunious that greatly reduce the sticker price at many universities). From this, PayScale estimates the financial returns of many different types of degree.

Hard Subjects Pay Off

Unsurprisingly, engineering is a good bet wherever you study it. An engineering graduate from the University of California, Berkeley can expect to be nearly $1.1m better off after 20 years than someone who never went to college. Even the least lucrative engineering courses generated a 20-year return of almost $500,000.

Arts and humanities courses are much more varied. All doubtless nourish the soul, but not all fatten the wallet. An arts degree from a rigorous school such as Columbia or the University of California, San Diego pays off handsomely. But an arts graduate from Murray State University in Kentucky can expect to make $147,000 less over 20 years than a high school graduate, after paying for his education. Of the 153 arts degrees in the study, 46 generated a return on investment worse than plonking the money in 20-year treasury bills. Of those, 18 offered returns worse than zero.

Colleges that score badly will no doubt grumble that PayScale's rankings are based on relatively small numbers of graduates from each institution. Some schools are unfairly affected by the local job market—Murray State might look better if Kentucky's economy were thriving. Universities that set out to serve everyone will struggle to compete with selective institutions. And poor colleges will look worse than rich ones that offer lots of financial aid, since reducing the cost of a degree raises its return.

All these caveats are true. But overall, the PayScale study surely overstates the financial value of a college education. It does not compare graduates' earnings to what they would have earned, had they skipped college (That number is unknowable). It compares their earnings to those of people who did not go to college—many of whom did not go because they were not clever enough to get in. Thus, some of the premium that graduates earn simply reflects the fact that they are, on average, more intelligent than non-graduates.

What is not in doubt is that the cost of university per student has risen by almost five times the rate of inflation since 1983, and graduate salaries have been flat for much of the past decade. Student debt has grown so large that it stops many young people from buying houses, starting businesses or having children. Those who borrowed for a bachelor's degree granted in 2012 owe an average of $29,400. The Project on Student Debt, a non-profit, says that 15% of borrowers default within three years of entering repayment. At for-profit colleges the rate is 22%. Glenn Reynolds, a law professor and author of "The Higher Education Bubble", writes of graduates who "may wind up living in their parents' basements until they are old enough to collect Social Security".

That is an exaggeration: Students enrolling this year who service their debts will see them forgiven after 20 years. But the burden is still heavy for many. It does not help that nearly a third of those who take out such loans eventually drop out of college; they must still repay their debts. A third transfer to different schools. Many four-year degrees drag on longer, and so cost more. Overall, the six-year graduation rate for four-year institutions is only 59%.

The lousy national job market does not help, either. A report by McKinsey, a consultancy, found that 42% of recent graduates are in jobs that require less than a four-year college education. Some 41% of graduates from the nation's top colleges could not find jobs in their chosen field; and half of all graduates said they would choose a different major or school.

Chegg, a company that provides online help to students, collaborated the study. Dan Rosensweig, its boss, says that only half of graduates feel prepared for a job in their field, and only 39% of managers feel that students are ready for the workforce. Students often cannot write clearly or organise their time sensibly. Four million jobs are unfilled because jobseekers lack the skills employers need.

Grading the Graders

For all their flaws, studies like PayScale's help would-be students (and their parents) make more informed choices. As Americans start to realise how much a bad choice can hurt them, they will demand more transparency. Some colleges are providing it, prodded by the federal government. For example, the University of Texas recently launched a website showing how much its graduates earn and owe after five years.

"Opportunity," said Mr. Obama on April 2nd, "means making college more affordable." In time, transparency and technology will force many colleges to cut costs and raise quality. Online education will accelerate the trend. In 2012, 6.7m students were taking at least one online course. Such courses allow students to listen to fine lecturers without having to pay for luxurious dormitories or armies of college bureaucrats. They will not replace traditional colleges—face-to-face classes are still valuable—but they will force them to adapt. Those that offer poor value for money will have to shape up, or disappear.

Task Q&A

Directions: Please answer these questions based on the article.

1. Is college education worth the price?
2. Are all degrees equally useful?
3. According to the article, what degrees have offered returns worse than zero?
4. What trend in education allows students to have access to classes without paying too much?

(2) Higher Education: Creative Destruction

(See:http://www.economist.com/news/leaders/21605906-cost-crisis-changing-labour-markets-and-new-technology-will-turn-old-institution-its.)

Vocabulary

entitlement	[ɪn'taɪtlmənt] *n.* 授权应得权益；命名，被定名
disruptive	[dɪs'rʌptɪv] *adj.* 分裂性的，破坏的，扰乱的
stagnant	['stægnənt] *adj.* 不流动的，不景气的；迟钝的，呆笨的
productivity	[ˌprɒdʌk'tɪvətɪ] *n.* 生产率，生产力
boost	[buːst] *vt.* 促进，提高；增加；吹捧；向上推起
accreditation	[əˌkredɪ'teɪʃn] *n.* 委派，信赖，鉴定合格
certified	['sɜːtɪfaɪd] *adj.* 被鉴定的；被证明的；有保证的；公认的
halt	[hɔːlt] *n.* 停止，中止 *vt. & vi.* 使停止；使中断；阻止；停止
prop up	支持，资助
welfare state	福利国家
pick up the slack	拯救颓势

Higher education is one of the great successes of the welfare state. What was once the privilege of a few has become a middle-class entitlement, thanks mainly to government support. Some 3.5m Americans and 5m Europeans will graduate this summer. In the emerging world universities are booming: China has added nearly

30m places in 20 years. Yet the business has changed little since Aristotle taught at the Athenian Lyceum: Young students still gather at an appointed time and place to listen to the wisdom of scholars.

Now a revolution has begun thanks to three forces: rising costs, changing demand and disruptive technology. The result will be the reinvention of the university.

Higher education suffers from Baumol's disease—the tendency of costs to soar in labour-intensive sectors with stagnant productivity. Whereas the prices of cars, computers and much else have fallen dramatically, universities, protected by public-sector funding and the premium employers place on degrees, have been able to charge ever more for the same service. For two decades the cost of going to college in America has risen by 1.6 percentage points more than inflation every year.

For most students university remains a great deal; by one count the boost to lifetime income from obtaining a college degree, in net-present-value terms, is as much as \$590,000. But for an increasing number of students who have gone deep into debt—especially the 47% in America and 28% in Britain who do not complete their course—it is plainly not value for money. And the state's willingness to pick up the slack is declining. In America government funding per student fell by 27% between 2007 and 2012, while average tuition fees, adjusted for inflation, rose by 20%. In Britain tuition fees, close to zero two decades ago, can reach £9,000 (\$15,000 a year).

The second driver of change is the labour market. In the standard model of higher education, people go to university in their 20s: a degree is an entry ticket to the professional classes. But automation is beginning to have the same effect on white-collar jobs as it has on blue-collar ones. According to a study from Oxford University, 47% of occupations are at risk of being automated in the next few decades. As innovation wipes out some jobs and changes others, people will need to top up their human capital throughout their lives.

By themselves, these two forces would be pushing change. A third—technology—ensures it. The Internet, which has turned businesses from newspapers through music to book retailing upside down, will upend higher education. Now the MOOC, or "Massive Open Online Course", is offering students the chance to listen to star lecturers and get a degree for a fraction of the cost of attending a university.

MOOCs started in 2008, and, as often happens with disruptive technologies, they have so far failed to live up to their promise. Largely because there is no formal system of accreditation, drop-out rates have been high. But this is changing as private investors and existing universities are drawn in. One provider, Coursera, claims over 8m registered users. Though its courses are free, it bagged its first \$1m in revenues last year after introducing the option to pay a fee of between $30 and $100 to have course results certified. Another, Udacity, has teamed up with AT&T and Georgia Tech to offer an online master's degree in computing, at less than a third of the cost of the traditional version. Harvard Business School will soon offer an online "pre-MBA" for $1,500. Starbucks has offered to help pay for its staff to take online degrees with Arizona State University.

MOOCs will disrupt different universities in different ways. Not all will suffer. Oxford and Harvard could benefit. Ambitious people will always want to go to the best universities to meet each other, and the digital economy tends to favour a few large operators. The big names will be able to sell their MOOCs around the world. But mediocre universities may suffer the fate of many newspapers. Were the market for higher education to perform in future as that for newspapers has done over the past decade or two, universities' revenues would fall by more than half, employment in the industry would drop by nearly 30% and more than 700 institutions would shut their doors. The rest would need to reinvent themselves to survive.

A New Term

Like all revolutions, the one taking place in higher education will have victims. Many towns and cities rely on universities. In some ways, MOOCs will reinforce inequality both among students (the talented will be much more comfortable than the weaker outside the structured university environment) and among teachers (superstar lecturers will earn a fortune, to the fury of their less charismatic colleagues).

Politicians will inevitably come under pressure to halt this revolution. They should remember that state spending should benefit society as a whole, not protect tenured professors from competition. The reinvention of universities will benefit many more people than it hurts. Students in the rich world will have access to higher education at lower cost and greater convenience. MOOCs' flexibility appeals to older people who need retraining: edX, another provider, says that the median age of its online students in America is 31. In the emerging world online courses also offer a way for countries like Brazil to leap-frog Western ones and supply higher education much more cheaply. And education has now become a global market: the Massachusetts Institute of Technology discovered Battushig Myanganbayar, a remarkably talented Mongolian teenager, through an online electronics course.

Rather than propping up the old model, governments should make the new one work better. They can do so by backing common standards for accreditation. In Brazil, for instance, students completing courses take a government-run exam. In most Western countries it would likewise make sense to have a single, independent organisation that certifies exams.

Reinventing an ancient institution will not be easy. But it does promise better education for many more people. Rarely have need and opportunity so neatly come together.

Task: Q&A

Directions: Please answer these questions based on the article.

1. What factors have caused the revolution of modern higher education?
2. Is the Internet helpful or harmful to the traditional way of education?
3. What kind of universities may suffer from the on-line courses?
4. What is the author's attitude towards the new model of learning and teaching?

Part 3 Listening and Speaking Practice

Pass 1 Helpful Tips in Choosing US School

(Difficulty: ★★★)

背景知识

美国大学录取方式

美国大学总体来说有三种录取方式，即早期录取 (Early Decision)、早期行动 (Early Action) 和常规录取 (Regular Decision)。前两者简单地说就是提前录取，最后一种是常规录取。

早期录取即在早期申请中获得录取，只可申请一所学校。被学校录取后不得申请其他学校。早期行动与早期录取相同，但是被录取后仍可申请其他学校。

这两种申请截止日期比较早，通常在每年的 11 月 1 日或 11 月中旬，录取结果在 12 月中旬就能知道，适合申请美国排名前 50 的大学的学生。一般来说，这些学生的中学平均成绩应达 85 分以上，托福 95 分左右（或雅思 6.5 ~ 7 分），SAT 成绩至少 1 800 分以上。

虽然早期录取和早期行动的申请时间和适用对象相近，但它们之间仍有较大差别。走早期录取途径的学生一旦被学校录取，就不能再选择其他学校了。也就是说，学生只能申请一所提供早期录取的学校，而且如果被录取的话，就必须选它，就算其他学校提供更好的条件，学生也没有权利更改决定。不过如果没被录取，依然可以正常申请常规录取。

早期行动的要求相对宽松，可以同时申请多所学校，录取结果不会绑定，遇到更好的可以更换。如果被学校拒绝，其他申请也不会受影响。不过有这种申请模式的学校并不是很多，而且通常要求比较高。学生可在次年的 4 月或 5 月答复学校是否会入学。

需要注意的是，同一个学校早期录取和早期行动两种方式不能同时进行，两者只能选其一。

常规录取一般 12 月底左右截止申请，次年 4 月录取，比较适合申请全美 50 名以后的大学的学生，一般来说，他们要达到托福 80 分或者雅思 6.5 分。如果通过常规录取申请美国前 50 名的学校，要求则比早期录取和早期行动高。申请全美前 50 名综合性大学的本科，拿到奖学金的概率都不高。

所以如果学生想申请奖学金，可以考虑文理学院。这类学校把所有资源都用在了本科生教育上，所以其本科教育质量并不亚于排名靠前的综合性大学，而它们一般都会为留学生提供高额奖学金。申请时同样可在以上三种途径中选择，跟综合性大学是一样的。

（资料来源：www.asarts.cn 2015-11-07。）

Task 1 General Understanding

Directions: Listen to the clip and then sum up its main idea. You may do this either in Chinese or English.

Task 2 True or False

Directions: Listen to the passage and tell whether the following statements are true or false (T/F).

1. ( ) Admission is very competitive for international students, so it's important to apply to as many institutions as possible to have a reasonable chance of acceptance.
2. ( ) To get admitted to an ideal American school, applicants can only refer to college rankings of the US.
3. ( ) The right school is the one that best meets your own personal needs and interests, as well as people's assessment of the institution's prestige.
4. ( ) Those who want to transfer to a new field must pass certain exams on the subject first.
5. ( ) It helps to limit the search to one region of the US, such as the east or the west coast, before looking for schools that match other requirements.

Task 3 Listening Comprehension

Directions: Choose the correct answers to the following questions based on your listening.

1. According to the passage, which of the following difficulties is NOT mentioned as faced by Chinese university students who want to go to the US for further study?
   A) Language efficiency exams.
   B) Choosing a suitable school.
   C) Financial circumstances.
   D) Academic scores.
2. In order to be admitted, the following advices are offered EXCEPT ________.
   A) applying to different institutions at the same time
   B) trying to apply to schools that are not too selective of students' performance
   C) making full use of the college rankings
   D) making sure the courses of your chosen subjects have been generally covered in your college period
3. When considering the schools, what condition among the following is the mostly helpful to your future study?
   A) A school of good prestige.
   B) A school that you like very much.

C) A department with some recognition, in whatever field.

D) A well-known professor who will be ready to assist you in your personal issues.

4. Among the following statements of US school, which one is NOT mentioned?

   A) The most important factors in choosing a location are climate and living costs.

   B) Living costs are higher in large cities like New York and Boston.

   C) Living costs in cities like Pittsburgh and Seattle are relatively lower.

   D) Cities in the south cost less.

5. Among the following popular states for international students, which are mentioned in the passage?

   A) California, Massachusetts, Ohio, and Missouri;

   B) Florida, Illinois, Michigan, and New Jersey;

   C) Massachusetts, Ohio, Missouri, and Texas;

   D) Oklahoma, Florida, Illinois, and New Jersey.

Task 4 Blank Filling

Directions: Listen to the leading part of the clip again and fill in the blanks in the following sentences.

For most (1) ___________, the US is (2) ___________ for further education. But apart from (3) ___________ such as the GRE and TOFEL exams, choosing a good graduate school is (4) ___________. Admission is (5) ___________ for international students, so it's important to apply to (6) ___________ to have (7) ___________. Since the application to most universities (8) ___________, Chinese students usually (9) ___________ according to (10) ___________.

To (11) ___________, at least (12) ___________ of the applications should be to (13) ___________. Applicants shouldn't (14) ___________ to (15) ___________. Furthermore, one (16) ___________ college rankings. The right school is the one that (17) ___________ your own (18) ___________, rather than someone else's (19) ___________ of an institution's (20) ___________.

Task 5 Retelling

Directions: Listen to the video clip again and retell the gist of the clip with the aid of words and phrases.

1. a favorite destination for further education

2. obstacles such as the GRE and TOFEL exams
3. competitive for international students
4. chance of acceptance
5. financial circumstances
6. limit their choices to
7. one's personal interests and academic background
8. transfer to a new field
9. some recognition
10. a well-known professor
11. match requirements

Task 6 Back Translation

Directions: Translate the following sentences into English based on your listening.

1. 对于多数中国大学生而言，美国是理想的继续深造的地方。

____

____

2. 不过除了 GRE 和托福考试，选择一所好的研究生院不是简单的事。

____

____

3. 入学遴选竞争激烈，所以有必要申请几所院校，以增加被接收的概率。

____

____

4. 有时，在寻找符合条件的学校之前，先将范围确定在某一个区域，如东岸或是西岸，会有所帮助。

____

____

Pass 2 Brain

(Difficulty: ★★★)

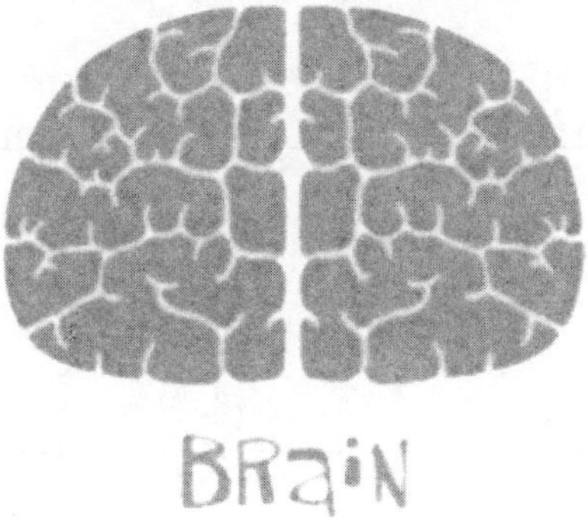

背景知识

你的大脑还有多少潜能？

在科幻电影《超体》中，“你的大脑只被使用了10%”这个由来已久的说法变成了“现实”。但事实又是怎样的呢？

福克斯帕金森氏症研究基金会于2013年在美国进行了一次调查，65%的人相信“你的大脑只被使用了10%”这个谬论，这比相信进化论的人还多5%。美国科普节目《流言终结者》在这个问题上也一改之前的否定态度，抛出新的理论：人们对大脑的利用率不是10%，而是35%。

跟所有的传言一样，这个谣言究竟从何而起已不可考，但是普林斯顿大学的神经科学家萨姆·王（Sam Wang）认为，这个理论应该是由促人自我提高的“成功学”推广起来的。20世纪初，现代最有影响力的思想家威廉·詹姆斯提出“人类还有未发挥的智力潜能”，这个说法大家都不陌生，也非常可信，但是后来有人胡乱篡改了这句话。

无论从哪个角度来说，所谓的只使用了10%都是荒谬的。大脑每时每刻都处于全体活跃状态，大脑作为一个器官是一个整体，其中的神经元及后勤细胞没有一分钟是停止运行的。这怎么能说只使用了10%呢？

纽约大学神经学及心理学教授乔·勒杜（Joe LeDoux）认为，现在的人可能被核磁共振成像拍摄出的大脑图片误导了，上面只标示出大脑活动剧烈的区域。通常所说的大脑的某些地方被激活了，就是指这种情况。

神经科学作为一个学科还未完全发展成熟，但是大众常常误以为它已经非常完备和高深了。各种谣言和谬论因此纷纷出炉，并长盛不衰。

（资料来源：http://zhidao.baidu.com/daily/view?id=3061。）

Task 1 Word Hunting

Directions: Try your best to spot the following words and expressions while listening to the news report.

1. 天才

____

2. 额外的空间

____

3. 凡夫俗子

____

4. 肌肉

____

5. 调查

____

6. 尚未发现的

____

Task 2 True or False

Directions: Listen to the video clip again and tell whether the following statements are true or false (T/F).

1. (   ) One of the speakers think geniuses are born.
2. (   ) Only 10 percent of your brain is used.
3. (   ) We can't increase the capacity of the brains.
4. (   ) We can train our brain muscles by climbing mountains.
5. (   ) There are still a lot of unknown things within our brain.

Task 3 Retelling

Directions: Listen to the video clip again and retell the gist of the clip with the aid of words and phrases.

1. geniuses
2. how much of the brain do we use
3. spare capacity

4. surplus
5. muscle
6. climb a mountain
7. things that people have never seen before
8. investigate
9. undiscovered

Task 4 Blank Filling

Directions: Listen to the video clip again and fill in the blanks in the following sentences.

Are geniuses born? Or (1) __________?

That's (2) __________. My feelings are that (3) __________. So how much of the brain(4) __________ every day?

I've no doubt that you use, oh, (5) __________, and you've got (6) __________.

But for us, mere (7) __________, we use all our brain (8) __________. There's no sort of (9) __________. But what you can do is (10) __________. It is (11) __________.

For me it's like (12) __________ and I'd say it's exactly (13) __________ I go to the mountains because you see things that (14) __________. When you (15) __________, that's how (16) __________ within it.

Task 5 Oral Practice

Directions: Prepare a mini-presentation on the following questions:

1. Do you think all the geniuses are born? Why or why not?
2. Have you encountered anyone who's a genius? What is his/her talent?
3. What is your suggestion to improve one's brain capacity in daily life?
4. How would you train your brain in the future?

Task 6 Back Translation

Directions: Translate the following sentences into English based on your listening.

1. 大脑的潜能就像肌肉一样，是可以通过锻炼来增强的。

____

2. 我们去爬山是因为那里有我们未曾见过的风景。

____

Pass 3 UK Report on Pronunciation

(Difficulty: ★★★)

背景知识

英语美语的发音变化

琼斯 (Daniel Jones) 的《英语发音词典》(*English Pronouncing Dictionary*) 自 1917 年问世以来，不得不每几年就修订一次。

琼斯在世时直接参与修改的最后一版发音词典是第 12 版，这已是四五十年前的事了。而后琼斯的接班人继续发音词典的修订，至今已出了第 15 版（截至 2001 年）。新近几版的发音词典反映了英国英语发音和美国英语发音的最新变化，具有极大的认识价值和应用价值。

英国伦敦大学语音学教授吉姆逊 (A.G. Gimson) 在 1967 年琼斯逝世前不久就修订了《英语发音词典》，出了第 13 版。10 年后吉姆逊再次修订了发音词典，出了第 14 版。人工排版的第 14 版的全部内容被转化为一个计算机数据库，并进行了更新和增补。

1997 年英国剑桥大学出版了由彼得·洛奇 (Peter Roach) 和詹姆斯·哈特曼 (James Hartman) 修订的第 15 版《英语发音词典》。编者在该版《前言》中指出，如果说第 15 版前的“标准英语 (RP)”指在英国依然广泛地被人们所接受、能被人们听懂的一种口音的话，第 15 版《英语发音词典》采用的英国发音典范具有更加广泛的基础，更普遍地被人们听到。此外，第 15 版《英语发音词典》还增加了一种普遍被人们所接受的美国英语发音，它所采用的典范和“通用美国发音 (General American)”很接近。

至于美国英语，其起源于英国殖民者在 17 世纪移入北美洲太平洋沿岸时带去的英语。美国的语言学家们一致认为：这些殖民者的英语就是当时英国的标准英语。现代美国英语在发音上仍保持着 17 世纪英国标准英语的一些特点。从近几十年美国英语发音变化中可以看到早期现代英语向现代英语发展的一段轨迹，还可以了解到美国英语与英国英语相互影响的内在原因：美国英语与英国英语是处在不同语音发展阶段的同一种语言。这从美国英语音素与英国英语音素的比较中就可以得知。

（资料来源：http://www.cnki.com.cn/Article/CJFD2001-LBJX200101006.htm。）

Task 1 General Understanding

Directions: Listen to the clip and then sum up its main idea. You may do this either in Chinese or English.

Task 2 Word Hunting

Directions: Try your best to spot the following words and expressions while listening to the news report.

1. 雷区

____

2. 社会语言学家

____

3. 大英图书馆

____

4. 就个人而言

____

Task 3 True or False

Directions: Listen to the video clip again and tell whether the following statements are true or false (T/F).

1. ( ) Now as any English speaker knows there are a whole range of ways to pronounce the language.
2. ( ) Researchers at the British Library are recording people to find out how English pronunciation evolves.
3. ( ) There is no right or wrong in terms of pronunciation.
4. ( ) Older dictionaries recommend certain pronunciation as the approved form of some word. But increasingly over time, modern dictionaries accepted more alternatives.

5. (　) The British Library wants as many people as possible to read Mr. Tickle to say how spoken English is changing.

Task 4　Listening Comprehension

Directions: Choose the correct answer to the following questions based on your listening.

1. Pronunciations of the following words were discussed in the video EXCEPT ________.
   A) say mischievous scallop "H"
   B) say eat scallop hatch
   C) ate scallop harass "H"
   D) says ate harass hatch
2. Among the following statements of "says", which is right?
   A) For English speakers, they have different ways of pronouncing the word.
   B) David Sillito believes /sez/ is right instead of /seiz/.
   C) Younger speakers are saying /sez/ due to the spelling.
   D) According to a socio-linguistic, /sez/ is the recommended way of pronouncing.
3. How do dictionaries cope with the shifting of pronunciation?
   A) If you pronounce "ate" as /eit/ instead of /et/, it's wrong.
   B) Dictionaries recommend /et/ as the approved form of "ate".
   C) Modern dictionaries accept /eit/ as well.
   D) Different dictionaries have different standards.
4. The script of "Another casualty of the combat, although a luxury, its inherent beauty, its pristine condition…" sounds odd, yet it was ________.
   A) all official BBC pronunciations in 1982
   B) all official CNN pronunciations in 1982
   C) all official BBC pronunciations in 1928
   D) all official CNN pronunciations in 1928

Task 5　Blank Filling

Directions: Watch the leading part of the video clip again and fill in the blanks in the following sentences.

Now as any English speaker knows there are (1) __________ to pronounce the language. …Well, (2) __________ at the British Library are (3) __________ to find out how (4) __________. David Sillito enters (5) __________.

……

So who is right? Meet Jonnie Robinson, (6) __________ from the British Library.

……

Well, interestingly you said right or wrong. Obviously, there is no right or wrong (7) __________. But certainly the dictionaries, older dictionaries recommend /et/ as (8) __________. But (9) __________, we've seen (10) __________ accepting /eit/ as (11) __________.

Task 6 Oral Practice

Directions: Start a discussion with your partners on the following topics.

1. Do you think there's right or wrong in pronouncing English for Chinese students?
2. What accent of English do you prefer to acquire as a language learner?
3. Have you ever been bothered with someone who's speaking non-standard English?
4. Do you think it's important for Chinese students to spend a lot of time and energy in training themselves with standard English?

Pass 4 South Korea's Silence

(Difficulty: ★★★★)

背景知识

韩国高考

韩国高考又称“大学修业能力考试”，每年的11月中旬举行，每年都有数十万名考生参加考试，而录取率只有50%。在高考当天，整个韩国的空气中似乎都弥漫着紧张气氛，曾有韩国学生形容本国高考是一场“核战役”。

韩国高考时间安排十分紧凑，考生要在一天内考完数理、语言、外语、社会探究或科学探究4门科目。与中国不同的是，韩国高考不计算总分，而是各科目分别打分，然后依据分数段确定各科目的等级以及综合等级。各大学将根据各科目考试等级、学生手册、面试成绩、学生专长等情况招收学生。

在大部分韩国人眼里，高考成绩会影响一个人的人生轨迹。勤奋学习的同时，他们也会通过一些奇葩的方式为高考求好运。高考前，会有不少考生偷走韩国现代索纳塔轿车或者三洋卡车上的金属标志牌，这两种车的标志上都有字母“S”，而“S”在韩国的高考季节代表着顶尖大学首尔国立大学。高考的当天，低年级学生会早早来到校门口，为赴考的学长学姐们呐喊、打气，红旗招展、锣鼓喧天，跪拜大礼齐上阵。亲朋好友也会送年糕和巧克力给考生，就是为了祈愿考生能像年糕一样榜上有名。在考前最忌讳的是海带，因为海带比较油腻，吃了会有落榜之嫌。考生也绝对不会吃有裂缝的鸡蛋，认为有裂缝的鸡蛋会带来坏运气。这些奇怪的考前习俗，对于希望通过高考改变人生轨迹的小伙伴来说只怕还不够多。

高考这一天，政府机构和企业都会把上班时间推迟两个小时，警察机构要求驾驶员不得在学校附近鸣喇叭，驻韩美军被要求停止实弹演习和航空任务。

（资料来源：http://learning.sohu.com/20150915/n421206576.shtml。）

Task 1 General Understanding

Directions: Listen to the clip then sum up its main idea. You may do this either in Chinese or English.

Task 2 Word hunting

Directions: Try your best to spot the following words and expressions while listening to the news report.

1. 为考生加油！

____

2. 必须保持安静，这是命令！

____

3. 不得鸣笛

____

4. 不能穿发出响声的鞋子

____

5. 大惊小怪

____

6. 薪水的多少

____

Task 3 True or False

Directions: Watch the video clip again and tell whether the following statements are true or false (T/F).

1. ( ) 70,000 South Korean high school students took the test last week.
2. ( ) The exam took 6 hours.
3. ( ) Government imposed strict restrictions on planes and cars on the day of the college entrance exam.
4. ( ) South Koreans believe the test can decide whom the students are going to marry eventually.

Task 4 Listening Comprehension

Directions: Choose the correct answer to the following questions based on your listening.

1. What measures does the society take on the day of the College Entrance Exam in South Korea?
   A) Younger kids cheered on the test-takers.
   B) Police motorcycles send the late ones to school.
   C) Relatives prayed outside the school gates for good results.
   D) All of the above.
2. Which of the following is NOT in the belief of South Korean people?
   A) The test determines which college a student will go to.
   B) The test determines which company they will not then work at.
   C) The test determines the size of their eventual paycheck.
   D) The test determines whom they will marry.

Task 5 Blank Filling

Directions: Watch the video clip again and fill in the blanks in the following sentences.

And now for the last look. Those of you (1) __________ saw (2) __________ of South Korean students. The culmination of that pressure was last week when (3) __________ took the test (4) __________ working toward.

It was (5) __________ outside (6) __________ as younger kids cheered on (7) __________ as they arrived. Police motorcycles even (8) __________. But when it came time for (9) __________ to (10) __________, silence was the order. Planes were (11)__________. Honking was (12) __________. And teachers refrained from (13) __________ for fear of (14) __________. Relatives (15) __________ for good results.

Why all the fuss? Well, it's widely believed in South Korea that this test (16) __________, which company (17) __________, the size of (18) __________, and even whom (19) __________. That's pretty (20) __________.

Task 6 Oral Practice

Directions: Start a discussion with your partners on the topic of whether the College Entrance Exam in South Korea is a "fuss".

Pass 5 Rural School in China

(Difficulty: ★★★★)

背景知识

世界的文盲与失学儿童现状

联合国教科文组织2004年公布：全世界被剥夺上学权利的儿童有1.26亿人，女童占56%；他们中超过1/3的孩子从来都没有进过教室。也就是说，全世界每六个儿童中，就有一个没在接受教育。

联合国教科文组织和联合国儿童基金会的报告指出：在这1.26亿失学儿童中，有1.1亿多失学儿童生活在发展中国家，尤其是最不发达国家，一半在亚洲。相比之下，在工业化国家里，只有200多万儿童没能上学。

另据世界劳工组织公布：当今世界上大约有2.56亿5至17岁不等的童工。他们中超过1亿的孩子不能上学，或是被剥夺了正常的儿童生活。

在中国，政府实施九年义务教育，各地均有"希望工程"基金会专门用来帮助失学儿童上学，"希望小学"也是风起云涌，努力争取让所有孩子不因没有钱而读不起书。很多名人公开或是私下赞助孩子们读书或是给学校捐款。他们的慷慨解囊，使一批批孩子重返校园。

国际上还有不少类似于中国的"希望工程"的慈善会，每年都有无数慈善人士慷慨解囊，帮助了很多由于经济原因失学的孩子重返校园。比尔·盖茨就是其中的一位，他几年内捐赠了几亿美元用于建学校，资助儿童上学，为生病的孩子们打疫苗。中国香港的李嘉诚等也数次为中国的教育事业捐赠大项基金。正因为他们的关注，大量失学儿童圆了他们的读书梦。

（资料来源：http://news.youth.cn/sh/201412/t20141202-6148275.htm。）

Task 1 General Understanding

Directions: Listen to the clip and then sum up its main idea. You may do this either in Chinese or English.

Task 2 Word Hunting

Directions: Try your best to spot the following words and expressions while listening to the news report.

1. 辍学

____

2. 奢侈的事情

____

3. 减免学费

____

4. 小学和初中

____

5. 生活补贴

____

6. 菜地和果园

____

7. 劳动课

____

8. 模范，示范

____

9. 额外资源

____

10. 光秃秃的岩石

____

Task 3 True or False

Directions: Listen to the video clip again and tell whether the following statements are true or false (T/F).

1. ( ) Many pupils in remote areas of China have to drop out of school because they are girls.
2. ( ) One school in Yunnan Province has found a way to keep its students in the classrooms.
3. ( ) The central government has made policies requiring the local government to scrap tuition fees for the senior high school students.
4. ( ) All students take at least one labor class a week.

Task 4 Listen and Order

Directions: Please listen and write down the order of the sense groups mentioned in this report according to your memory.

( ) Many pupils in remote areas of China have to drop out of school.
( ) Education for children is a luxury.
( ) The money a girl saves can help her brother to go to school.
( ) Many students want to go to the outside world.
( ) As educators we're very sad to see students dropping out because of money.

Task 5 Blank Filling

Directions: Watch the video clip again and fill in the blanks in the following sentences.

For farmers who (1) __________, education for their children is (2) __________. The central government has made policies (3) __________ to (4) __________ for (5) __________ and (6) __________ students in (7) __________. The students are also (8) __________. But (9) __________ are still a large amount of money for poor families that earn (10) __________ a year.

……

It's not just (11) __________. They can use (12) __________ they have learned if they don't (13) __________ after graduation.

The way that Xijiekou School has followed (14) __________ for other schools in our county. It helps students (15) __________ in school without (16) __________ from the government.

Many students told me they want to (17) __________. But first thing's first. That means going to school to (18) __________ and then they can (19) __________ and get away (20)__________.

Feng Jintao, CCTV, for CNN World Report.

Task 6 Oral Practice

Directions: Start a mini-presentation on the following topics.

1. Why do many pupils in remote areas of China have to drop out of school?
2. What policies has the central government made to keep school students in the western regions?

3. According to CCTV reports, what solution has one school in Yunnan Province found to keep its students in the classrooms?
4. What are the advantages of keeping vegetable gardens and orchard near the classrooms?
5. At the end of this video, as what has been mentioned, what is the first priority of the students from rural families?

Task 7 Back Translation

Directions: Please watch the clip attentively and then translate the following Chinese sentences into English.

1. 经过多年探索之后，我们找到了一种帮助贫困学生们减少生活开支的方法。

____

2. 他们种植水果和蔬菜，收获了就可以自己食用了。

____

3. 很多学生愿意留在学校里，因为在家里不会吃得这么好，也没这么便宜。

____

4. 不仅是省钱。如果他们毕业后不继续接受教育的话，这些种植技能可以学以致用。

____

Pass 6 The Choosy in China

(Difficulty: ★★★★)

背景知识

大学生毕业等于失业吗?

毕业即失业，就目前来看，并非危言耸听。从 1999 年起，我国连续扩大招生规模，高等教育的发展从此进入新的阶段：平民化教育阶段。据相关统计，2001 年全国高校毕业生为 115 万人；而到了 2010 年，全国普通高校毕业生人数已经达到 631 万人；2012 年达到 680 万人；2013 年，全国普通高校毕业生规模已高达 699 万人。对于如此迅猛的毕业生增幅而言，工作岗位的增加则显得有限。毕业生就业面临的形势复杂而严峻。

大学生“毕业等于失业”的原因有以下几点：

1. 对工作的期望值太高：很多大学生毕业后找工作的期望值过高，或者说不能深入了解市场行情；对于工作存在幻想，容易将自己的工作定位为电视剧中的理想工作。

2. 缺乏工作经验：工作经验的缺乏是应届毕业生的最大诟病，被阻挡在职场门槛外的毕业生往往都是因为工作经验达不到企业的要求。

3. 专业知识、技术不过关：虽说工作内容往往与大学所学知识没有必要联系，但很多工作还是需要过硬的专业知识和技术，如医学、IT、设计、文学等领域的工作。如果大学期间专业知识和技术掌握不牢固，则是难以胜任的。

4. 行业选择不明确：很多学生迫于就业难、“断奶”生存等压力，在选择行业时来不及慎重考虑而盲目就业，导致很快辞职，陷入失业。

5. 工作岗位提供量与毕业生数量的差距：就业岗位数与毕业生人数的差距是毕业生找工作难的一个客观因素。随着每年毕业生人数的急剧增加，毕业生就业面临着一职难求的现象。

6. 供与求的错位和失衡：近年来，由于“热门专业”与“冷门专业”的选择导致相关专业人数的人满为患或人才匮乏；在职场中，“热门专业”人才过剩，而“冷门专业”却人才不足。

应该说，成功与否往往在于自己的心态，眼光不能只看重眼前的高工资、高待遇，应着眼于长远的职业规划，注重各方面的积累，包括人脉、经验、口碑、人际关系等对今后发展有利的东西。

（资料来源：http://www.studentboss.com/html/news/2013-12-12/142183.htm。）

Task 1 General Understanding

Directions: *Listen to the clip and then sum up its main idea. You may do this either in Chinese or English.*

Task 2 Word Matching

Directions: Match the English phrases on the left with those Chinese phrases on the right.

turn nose up	为……坚持/拖延着
hold out for	对……无动于衷

Task 3 Word Hunting

Directions: Try your best to spot the following words and expressions while listening to the news report.

1. 求职的毕业生
____

2. 噩梦
____

3. 过多的，富余的
____

4. 就业中心
____

5. 服务业
____

6. 高技术机械业
____

7. 技术人才
____

8. 制造业
____

9. 金融业
____

10. 劳动密集型的工作
____

11. 较高的社会地位

____

12. 低收入职位

____

13. 劳动与社会保障部

____

14. 谨慎的选择

____

15. 基本的生活保障

____

Task 4 True or False

Directions: Watch the video clip again and tell whether the following statements are true or false (T/F).

1. ( ) Some 6 million students have flooded into the job market in recent years.
2. ( ) This March, Chinese top officials warned that for some of the city's graduates there's a high possibility of unemployment.
3. ( ) It can be inferred from the video that girls are preferred to boys in the job market.
4. ( ) Job centers in Shanghai report that some industries like hotels, restaurants and high-tech machinery still can't find enough job-seekers.
5. ( ) Most students prefer positions such as finance.

Task 5 Listening Comprehension

Directions: Choose the correct answer to the following questions based on your listening.

1. Which of the following is NOT mentioned in this video?
   A) China has the largest number of college graduates in the world.
   B) 2 thirds of Chinese college graduates haven't found jobs so far this year.
   C) For most job-seekers 7 thousand *yuan* per month is not enough.
   D) The job-seekers can find job easily in Shanghai and Beijing.

2. Which of the following is a FALSE statement?
   A) What Shanghai needs most are technical talents.
   B) Most manufacturing industries can't find suitable candidates for the moment in China.
   C) The finance sector is welcomed among graduates.
   D) According to the Ministry of Labor and Social Security, over 75 percent of these jobless youngsters are unemployed for more than one year.
3. Which of the following can be inferred from the video?
   A) Educational authorities suggest both students and parents make prudent choices.
   B) The academic courses are not helpful in finding jobs.
   C) Students and parents have had unrealistic expectations of employment.
   D) Being employed in a low-end position is not encouraged by any parent.

Task 6 Blank Filling

Directions: Watch the leading part of the video clip again and fill in the blanks in the following sentences.

And China is (1) __________ by the millions. Some (2) __________ students (3) __________ so far this year. But as SBN explains many are turning their noses up at (4) __________ and holding out for (5) __________.

This March, Chinese top officials (6) __________ that the country will be having (7) ____________________________________. A season later such warnings (8) __________ for (9) __________ as graduation brings only (10) __________.

Except for some (11) __________ in our class, most boys haven't found jobs.

Our class has more than (12) __________, but even after a year of graduation, (13) __________ of them still remain (14) __________.

But the (15) __________ of job-seekers hasn't led to (16) __________. Job centers in Shanghai report some industries like (17) __________ and (18) __________ still can't find (19) __________ job-seekers even with wages as high as (20) __________.

Task 7 Oral Practice

Directions: Start a discussion with your partners on the following topics:

1. What is your expectation of jobs?
2. To start with, how much is your ideal salary?

3. Will you accept a job in the labor-intensive sector? Why and why not?
4. In order to find a suitable job, what should you do?
5. If you are temporarily unemployed, what would you do?

Task 8 Back Translation

Directions: Please watch the clip attentively and then translate the following Chinese sentences into English.

1. 对于很多人来说，毕业意味着失业。

____

2. 很多人对某些工作不屑一顾，却一心期望着赚大钱。

____

3. 对于有些毕业生而言，劳动密集型的工作意味着无聊、肮脏和没什么回报。

____

4. 有的毕业生宁愿待在家里等着好工作上门。

____

5. 教育部人士建议学生及家长谨慎选择学习课程以及就业方向，以符合市场需求。

____

Pass 7 Fisherman's Secret

(Difficulty: ★★★★)

背景知识

国际扫盲日

9 月 8 日是国际扫盲日。联合国教科文组织于 2011 年公布的调查报告显示，全球约有 7.93 亿成年人是文盲，他们既不会阅读，也不会书写。

总部设于法国巴黎的教科文组织称，成年人文盲中大部分是女性，而且分布非常集中，其中超过七成分布在撒哈拉以南的非洲、南亚和西亚等贫困地区。此外，全球约有 6 700 万适龄儿童无法接受小学教育，超过 7 200 万青少年无法接受中学教育。

文盲率指标除按两性合计人口计算外，按男女分别计算也具有重要意义，许多国家女性不识字或识字很少的比重超过男性。归根结底，是政治、社会、经济、伦理、习俗等多种因素导致。文盲率的高低不仅标志着一个国家的文化教育普及程度和发达程度，而且反映一个国家的经济发展程度。

文盲率在世界各国的差距比较大。虽然欧洲国家的扫盲率一直维持在较高水平，但一些中东欧国家依然存在大量文盲，对社会和经济的发展造成了负面影响。2008 年度《全民教育全球监测报告》的统计数据显示，在中东欧地区大约有 900 万成人文盲。此外，在欧洲的文盲当中，大部分人都不具备基本的生存技能，这给他们个人的生活和国家的发展都带来了很多不利影响。而这一点在一项调查中也得到过验证：在德国和斯洛文尼亚等国，文盲的失业率是受教育者的近 2 倍。

联合国教科文组织于 1965 年 11 月设立国际扫盲日，日期定为每年的 9 月 8 日，旨在动员世界各国及相关国际机构重视文盲现象，努力扫盲，促进世界各国普及初等教育，使适龄儿童都能上学，达到能够识字的基本水平，最终达到增进人际沟通，消除歧视，促进文化传播和社会发展的目标。

（资料来源：http://news.xinhuanet.com/gongyi/2011-09/06/c_121985359.htm。）

Task 1 General Understanding

Directions: Listen to the clip and then sum up its main idea. You may do this either in Chinese or English.

Task 2 Word Hunting

Directions: Try your best to spot the following words and expressions while listening to the news report.

1. 承认，招认

____

2. 出海的岁月

____

3. 捕龙虾的人

____

4. 渔船船长

____

5. 葡萄牙的，葡萄牙语

____

6. 退学

____

7. 生活智慧

____

8. 怀疑

____

9. 文盲

____

10. 学习障碍

____

11. 开发，利用

____

12. 慢性失眠

____

13. 副作用

____

Task 3 Listen and Order

Directions: Please listen and write down the order of the sense groups mentioned in this report according to your memory.

( ) His teachers kept promoting him to the next grade.

( ) Some night it's tempting to sacrifice sleep, but grab that rest if you can.

( ) It has become very popular, especially among people with learning disabilities.

( ) Studies show as the human brain ages, it becomes more difficult for someone to learn a new skill.

Task 4 Listening Comprehension

Directions: Choose the correct answer to the following questions based on your listening.

1. Among the following statements of Jim Henry, which one is NOT true?
   A) He is 90 years old.
   B) He was a lobsterman and fishing boat captain.
   C) He has a Portuguese origin.
   D) His family and friends didn't know he was illiterate.
2. What did Jim Henry do in his 90s?
   A) With the help of his family and friends, Henry began to teach himself.
   B) He went through the entire dictionary from back to front, reading and writing.
   C) He hired a tutor to look after him after his wife was ill.
   D) It took him 5 years to learn how to read and write.
3. Which statement of Jim Henry's book is WRONG?
   A) He had three stories stuck inside his head with no way to pass them along.
   B) His book is called "*In a Fisherman's Language*."
   C) It is a biography of him.
   D) It's a reflection of his life.
4. When is Jim Henry's birthday?
   A) On Sunday, April 19.
   B) On Monday, April 29.
   C) On Sunday, April 29.
   D) On Monday, April 19.
5. What can we learn from Jim Henry's longevity?
   A) Always get 8 hours of sleep every single night.
   B) Sleep deprivation has side effects.
   C) Sleep-deprived people need to consume more energy per day.
   D) All of the above.

Task 5 Blank Filling

Directions: Listen to the leading part of the video and then fill in the blanks.

Imagine (1) __________ from (2) __________ your whole life, something you know will (3) __________. And then one day (4) __________ you decide to (5) __________.

For (6) __________ years, Jim Henry (7) __________ —the lobsterman and fishing boat captain (8) __________.

I was so (9) __________ that I never (10) __________.

Growing up with a (11) __________, Henry was (12) __________ as a young child. His father (13) __________, so Henry (14) __________.

I didn't learn a thing. I didn't know nothing, (15) __________.

Task 6 Oral Practice

Directions: Start a mini-lecture on the following topic.

The Inspiring Story of Jim Henry.

Task 7 Back Translation

Directions: Please watch the clip attentively and then translate the following Chinese sentences into English.

1. 多年以来，他始终保守着一个秘密。

____

2. 亨利很小就出来工作了。

____

3. 他将整本字典从头到尾逐页读过。

____

4. 研究表明，随着年岁的增长，人的大脑会退化。

____

5. 亨利担心时间不够用了，所以他请了一个导师协助他。

____

6. 他有好多故事放在心里，但是没办法传达出来。

____

7. 现在有文字帮助了，他写了一本书，叫做《一名渔夫的话》，是对他人生的回顾。

____

8. 他说这是一条独特的道路。

____

9. 吉姆力图活过百岁，他的目标即将达成。

10. 睡眠少的人平均每天需要多摄入 300 卡路里。

Pass 8　Drugs Are Rampant in Schools

(Difficulty: ★★★★★)

背景知识

澳洲校园平均每周有 20 名学生因毒品问题被停学

据澳大利亚“新快网”报道，澳大利亚新州服用或持有毒品的学生数量已创新高，平均每周有 20 名学生因被搜出违禁药物而被要求停学。一些校长声称这是危机。

2013 年，新州学校对毒品犯罪的学生实施过 790 次长期停学处罚，几乎是 10 年来的最高值。新州教育及社区厅的数据显示，在 2012 年和 2013 年，涉嫌违禁品犯罪的学生被处以总计 1 539 次长期停学惩罚。

据报道，虽然许多吸毒或饮酒行为发生在校园外，但也有部分学生会在课室或操场变得病入膏肓，需要被送到医院接受治疗。一份调研显示，200 多名高中校长声称酒精和毒品对学生的学业有巨大的负面影响，迫使教师要花大量的时间帮助受影响的学生。

年轻人服食的毒品和酒精被指与精神健康问题及网络霸凌有关系。毒品问题委员会认为，学校需要政府、社区及药物酒精产业的大力支持。

（资料来源：http://news.xgo.com.cn/109/1093622.html。）

Task 1　General Understanding

Directions: Listen to the clip and then sum up its main idea. You may do this either in Chinese or English.

Task 2 Word Hunting

Directions: Try your best to spot the following words and expressions while listening to the news report.

1. 一小撮 ____________________
2. 大麻 ____________________
3. 处方药 ____________________
4. 药丸 ____________________
5. 藏匿 ____________________
6. 流行，瘟疫 ____________________
7. 因……成患的 ____________________
8. 市场 ____________________
9. 毒品和药物滥用国家研究中心 ____________________
10. 同伴 ____________________
11. 可卡因 ____________________
12. 毒品（口语） ____________________

Task 3 True or False

Directions: Watch the video clip again and tell whether the following statements are true or false (T/F).

1. ( ) Drugs have become a wide problem in American schools.
2. ( ) The students took some drugs out of adults' medicine cabinets.
3. ( ) Drug problem occurs both in juror high and senior high school.
4. ( ) Since 2002 the number of kids attending schools where drugs are used has jumped 29% in high school, up 36% in middle school.
5. ( ) Luckily, only below-average public high schools are affected with drug and alcohol abuse now.

Task 4 Listening Comprehension

Directions: Choose the correct answer to the following questions based on your listening.

1. At the beginning scene of this video, in a raid by policemen, we've discovered the following drugs in the high school EXCEPT ________.

   A) marijuana　　　　B) prescription drugs

C) coughing syrup　　D) pills

2. Among the following statements, which one is NOT true?
   A) Kids' getting high inside middle and high school is a very common scene now.
   B) The middle and high schools are really impacted by drugs.
   C) Most children in school have witnessed someone getting high.
   D) According to the video, these 6 teenagers are all student leaders at Whitewater Middle School.
3. Among the following statements of Whitewater School, which one is NOT true?
   A) It is located in Fayette County, Georgia just south of Atlanta.
   B) It is one of the premier public high schools in the country.
   C) Even here drug and alcohol abuse is an issue.
   D) Most of its student leaders are involved in drug abuse.
4. Which statement is statistically INCORRECT?
   A) In 1978 the school faced primarily alcohol and marijuana problem.
   B) According to a study 70% of high school students say they could buy marijuana somewhere on campus in an hour.
   C) In 2007, apart from marijuana, the school administration are facing cocaine and high levels crack, alcohol.
   D) 37% students say they could get a hand of the drugs in a day.

Task 5　Listen and Order

Directions: Please write down the order of the sense groups mentioned in this report according to your memory.

(　) That's one stash from one high school seized in one day.
(　) A show of hands if you've ever known anyone to be high in school, everybody.
(　) Pills are a favorite; they take them out of their parents' medicine cabinets.
(　) Our middle and high schools are really infested with drugs.

Task 6　Blank Filling

Directions: Watch the middle parts of the video clip and fill in the blanks in the following sentences.

This (1) ________ about the National Center on Addiction and Substance Abuse found that (2) ________ the number of kids attending schools (3) ________ has jumped (4) __________ up to 63% in middle school.

A (5) __________ if you've ever known anyone (6) __________, everybody.

But then again it's so hard (7) __________ it because it's so common now.

These 6 teenagers are (8) __________ at Whitewater High School in Fayette County, Georgia just (9) __________.

There's no benefit to (10) __________ to be (11) __________. Zero.

Whitewater is (12) __________ in the country.

Yet even here (13) __________ is an issue.

What would (14) __________ in 1978 face versus (15) __________?

……

Task 7 Oral Practice

Directions: Look at the following topics carefully and then choose one topic and deliver a short (1–3 minutes) presentation.

1. How serious is the drug problem in US school now?
2. What are the reasons behind?
3. What measures should we take to avoid such a situation?

Task 8 Back Translation

Directions: Please watch the clip attentively and then translate the following Chinese sentences into English.

1. 有的学校成了大麻市场和药丸的宫殿。

   ____

2. 对于你和你的同伴来说，跟毒品与酒精打交道没有好处。完全没有！

   ____

3. 专家们说，无论是孩子的肤色还是孩子的种族和居住地，这都是一个问题。

   ____

4. 如果家长们能更多地参与孩子们的生活，和他们多聊聊，即使这样不能解决全部问题，也意味着解决问题的开始。

   ____

Pass 9 Cool at School

(Difficulty: ★★★★★)

背景知识

加拿大学校允许学生上课使用移动电子设备

几年前，加拿大中小学系统还曾试图“对抗”学生带手机上课这一现象，在2007—2011年间，多伦多教育局禁止学生们在课堂上用手机，美国纽约市也曾有过类似禁令。然而，随着移动设备的大普及，此类禁令也越来越行不通，中小学系统意识到，不如利用新媒体的优势来促进教学。

位于魁北克省南部的东镇学区是整个北美最早采取这一做法的学区之一。从2003年开始，这个学区内3~11年级的学生每人都得到了一部笔记本电脑。

特里·卡森提(Thierry Karsenti)是蒙特利尔大学的教授，他对东镇学区实行1∶1项目的情况进行了评估。卡森提的研究(Karsenti's study)发现了许多令人鼓舞的数据，在实行1∶1政策后，该学区的辍学率从近40%下降到20%以下，学校在全省的排名上升，学生们上课更专心，也更主动。但卡森提也指出，别以为把平板电脑发到学生手里，他们就会开始学习了，学校必须提前培训教师，跟进新的教学方式，引导学生对自己负责，否则可能出现灾难性局面。他说，东镇学区的学校首先花了大量时间来培训教师，以确保学生们在课堂上用电脑来学习，而不是去干别的。

温哥华的一位家长表示，移动电子设备向孩子敞开了世界，有些父母感到紧张，但这也给孩子们打开了教育的空间，他们上课能学到更多东西，学习也更主动。

不列颠哥伦比亚省的教育部长彼得·法斯本德(Peter Fassbender)表示，技术是强大的工具，如果使用得当，将有助于学生的探索和学习。

（资料来源：http://www.bcbay.com/news/2015/09/02/360723.html。）

Task 1 General Understanding

Directions: Listen to the clip and then sum up its main idea. You may do this either in Chinese or English.

Task 2 Word Hunting

Directions: Try your best to spot the following words and expressions while listening to the news report.

1. 即将上大学 ______________________
2. 必备的高科技产品 ______________________
3. 完全安装所有需要的程序 ______________________
4. 学生折扣 ______________________
5. 划算的事情 ______________________
6. 闹钟没响 ______________________
7. 黑莓手机 ______________________
8. 保持与外界的联系 ______________________
9. 拍摄，记录 ______________________
10. 可兼容的存储卡 ______________________

Task 3 True or False

Directions: Watch the video clip again and tell whether the following statements are true or false (T/F).

1. ( ) Since you are heading off to college, it's time for you to give up toys.
2. ( ) The best thing about Mac is you can save up to 200 dollars using a student discount.
3. ( ) If you buy a Mac before September 6th, hopefully you will get an iPod for free.
4. ( ) You can use iPod to download classes and lectures.
5. ( ) An Apple iPhone and an LG envoi are both expensive.

Task 4 Listening Comprehension

Directions: Choose the correct answer to the following questions based on your listening.

1. What did the show recommend the college students to buy?
   A) Cell phones and computers.
   B) Cell phones, computers, and cameras.
   C) Cell phones, computers, cameras, and iPod.
   D) Cell phones, computers, cameras and printers.
2. According to the show, among the following tech toys, which is of No. 1 importance?
   A) A cell phone.
   B) A computer.
   C) A website.
   D) An alarm.
3. The procedures of printing photos in your dorm room include the following EXCEPT ________.
   A) insert a compatible memory card
   B) preview your shots
   C) make any adjustments using the colour LCD display
   D) apply digital frame

Task 5 Matching

Directions: Watch the video clip and match the brand names with their features as mentioned.

A. Mac
B. iPod
C. LG envoi
D. LG chocolate or Motoslvr
E. Canon powershot SD 1000 digital ELPH
F. A core photo printer also from Canon
G. a digital frame

1. ( ) You can save up to 200 dollars using a student discount.
   If you buy it before certain date, hopeful you'll get an ipod for free.
2. ( ) It has everything you will need to stay well-connected.
   It has a full keyboard.

The screen is great for picture and video over all a great phone.
It is not too expensive.

3. ( ) It is a phone that's also an MP3 player.
4. ( ) It is tiny enough to fit in your packet or your smallest purse.
   It's easy to use.
   The red-eye is automatically corrected when you take the picture.
5. ( ) It's easy to use.
   The quality of photos printed will last for a very long period of time.
6. ( ) It saves room.
   It's handy to use by just plugging.
   It can slid show of all your favorite pictures.
7. ( ) You can put it to good use.
   You can use it to download classical lectures at i-Tunes U.

Task 6 Blank Filling

Directions: Watch the concluding parts of the video clip and fill in the blanks in the following sentences.

When it comes to phones, enjoy (1) ___________ while you still can. If you can't (2) ___________, then what students can? Here is a few that (3) ___________. The LG envoi has everything you will need to (4) ___________. The (5) ___________ makes (6) ___________ easy and if you like to (7) ___________ all the time. Plus (8) ___________ for picture and video over all a great phone and (9) ___________. If you want a phone that's (10) ___________, the LG chocolate and Motoslvr are (11) ___________. Now (12) ___________ is not complete (13) ___________ to capture all your friends' (14) ___________. The Canon powershot SD 1000 digital ELPH camera is tiny enough to (15) ___________ or your (16) ___________. It's (17) ___________ and red-eye is (18) ___________ when you (19) ___________. Now smile and (20) ___________.

Task 7 Oral Practice

Directions: Look at the following topics carefully and then choose one topic and deliver a short (1–3 minutes) presentation.

1. Do you often use electronic devices?
2. If you can bring only one with you, which will you get?
3. Which brand of cell phone are you using right now?

4. Can you list the advantages and disadvantages of using tech toys for college students? Your reasons?

Task 8 Back Translation

Directions: Please watch the clip attentively and then translate the following Chinese sentences into English.

1. 如果你的妈妈处于空巢期，又远在德国，内置摄像头可以非常便捷地让她知道你正在大学生活中挣扎。

____

2. 你不可以因为睡过头而逃课。

____

3. 这些电子设备不至于贵到负担不起。

____

4. 打印的照片可以一百年不褪色。

____

5. 如果你没有足够的空间来收纳大部头的相册，用电子相框就可以看到你最喜欢的照片被逐一播放。

____

Pass 10 What Women Want: Affordable Child Care

(Difficulty: ★★★★★)

背景知识

各国的产假

国际劳工组织的《生育保障公约》规定，妇女产假应该不少于14周。如果妇女的产假被用人单位剥夺，应采取协商的方式来解决。生育保障应该反映在劳动合同以及工会代表工人和资方达成的协议中。如果用人单位有工会组织的话，女员工应该要求该工会代表与雇主协商获得应有的生育保障权利。如果妇女的权益被侵犯了，应该以"就业歧视"向相关政府劳工部门起诉。

事实上，在产假方面，瑞典是最慷慨的国家。瑞典法律规定，所有工作的父母每生育一个子女享有16个月（480天）的带薪产假，费用由国家和雇主分摊。在挪威，父母双方一共可以休47周的育儿假，拿全额工资；也可休57周，拿原来工资的80%，全部费用都由国家承担。在英国，从2010年4月开始，女性产假（包括流产、难产）可以申请52周，即一年的时间。产假的前6个星期，妈妈可以领取90%的工资，以后的33个星期，每周最多可以领取112.75英镑，再以后的13个星期，不领取工资。

同样是发达国家，在美国，没有母亲带薪产假这一说，只有母亲不带薪产假12周，父亲也是如此。这是所有工业化国家中最短的产假，而且还有一些限制，比如之前必须受雇于特定雇主12个月，其间至少工作1 250个小时等。

人权观察组织女权部门副主任华珍妮表示：虽然美国一直强调家庭，但在确保工薪家庭的福利方面却一直落后于其他发达国家。人权观察组织甚至在报告中称，缺乏带薪产假或事假可能导致诸多有害的结果，诸如产后抑郁症、母亲提前停止哺乳，甚至会迫使一些家庭陷入债务危机中。

（资料来源：http://insurance.cngold.org/c/2016-03-09/c3953600.html。）

Task 1 General Understanding

Directions: Listen to the clip and sum up its main idea. You may do this either in Chinese or English.

Task 2 Word Matching

Directions: Match the English phrases on the left with those Chinese phrases on the right before listening.

1. au pair 选择

2. opt for　　实现潜能，释放全部潜能
3. realize full potential; fully unleash the power　　平等的；互惠的

Task 3 Word Hunting

Directions: Try your best to spot the following words and expressions while listening to the news report.

1. 影响

____

2. 可以负担的幼儿托管服务

____

3. 房屋的按揭

____

4. 房屋的月租

____

5. 托管服务的候补名单

____

6. 划算

____

7. 根据情况作出调整

____

8. 带薪产假

____

9. 带薪病假

____

10. 打破了的壁垒

____

Task 4 True or False

Directions: Watch the video clip again and tell whether the following statements are true or false (T/F).

1. ( ) Unaffordable child care keeps some women from realizing their full potential.
2. ( ) One of the reasons why a woman might leave the work force is economic concern.
3. ( ) Child care in the States can be incredibly expensive and hard to find.
4. ( ) The wait lists were generally long in several day care centers.
5. ( ) According to Becky and Nick's experience, in order to get into a priority list, you need to put in nonrefundable deposit.
6. ( ) Nannies are getting paid like $50,000 a year.
7. ( ) Among readers of *Parents* magazine who use child care, 48 percent found it either challenging, very hard, or impossible to find quality care.
8. ( ) The advocacy group Child Care Aware says infant care at a day care center can cost as much as $15,000 a year for one child.

Task 5 Listening Comprehension

Directions: Choose the correct answer to the following questions based on your listening.

1. How does a temporary break impact a working woman?
   A) It is not that hard for a woman to get back in the labor force.
   B) It affects her career track slightly.
   C) She can continue the upward climb if she works hard enough.
   D) It hinders her career development.
2. Among the following statements of Dina Bakst, which one is NOT true?
   A) She works for a group of better balance.
   B) According to Dina's opinion, employers need to adjust to the current situation as well.
   C) Her group wants the federal government to expand the Family Medical Leave Act.
   D) The family medical leave act includes paid maternity leave and paid sick leave.
3. Which of the following condition is most logical?
   A) When women take the leave and have support, it makes child care costly yet keeps women on the job.

B) When women take the leave and have support, it makes child care less costly and also keeps women on the job.

C) When women take the leave and have no support, it does not make child care less costly and keep women on the job.

D) When women take the leave and have no support, it both makes child care costly yet can't keep women on the job.

4. According to the House minority leader, Nancy Pelosi, what social achievement is Not women have made so far?

A) Women have won the right to vote.

B) Women have broken barriers in education.

C) Women have won a place in the corporate board rooms.

D) Women have chance to work to their full potential.

5. What is the constructive advice to solve the problem so far?

A) To get an au pair instead of a full-time nanny.

B) To work from home sometimes.

C) To change the school day schedule 9:00 a.m. to 5:00 p.m.

D) To make the summer break a little shorter.

Task 6 Blank Filling

Directions: Watch the leading and concluding parts of the video clip and fill in the blanks in the following sentences.

CNN is looking at (1) __________, our Special Reporting on (2) __________ from (3) __________. Today, an issue that impacts (4) __________ out there is (5) __________. CNN's Lisa Sylvester is here. She's been looking it to the story for us. What do you find there?

Well, Wolf. You know, if you talk to (6) __________, one of the main reasons why (7) __________ is because of (8) __________. It can be (9) __________, and in some cases families are paying more for (10) __________ than for (11) __________. So, what do women want? Well, how about (12) __________, (13) __________?

……

And that goes a long way, having (14) __________. One complaint you hear a lot from parents is why is the school day (15) __________, when the work day is (16) __________? Other parents have suggested, how about making (17) __________ a little shorter? Then maybe, it won't (18) __________ and (19) __________. So, all of this, Wolf, just a little (20) __________.

Task 7 Oral Practice

Directions: Look at the following topics carefully and then choose one topic and deliver a short (1–3 minutes) presentation.

1. Why does child care become unaffordable for working parents in the States?
2. Why do most moms stay at home to take care of the kids?
3. What measures should the government and company heads take to relieve this pressure?

Task 8 Back Translation

Directions: Please watch the clip attentively and then translate the following Chinese sentences into English.

1. 女性离职的主要原因之一是孩子的托管问题。

   ____

2. 据说有一个地方，你付 500 美金不可退还的押金，才有可能上候补优先名单。

   ____

3. 我们终于获得候补机会的时候，索菲亚已经两岁了。

   ____

4. 如果这件事听起来很耳熟，那是因为多数父母都处于同样的局面。

   ____

5. 在美国的 36 个州，婴儿托管中心的费用比大学一年的学费还要高。

   ____

6. 即使是暂时离职，也会让一名女性很难回到工作行列，继续其职业上升道路。

   ____

7. 我们能有弹性工作制，运气真是不错。

   ____

Part 4 英语听说秘籍之吞音（Omission）

(Difficulty: ★★★★★)

英语中的吞音现象往往和连读一起出现。通常连读的情况有：(1)"辅音 + 元音"型连读（如 Not~at~all）；(2)"r/re+ 元音"型连读（如 Here~is a letter for you）；(3)"辅音 + 半元音"型连读（如 Thank~you）；(4)"元音 + 元音"型连读（如 How~and why did you come here?）

典型的吞音则在失去爆破的时候经常出现。

对此，我们需要知道，爆破音有 3 对 /p/ 和 /b/，/t/ 和 /d/，/k/ 和 /g/，一共是 6 个。失去爆破，又叫不完全爆破，指的是在某些情况下（特别是快速流利地说英语的时候），只做出发音的准备，但并不发音，稍稍停顿后就发后面的音。

这种失去爆破造成的吞音现象又可以分为两种：

第一种是"爆破音 + 爆破音"型。

当 6 个爆破音（/p/，/b/，/t/，/d/，/k/，/g/）中的任意两个相临时，前一个爆破音会失去爆破，即由相关的发音器官做好这个发音的姿势，稍做停顿后即发后面的爆破音。例如：The bi(g) bus from the fa(c) tory is full of people.

第二种是"爆破音 + 摩擦音"型。

如果前面是爆破音，其后紧跟着某些摩擦音（如 /f/，/s/，/w/，/t/ 等），那么前面那个爆破音仅有十分轻微的爆破，而后面那个摩擦音则要完全爆破。例如，Goo(d) morning, Mr. Bell. I wen(t) there alone a(t) nine las(t) night.

以下练习中，可以仔细根据录音中的 1、2、3 段进行模仿和跟读，感受吞音现象。方括号中的"[d]"和"[k]"等表示失去爆破，没有完全发音。

Whether the weather be fine, or whether the weather be not. Whether the weather be cold, or whether the weather be hot. We'll weather the weather whatever the weather whether we like i[t] or not.

How much woo[d] would a woodchuc[k] chuc[k] if a woodchuc[k] coul[d] chuc[k] woo[d]?

He'd chuck as much woo[d] as a woodchuc[k] coul[d] if a woodchuc[k] coul[d] chuc[k] woo[d].

Peter Piper picke[d] a peck of pickle[d] peppers. A peck of pickled peppers Peter Piper picke[d].

If Peter Piper picked a peck of pickled peppers, where's the peck of pickle[d] peppers Peter Piper picke[d]?

English Listening-and-Speaking Learning Planner

Monday Practicing Hour: ______ Tape Hour: ______ Commitment: ______	**Tuesday** Practicing Hour: ______ Tape Hour: ______ Commitment: ______	**Wednesday** Practicing Hour: ______ Tape Hour: ______ Commitment: ______	**Thursday** Practicing Hour: ______ Tape Hour: ______ Commitment: ______	**Friday** Practicing Hour: ______ Tape Hour: ______ Commitment: ______
Saturday Practicing Hour: ______ Tape Hour: ______ Commitment: ______	**Sunday** Practicing Hour: ______ Tape Hour: ______ Commitment: ______	**General Performance for Week ______:** (vocabulary, long sentence, background information, etc.) ______ Self-rating ☆☆☆☆☆		
Monday Practicing Hour: ______ Tape Hour: ______ Commitment: ______	**Tuesday** Practicing Hour: ______ Tape Hour: ______ Commitment: ______	**Wednesday** Practicing Hour: ______ Tape Hour: ______ Commitment: ______	**Thursday** Practicing Hour: ______ Tape Hour: ______ Commitment: ______	**Friday** Practicing Hour: ______ Tape Hour: ______ Commitment: ______
Saturday Practicing Hour: ______ Tape Hour: ______ Commitment: ______	**Sunday** Practicing Hour: ______ Tape Hour: ______ Commitment: ______	**General Performance for Week ______:** (vocabulary, long sentence, background information, etc.) ______ Self-rating ☆☆☆☆☆		

Chapter 3

Marriage

Part 1 Famous Quotes

A wise woman likes but doesn't love, listens but doesn't believe and leaves before she is left.

—Marilyn Monroe

聪明的女人会喜欢但不会深爱，会倾听但不会相信，会在被抛弃以前离开。

——玛丽莲·梦露

Women are made to be loved, not understood.

—Oscar Wilde

女人生来是被爱的，而不是被理解的。

——奥斯卡·王尔德

If you love somebody, let them go. If they return, they were always yours. If they don't, they never were.

—Anonymous

如果你真的爱上谁了，就放他走。如果他回来了，他永远是你的，如果没回来，他就从来未属于过你。

——匿名

Part 2 Background Knowledge

(1) Economist: One-Child Policy Changes Chinese Weddings

(Extracted from: *Economist*)

Vocabulary

personalized	['pɜːs(ə)n(ə)laɪzd]	*adj.*	个性化的
kowtow	[ˌkaʊ'taʊ]	*vi.*	叩头；顺从；唯命是从；（对……）卑躬屈膝
opulent	['ɒpjələnt]	*adj.*	富裕的；豪华的
frugality	[frʊ'gælətɪ]	*n.*	节约，朴素，节俭
extravagance	[ɪk'strævəgəns]	*n.*	奢侈，挥霍
nuptials	['nʌpʃlz]	*n.*	婚礼
swap	[swɒp]	*vt.*	用……替换；把……换成
dowry	['daʊrɪ]	*n.*	嫁妆；陪嫁
frippery	['frɪpərɪ]	*n.*	俗丽的装饰；无用的玩意儿
peripheral	[pə'rɪfərəl]	*adj.*	次要的
cupid	['kjuːpɪd]	*n.*	丘比特的画像或雕像
heart-shaped		*adj.*	心形的
fork out			付钱
one-child policy			独生子女政策

Oversized cupids in pink, furry outfits hand out heart-shaped balloons with "I Do" written on them in English at a wedding-theme trade fair in Beijing. Vendors offer romantic photo-shoots of couples under water or at a racetrack, personalized wedding cigarettes, and biscuits with names such as "Date & Fate". An emphasis on love is a new addition to Chinese weddings—and shines a pink-filtered spotlight on social change.

For centuries, marriage in China was about ensuring heirs for the groom's family. Ceremonies centered on the groom's kin: couples kowtowed to the man's parents but the woman's relatives were absent. Unusually, both the groom's and the bride's family exchanged money or goods. The more money changed hands, the more opulent the wedding.

After it came to power in 1949, the Communist Party imposed frugality. Dowries consisted of necessities like bed linen or a bicycle; guests brought their own food coupons. But since the 1980s the extravagance of nuptials has matched the country's rise. Celebrations moved out of homes into hotels. Brides swapped traditional red dresses for white, flouncy meringue-like ones (some now wear both, in sequence).

A large industry has emerged to serve the 13m couples who marry each year. Wedding planners are increasingly common, particularly in cities. A decade ago *Cosmo*

Bride, an American-owned lifestyle magazine, launched a Chinese-language edition in China. An average wedding cost $12,000 in 2011 (the latest year for which such data exist)—the equivalent of more than two years income for the average urban household. An increase in the average marriage age by 2.5 years since 1990 has given parents (who still usually pay for wedding, despite the earning power of their children) more time to save up.

The change in wedding frippery also reflects a fundamental shift in society. For the first time in the history of Chinese family life, the child—rather than ancestors or parents is regarded as the center of the family, says Yan Yunxiang of the University of California, Los Angeles. Most newly-weds now are single children, born since the one-child policy was introduced more than 30 years ago. Parents have more to spend if they only have to fork out for one wedding (they usually share costs with the spouse-to-be's family).

William Jankowiak of the University of Nevada, Las Vegas, who has documented relationship in China for 30 years, says love plays a larger part in young people's lives—both in choice of partners and in their relationships with parents. Love is far more often spoken about. The result is evident in weddings, which now focus on the couple. Both sets of parents are represented, but their position is peripheral. Wedding often feature a day of wedding photos, shot before the event, with the couple in a range of outfits against romantic backgrounds, but with no family members.

Task Q&A

Directions: Read the above material and answer the following questions.

1) What caused the extravagance in weddings nowadays?
2) What can people expect from the boom in extravagant weddings?

(2) Economist: The Ruling for Divorced Couple

(Extracted from: *Economist*)

Vocabulary

idle	['aɪdl]	*adj.*	懒惰的
jurisdiction	[ˌdʒʊərɪs'dɪkʃn]	*n.*	权限
ruling	['ruːlɪŋ]	*n.*	判决
bespoke	[bɪ'spəʊk]	*adj.*	定做的；预定的

wrangling	['ræŋgəlɪŋ] *n.*	争吵，争论，口角
tilt the balance		向……倾斜
lose on appeal		上诉失败
taper off		逐渐停止
dent one's attraction		削减……的吸引力

England becomes a slightly worse place for idle-ex-wives.

England has long been the jurisdiction of choice for wives who have the luxury of being able to choose where they divorce. English law (Scotland is different) tries to balance lifelong need and fairness. The poorer partner—typically a wife bringing up children—can expect housing and many years of income, especially if she has sacrificed her career for the marriage.

A court ruling on February 23rd has nonetheless continued a recent trend of tilting the balance a little towards husbands. Tracey Wright objected to her ex-husband's bid to cut her 75,000 ($116,000) annual maintenance, awarded after an 11-year marriage failed in 2008. She argued that she was too busy with the two children (one at boarding school, the other, aged ten, at home) even to look for work. She lost on appeal. Lord Justice Pitchford said Mr. Wright's payments should taper off as he neared retirement and that his ex-wife should get a job.

The ruling is a legal landmark chiefly because it sets out a mother's duty at least to have to seek a job as her children grow older. As David Hodson, a specialist lawyer, notes, that principle has long applied to poor women when it comes to claiming welfare benefits. But an ex-wife will still be able to argue that no suitable work is available for her and that she needs her ex-husband's help in order to keep up her own and her children's living standards. Such arguments would cut little ice in most other countries.

The ruling will not dent London's attraction as a global center for divorce. English divorce law, with its bespoke solutions reached after costly legal wrangling, is also likely to remain a luxury service, out of reach to all but the very rich.

Task Q&A

Directions: Read the above material and answer the following questions.

1) What is the duty that an ex-wife should fulfill before the ruling?
2) How does the ruling influence the divorced mother?

Part 3 Listening and Speaking Practice

Pass 1 Temporary Marriage

(Difficulty: ★★★)

背景知识

期限婚姻是对传统婚姻一纸定终身的挑战，由于种种原因，有些人结婚几年、十几年甚至几十年后，还是会闹离婚。有时，若另一方执意不离，则对其施以暴力胁迫，甚至会出现危及生命的家庭暴力，受害者又很少能得到及时的救助。因此，有人提出期限婚姻，即在结婚前签订协议，在规定的期限内结婚，期满后离婚，若想继续就续婚，期满后再离，如此反复。

由于并非所有国家都承认这类协议的法律效力，因此期满后若一方不履行协议，另一方也不能受到法律保护，所以依然无法保证协议的有效实施。实施期限婚姻的国家爱尔兰是一个信奉天主教的国家，该国禁止离婚。因此，爱尔兰人无不对婚姻大事格外慎重。爱尔兰人以高度的智慧，创造了一种兼顾传统和自由的婚姻制度。男女双方在结婚时，可以协商婚姻关系的期限，从 1 年到 100 年不等。办理结婚登记的费用，也因婚期的长短而不同，婚期越短，登记费用就越高，婚期越长，登记费用就越低。如果婚期为 1 年，需要 2 000 英镑；如果婚期为 100 年，则只需要 0.5 英镑。最高收费是最低收费的整整 4 000 倍，政府鼓励长久婚姻的政策一览无余。

Vocabulary

essential	[ɪ'senʃl]	*adj.* 基本的，必不可少的
vow	[vaʊ]	*n.* 誓言
expire	[ɪk'spaɪə(r)]	*vi.* 满期；终止
extension	[ɪk'stenʃn]	*n.* 延期
heartache	['hɑːteɪk]	*n.* 心痛，悲伤，伤心

Task 1 Matching

Directions: Match the English phrases on the left with those Chinese phrases on the right before listening.

1. the 7-year itch　　至死不渝
2. till death do us part　　七年之痒

Task 2 General Understanding

Directions: Listen to the clip and then sum up its main idea. You may do this either in Chinese or English.

Task 3 Word Hunting

Directions: Try your best to spot the following words and expressions while watching the video clip.

1. 离婚率 ________________
2. 转折点 ________________

Task 4 True or False

Directions: Watch the video clip again and tell whether the following statements are true or false (T/F).

1. ( ) The German politician's solution is radical.
2. ( ) The proposal has been approved by church.
3. ( ) Based on the proposal, marriages are time-based.

Task 5 Re-organizing Sentence Groups

Directions: Watch the video clip again and reorganize the sentence groups in order to retell the story.

1. a 7-year limit
2. church leaders
3. experience
4. financial and emotional heartache
5. divorce rate
6. to end in divorce
7. to last 7 years
8. second marriage

Task 6 Blank Filling

Directions: Watch the video clip again and fill in the following blanks.

I (1) __________ marriages to (2) __________ after 7 years.

That means in future people would (3) __________ only on a time-limited basis and would then (4) __________ say "yes" to (5) __________.

Task 7 Oral Practice

Directions: Look at the following topics carefully and then deliver a short (1–3 minutes) presentation on them.

1. Should we set a time-limit to marriage?
2. Should marriage be meant for a life time?

Task 8 Back Translation

Directions: Please watch the clip attentively and then translate the following Chinese sentences into English.

1. 7 年能免去诸多经济上和感情上的痛苦，还能够降低该国的离婚率。

____

2. 旧的体制是最好的，我们为什么不能好好地结婚并为美好的婚姻而努力呢？

____

Pass 2 Wedding Customs

(Difficulty: ★★★)

背景知识

目前塔吉克斯坦 (Tajikistan) 的男女比例是 1∶7，这说明在塔吉克斯坦出现了“男人稀缺”的现象。塔吉克斯坦总人口约为 700 万，其中近 100 万人由于贫困和失业而流亡到国外，大多数是去了俄罗斯。另外，1992 年至 1997 年的塔吉克斯坦内战造成了近 50 万人死亡，其中大多数为男性。这些原因对塔吉克斯坦的人口影响是巨大的，特别是造成了男女比例严重失衡。

在塔吉克斯坦，由于男少女多，使得一夫多妻现象非常普遍，尽管这是政府禁止的。在塔吉克斯坦，连说三遍“休妻”(divorce a wife) 是一种习俗化的表达方式。按照传统的做法，要想离婚，在证人面前说出这句话就足够了。对于男人来说，没有什么比这更简单的了。而对于女人来说，离婚则要困难得多，妻子必须要求丈夫说出这句话。

（资料来源：http://news.jqgc.com/guojixinwen/53848.html。）

Vocabulary

bride	[braɪd] *n.* 新娘，即将（或刚刚）结婚的女子
groom	[gruːm] *n.* 新郎
tab	[tæb] *n.* 账单；标签；制表
extravaganza	[ɪkˌstrævə'gænzə] *n.* 盛大的演出；盛大的活动
bankruptcy	['bæŋkrʌptsɪ] *n.* 破产
proceedings	[prə'siːdɪŋz] 进程（proceeding 的名词复数）

symbolic	[sɪm'bɒlɪk]	*adj.*	象征的，象征性的
Tajikistan	[tɑːˌdʒɪkɪ'stɑːn]	*n.*	塔吉克斯坦
be in full swing	活跃；蓬勃高涨		

Task 1 General Understanding

Directions: Listen to the clip and then sum up its main idea. You may do this either in Chinese or English.

Task 2 Word Matching

Directions: Match the English phrases on the left with those Chinese phrases on the right before listening.

1. stage huge wedding celebrations　　　增强团队意识
2. to bring a greater sense of community　　　举行盛大的婚礼庆典

Task 3 Word Hunting

Directions: Try your best to spot the following words and expressions while watching the video clip.

1. 防止人们陷入债务

____

2. 承担大部分费用

____

Task 4 True or False

Directions: Watch the video clip again and tell whether the following statements are true or false (T/F).

1. ( ) Tajikistan is one of the poorest countries in the former Soviet Union.
2. ( ) Families used to be on the verge of bankruptcy to stage huge wedding celebrations.
3. ( ) Government imposed strict restriction on the wedding proceedings to make it an extravaganza.

Task 5 Listening Comprehension

Directions: Listen again and choose the best answer from the choices marked A), B), C) and D).

1. Which of the following is TRUE?
   A) The bride's father is happy but helpless.
   B) The bride's brother is employed but her father unemployed.
   C) The bride's neighbors are in need of help.
   D) The bride's family managed to prepare the wedding independently.
2. Which of the following is FALSE about the new wedding law?
   A) It allows the wedding to last less than 3 hours.
   B) Only 150 guests should be invited at the wedding banquet.
   C) It challenged and changed the wedding tradition.
   D) There should be more than one dish to be served.
3. Which of the following is UNTOLD?
   A) The 18-year-old bride has been arranged to marry.
   B) The bride has known her bridegroom very well.
   C) Power supply can be guaranteed with a rented generator.
   D) There is no television, radio or tape recorder in the neighborhood.

Task 6 Blank Filling

Directions: Watch the video clip again and fill in the following blanks.

(1) ___________, Faridun, is followed by an official marriage ceremony. And while the guests are celebrating, the bride says her last goodbyes, not just to her parents but also to her childhood. This is the (2) ___________ and the home of her new husband's family. Zebo's first task is to show them her cooking skills by making symbolic dough. And it's only the beginning of her (3) ___________. Life is hard in rural Tajikistan but wedding parties give people (4) ___________.

Task 7 Oral Practice

Directions: Look at the following topics carefully and then deliver a short (1–3 minutes) presentation on them.

1. Will an expensive wedding be necessary?
2. What are the essentials for the nuptials?

Task 8 Back Translation

Directions: Please watch the clip attentively and then translate the following Chinese sentences into English.

1. 世界各国的传统婚礼上，费用是个大问题。

____

2. 除了重要的社会和文化活动，在塔吉克斯坦的农村，婚礼是主要的娱乐活动。

____

Pass 3 A Forbidden Romance

(Difficulty: ★★★)

背景知识

莉莉安·梅伊·戴维斯出生在英国威尔士斯旺西的一个普通家庭，16 岁时，从威尔士移居到伦敦从事模特工作，随后嫁给了英国男演员伊万·克雷格。1943 年，莉莉安在庆祝自己的 28 岁生日时，邂逅了来伦敦访问的瑞典王子、哈兰公爵 (Prince Bertil, Duke of Halland) 贝蒂尔亲王。当时两人一见钟情，迅速陷入热恋，两年后，莉莉安与丈夫克雷格离婚。但当时瑞典国王担心莉莉安一介民女并且又离过婚的身份会威胁到瑞典“贝尔纳多特王朝”(Bernadotte Dynasty)，因此坚决不同意她与儿子结婚，两人的关系也成为禁忌话题。1973 年，老国王古斯塔夫六世逝世后，贝蒂尔的侄子、时年 27 岁的卡尔·古斯塔夫于同年 9 月 15 日正式登基继承王位，他们长达 30 多年的苦恋这才修成了正果。并于 1976 年 12 月 7 日在瑞典王室的私人宫殿卓宁霍姆宫 (Drottningholms slott) 正式举行婚礼。虽然获得了王室祝福，但是此时的新郎和新娘均已是年过花甲的老人。婚后，莉莉安获哈兰公爵夫人的头衔，夫妇俩在瑞典社交圈深受欢迎。2013 年 3 月 10 日，这位瑞典王室曾经最禁忌的话题人物在瑞典首都斯德哥尔摩的家中安详去世，享年 97 岁。莉莉安王妃生前被瑞典媒体称为“真实版灰姑娘”，她与王子贝蒂尔的浪漫故事感动了无数人。

（资料来源：http://news.sina.com.cn/w/p/2013-03-12/025626501310. shtml。）

Vocabulary

forbidden	[fə'bɪdn]	*adj.*	不允许的，被禁止的；禁用的
eventful	[ɪ'ventfl]	*adj.*	充满变数的
outbreak	['aʊtbreɪk]	*n.*	突然发生，爆发
blossom	['blɒsəm]	*vi.*	发展
commoner	['kɒmənə(r)]	*n.*	平民；无贵族称号的人
divorcee	[dɪˌvɔː'siː]	*n.*	离婚者
jeopardize	['dʒepədaɪz]	*vt.*	危及，损害；使陷入险境或受伤
to be stationed	安置，派驻		

Task 1 General Understanding

Directions: Listen to the clip and then sum up its main idea. You may do this either in Chinese or English.

Task 2 Word Hunting

Directions: Try your best to spot the following words and expressions while watching the video clip.

1. 回顾其充满变数的一生

____

2. 浪漫小说的情节

____

Task 3 True or False

Directions: Watch the video clip again and tell whether the following statements are true or false (T/F).

1. ( ) Lilian Davies used to be a housewife after her first marriage.
2. ( ) Prince Bertil of Sweden agreed to pick her up in her neighbor for a date.
3. ( ) Princess Lilian outlived her husband and died at the age of 97.

Task 4 Listening Comprehension

Directions: Choose the correct answer to the following questions based on your listening.

1. What is it that made them regret?
   A) Inability to be approved by the Swedish King.
   B) Inability to get financial support from parents.
   C) Inability to get married.
   D) Inability to have any child.
2. Which of the following is UNTOLD?
   A) Prince Bertil was 3 years older than Lillian.
   B) Swedes were overwhelmed by the dedicated couple.
   C) The couple made many appearances in public.
   D) Princess Lillian withdrew from public after the death of her husband.

Task 5 Blank Filling

Directions: Watch the video clip again and fill in the following blanks.

After the (1) __________ of WWⅡ she met Prince Bertil of Sweden who was (2) __________ in London. He was the third son of the Swedish King. And romance (3) __________ when he picked her up in his car after her neighborhood was bombed.

The Swedish Royal Family (4) __________ Bertil for marrying Lillian who as a commoner and divorcee might (5) __________ of their dynasty.

Task 6 Oral Practice

Directions: Start a discussion with your partners to find out what might enable the couple to keep on loving each other despite all the frustration.

Task 7 Back Translation

Directions: Please watch the clip attentively and then translate the following Chinese sentences into English.

1. 他们相遇后的第 33 个年头，瑞典国王才允许他们结婚。

____

2. 他们为彼此付出的故事融化了瑞典人的心。

____

Pass 4 Same-Sex Marriage

(Difficulty: ★★★★)

背景知识

同性婚姻是指生理性别或性别认同相同的两人之间的婚姻关系。由同性恋权利支持者使用的婚姻的定义是：一个获得社会承认的、自愿的、忠贞的、单配的、合法的两个成年人之间的契约结合，由政府和（或）社会通过给予特定的权利、待遇和责任表示认可。这些权利包括经济、税收、遗产、家庭（如子女的监护权，部分同性伴侣会领养子女）、社会（如医疗保险、探视、代做医疗决定、代行权利、移民）以及做出医疗决定的权利。

对同性婚姻的法律认同的缺乏也同样给同性恋情侣领养子女带来了阻力。通常反对同性婚姻的反对者都有宗教背景，他们认为同性婚姻有可能破坏传统的婚姻价值观。在一些适应一夫一妻制度的国家，人们担心允许同性婚姻将可能重新打开对多夫多妻制度的立法，或其他很多令他们不愉快的形式。

2015 年 6 月 26 日，美国最高法院裁决同性伴侣在美国具有婚姻权，使得同性婚姻在美国全境合法化。总统奥巴马在 Twitter 发文，指这次裁决是迈向平等的一大步。全美有 36 个州以及首都华盛顿哥伦比亚特区准许同性婚姻，但最高法院的裁决意味其余 14 个州不能再禁止同性伴侣结婚。

（资料来源：http://www.calaw.cn/article/default.asp?id=10830。）

Vocabulary

elicit	[ɪ'lɪsɪt]	*vt.*	引出
historic	[hɪ'stɒrɪk]	*adj.*	历史性的；具有历史意义的
deride	[dɪ'raɪd]	*vt.*	嘲笑，愚弄；嘲弄
spur	[spɜː(r)]	*vt.*	加速；鞭策
endorse	[ɪn'dɔːs]	*vt.*	支持；赞同；认可
presumptive	[prɪ'zʌmptɪv]	*adj.*	可据以推定的
skyrocket	['skaɪrɒkɪt]	*vi.*	突升，猛涨
gay rights			同性恋者的权利

Task 1 Word Hunting

Directions: Try your best to spot the following words and expressions while watching the video clip.

1. 婚姻是一个男人和一个女人的结合。

____

2. 急需增加就业机会和拉动经济增长。

____

Task 2 True or False

Directions: Watch the video clip again and tell whether the following statements are true or false (T/F).

1. ( ) All republicans are not in favor of same-sex marriage and call for more jobs and stronger economy.
2. ( ) Religious leaders might oppose gay rights presumably.
3. ( ) President Obama's reelection campaign will make use of the benefits of gay rights movement.

Task 3 Listening Comprehension

Directions: Choose the correct answer to the following questions based on your listening.

1. What CANNOT be said about the Republicans?
   A) House speaker John Boehner wants to focus on economy and job creation.
   B) Representative Pelosi opposed gay rights across the country.
   C) Most republican senators are silent on same-sex marriage.
   D) Not all republicans derided the president's comment on same-sex marriage.
2. What CANNOT be said about the Democrats?
   A) Most of them support same-sex marriage.
   B) Democratic Party platform will back marriage rights for gays and lesbians.
   C) President Obama's reelection campaign will point out the benefits of same-sex marriage.
   D) President Obama's announcement has been welcomed and supported by gays and lesbians financially.

Task 4 Blank Filling

Directions: Watch the video clip again and fill in the following blanks.

President Obama's (1) ________________, "I think same-sex couples should be able to get married," elicited a (2) ________________ at the capital. House Democratic leader Nancy Pelosi had nothing but (3) ________________. "Yesterday was quite (4) ________________ all of us. America's children and families, workers saw history being made right before their very eyes—the president of the United States (5) ________________ in our country."

Task 5 Oral Practice

Directions: Look at the following topic carefully and then deliver a short (1–3 minutes) presentation on them.

Should same-sex couples be able to get married?

Task 6 Back Translation

Directions: Please watch the clip attentively and then translate the following Chinese sentences into English.

1. 共和党的立法者们对总统的意见予以嘲笑，认为这是在错误的时间发表的错误言论。

____

2. 在参议院的共和党人对此事闭口不提。

____

Pass 5　Anne Hathaway

(Difficulty: ★★★★)

背景知识

安妮·海瑟薇 (Anne Hathaway) 15 岁时就知道哥哥 Michael 是一名同性恋，安妮的整个家庭为了支持 Michael 的选择决定集体退出当地的天主教会。安妮与哥哥关系亲密，她因此也对同性恋者及同性婚姻公开支持。安妮说：“我为什么要支持一个对我的哥哥持有限制意见的组织呢？”安妮·海瑟薇将售卖其结婚照的部分所得捐献给倡导同性恋婚姻的非营利组织，以表示支持。

LGBT 是用来指女同性恋者 (Lesbian)、男同性恋者 (Gay)、双性恋者 (Bisexual) 与跨性别者 (Transgender)。20 世纪 90 年代，由于“同性恋社群”一词无法完整体现相关群体，LGBT 的用法便应运而生，并逐渐普及。在现代用语中，“LGBT”一词十分重视性倾向与性别认同文化多样性，除了指同性恋、双性恋或跨性别族群，还可广泛指代所有非异性恋者。另外，也有人在该词后面加上字母“Q”，代表酷儿（Queer）或对其性别认同感到疑惑的人（例如：“LGBTQ”）。LGBT 现今已获得了许多英语系国家中多数 LGBT 族群和 LGBT 媒体的认同及采用，成为一种非常主流的用法。

（资料来源：http://www.haibao.com/article/1469992.htm。）

Vocabulary

humble	['hʌmbl]	*vt.*	使感到卑微；使低声下气
empathetic	[ˌempə'θetɪk]	*adj.*	有同感的，感同身受的
alternative	[ɔːl'tɜːnətɪv]	*adj.*	另类的
ally	['ælaɪ]	*n.*	同盟；盟友；支持者
no big deal	没什么大不了的		
come out	公开同性恋身份		
come out of the closet	出柜		

Task 1 Matching

Directions: Match the English phrases on the left with those Chinese phrases on the right before listening.

1. alternative family lifestyle　　　　对同志社群很友善
2. be empathetic to the LGBT community　　　　另类家庭

Task 2 Word Hunting

Directions: Try your best to spot the following words and expressions while watching the video clip.

1. 我还有很大的进步空间。

____

2. 重大事件

____

Task 3 True or False

Directions: Watch the video clip again and tell whether the following statements are true or false (T/F).

1. ( ) This award was given to Anne Hathaway simply because of what she has done for the community.

2. (　) Anne Hathaway was born in a gay family and raised by two men.
3. (　) Anne's family hugged her gay brother and showed understanding.

Task 4 Blank Filling

Directions: Watch the video clip again and fill in the following blanks.

We had no idea that I would become (1) ________________ because of my work and that we would become (2) ________________ as having an "alternative family lifestyle". Just for the record, we don't feel that there's actually anything alternative about our (3) ________________.

So for semantic reasons only, it's (4) ________________ that I accept the HRCLI award. I don't consider myself just an ally to the LGBT community, I consider myself your family; and so, I'm doing, what we should all do, with our families, I'm loving you, I support you, I completely accept you as you are as I hope you do me, and if anyone, ever, tries to hurt you, I'm gonna (5) ________________!

Task 5 Oral Practice

Directions: Look at the following topics carefully and then deliver a short (1–3 minutes) presentation on them.

Should gay couples be allowed to adopt kids?

Task 6 Back Translation

Directions: Please watch the clip attentively and then translate the following Chinese sentences into English.

1. 你们今晚给我的殊荣多少让我觉得我还担当不起。

____

2. 在我们家，同性恋身份从来不是个问题。

____

Pass 6　Zach Wahls

(Difficulty: ★★★★)

背景知识

在美国，同性恋家庭的子女或亲生、收养，或由人工受孕方式所生，他们的成长都面临着几大挑战：（1）同性恋父母性侵孩子的可能性更大；（2）遭受的嘲笑会给自己造成严重的心理伤害；（3）同性恋家庭的孩子会变成同性恋；（4）孩子在“不自然”的家庭中成长不健康等。但也有研究显示，父母性侵孩子与性取向没有明显关系，在同性恋家庭长大的孩子在各个方面都和在异性恋家庭长大的孩子一样。此外，单亲异性恋家庭的问题比双亲同性恋家庭的问题更严重。在某些方面，同性恋家庭长大的孩子或许表现更为出色，比如，自律、自尊，较少出现心理问题。同性恋的子女确实会因父母的“特殊”而遭受一些嘲笑，但是他们的自尊水平不比异性恋家庭长大的孩子的自尊水平低。由同性恋父母抚养长大的孩子变成同性恋的概率不比异性恋父母抚养长大的孩子大。同性恋家庭抚养的孩子与异性恋家庭抚养的孩子并无明显不同，父母对子女的尊重和支持比父母的性取向重要得多。父母对子女的关爱、耐心、支持、理解才是子女健康成长的必备要素。

（资料来源：http://tieba.baidu.com/p/4380075443。）

Vocabulary

infantile	['ɪnfəntaɪl] *adj.* 婴儿（期）的
anonymous	[ə'nɒnɪməs] *adj.* 匿名的
sibling	['sɪblɪŋ] *n.* 兄弟，姐妹
sclerosis	[sklə'rəʊsɪs] *n.* 硬化症
codify	['kəʊdɪfaɪ] *vt.* 把（法律）编成法典
Iowa	['aɪəwə] *n.* 爱荷华州（美国中西部的一个州）

break down	消除，破除（障碍或偏见）
A.C.T.	美国大学入学考试
Eagle Scout	鹰级童军（美国童子军年龄最高的一级组织），童子军的最高级别；（得过21次奖章的）最高级童子军

Task 1 Word Matching

Directions: Match the English phrases on the left with those Chinese phrases on the right before listening.

1. biological mother	度假
2. artificial insemination	亲兄妹
3. full siblings	生母
4. go to church	争吵
5. go on vacation	人工受孕
6. to get in fights	（去教堂）做礼拜

Task 2 Word Hunting

Directions: Try your best to spot the following words and expressions while watching the video clip.

1. 被诊断出有硬化症

____

2. 归结起来（为……）

____

3. 得到政府合理、平等的待遇

____

4. 通过……实现价值

____

5. 家庭的价值

____

6. 修宪

____

7. 二等公民

____

Task 3 True or False

Directions: Watch the video clip again and tell whether the following statements are true or false (T/F).

1. ( ) Wahls' grandparents were empathetic to gay movement and rights.
2. ( ) Wahls' family underwent difficulties and unfair treatment from the government.
3. ( ) Wahls is not ashamed of the family he was born and raised.
4. ( ) Wahls' younger sister is a lesbian.
5. ( ) Wahls' growing up is mixed with difficult and hard times.
6. ( ) Wahls' family should be very proud of him.

Task 4 Blank Filling

Directions: Listen to the video clip again and fill in the following blanks.

Good evening, Mr. Chariman. My name is Zach Wahls. I'm a (1) __________ Iowan and an engineering student at the University of Iowa. I was (2) __________. (3) __________ Terry told my grandparents that she was pregnant that the artificial insemination had worked, and they wouldn't even (4) __________ it. It actually wasn't until I was born and they (5) __________ that they broke down and told her that they were (6) __________ to have another grandson. Unfortunately, neither of them lived to see her marry her partner Jackie of 15 years when they (7) __________ in 2009. My younger sister and only sibling was born in 1994. We actually have (8) __________ so we're (9) __________ siblings, which is really cool for me.

Task 5 Oral Practice

Directions: Look at the following topic carefully and then deliver a short (1–3 minutes) presentation on them.

How does a kid from a gay family differ from a kid from a straight family?

Task 6 Back Translation

Directions: Please watch the clip attentively and then translate the following Chinese sentences into English.

1. 我们不指望有谁能替我们解决问题。

____

2. 我们为自己奋战。

____

3. 家庭的意义来自于家庭成员彼此承诺。

____

4. 有福同享，有难同当。

____

5. 它来源于牵绊我们彼此的爱。

____

6. 你有权与你爱的人结婚。

____

7. 父母的性取向对我的性格发展毫无影响。

____

Pass 7 A Man's Families

(Difficulty: ★★★★)

背景知识

一夫多妻是一种一个男人同时有多于一位妻子的婚姻习俗。它始于母权制 (matriarchy) 后期，为父权制婚姻形式的特点，是生产资料私有制的产物。合法的一夫多妻婚姻多存在于伊斯兰教国家当中。

南非的一夫多妻制最为著名，而为这种婚俗提高世界知名度的就是今年 73 岁的南非现任总统祖马。祖马先后迎娶了六位妻子，其中原配夫人选择了离婚，另外一位妻子因抑郁而自杀，祖马的妻子和情人们为他生育了超过 20 个子女。祖马是祖鲁族人，南非有将近 5 000 万人，祖鲁族是最大的土著部族，人口比例超过全国人口的 1/5。

但现代生活对古老的习俗不断产生着冲击。在约翰内斯堡这样的国际大都市里，大多数具有体面工作的祖鲁族男士这样回答：自己坚决支持一夫一妻，一夫多妻只是村落里面少数人采取的生活方式而已。

（资料来源：http://www.dooland.com/magazine/article_586698.html。）

Vocabulary

polygamy	[pə'lɪgəmɪ]	一夫多妻（制）或一妻多夫（制）
Sheikh	[ʃeɪk] *n.*	（阿拉伯的）酋长；族长
Zulu	['zuːluː] *n.*	祖鲁人

Task 1 Matching

Directions: Match the English phrases on the left with those Chinese phrases on the right.

1. 说唱歌手	show off
2. 邻家女孩	rap singer
3. 炫耀	the girl next door

Task 2 True or False

Directions: Watch the video clip again and tell whether the following statements are true or false (T/F).

1. ( ) To practice polygamy is rarely seen in South Africa.
2. ( ) Milton Mbele is 43 and has married four times.
3. ( ) Milton Mbele made a plan of 4 families beforehand.

Task 3 Listening Comprehension

Directions: Choose the correct answer to the following questions based on your listening.

1. His four wives are found ________.

   A) purposefully

B) accidentally

C) purposelessly

D) naturally

2. Which of the following is FALSE?

A) Milton didn't plan on having multiple families.

B) It's customary for any man in South Africa to have multiple wives.

C) It's rare for a Zulu to have only one wife.

D) Multiple families are a sign of masculine price.

3. Which of the following is NOT mentioned?

A) Milton has to divide his time equally among his 4 families.

B) Polygamy is relatively common in West Africa.

C) Polygamy is relatively common in South Africa.

D) People who practice polygamy can be either men or women.

Task 4 Blank Filling

Directions: Watch the video clip again and fill in the following blanks.

But he jokes that having all these wives (1) ________________.

Or they'll say that if you only have one wife there is (2) ________________.

Milton is a Zulu. He says it's (3) ________________ for men in his tribe to take many wives and have many children, and that it's a sign that he is (4) ________________. So Milton says he tries to (5) ________________ between 4 of his families.

Task 5 Oral Practice

Directions: Look at the following topic carefully and then deliver a short (1–3 minutes) presentation on them.

If you were given the chance to practice polygamy, would you?

Task 6 Back Translation

Directions: Please watch the clip attentively and then translate the following Chinese sentences into English.

1. 你不一定非得是个国王或者酋长才能一夫多妻。

____

2. 自己的父亲有多位妻子，在这样的环境中长大是怎样的呢？

____

Pass 8 Children from Polygamy

(Difficulty: ★★★★)

背景知识

随着城市化进程的加速，南非祖鲁族的圆顶棚屋被放进了民俗村，并当成文物保护了起来。人们都住进了新式的住宅，一夫多妻制也正在逐步走向没落。据 2010 年的一项调查显示，将近 3/4 的南非人反对一夫多妻制，特别是妇女，有 83% 的受访者表示反对。

2012 年 11 月，曾有机构要求南非宪法法庭规定，不管源自何种非洲文化，一个男人若想娶第二个妻子，必须得到第一任妻子的同意。因为南非宪法规定了公民的平等和尊严，未经许可的再婚是父权制的一种形式，是违宪的行为。

（资料来源：http://epaper.tianjinwe.com/mrxb/mrxb/2015-02/15/content_7243064.htm。）

Vocabulary

outspoken	[aʊt'spəʊkən]	*adj.*	直言的；坦率的；毫无保留的
polygamist	[pə'lɪgəmɪst]	*n.*	多配偶的人；多配偶论者
illegal	[ɪ'liːgl]	*adj.*	不合法的，违法的

Task 1 Word Hunting

Directions: Try your best to spot the following words and expressions while watching the video clip.

1. 跟随父母的步伐

____

2. 传统让你感觉很自在

____

Task 2 True or False

Directions: Watch the video clip again and tell whether the following statements are true or false (T/F).

1. ( ) Daughters of Milton are very outspoken and comfortable with traditions.
2. ( ) Daughters of a polygamist are willing to follow in their parents' footsteps.
3. ( ) Daughters of Milton have no idea about what polygamy is.

Task 3 Listening Comprehension

Directions: Choose the correct answer to the following questions based on your listening.

1. Which of the following CANNOT be said about his daughters?
   A) Outspoken.
   B) Amazing.
   C) Understanding.
   D) Traditional.
2. Which of the following is TRUE?
   A) Children of a polygamist are bound to follow the tradition.
   B) Children of Milton are comfortable with tradition and proud of him.
   C) There are some differences among children of different mothers.
   D) Children of a polygamist live in separate families.

3. Which CAN be described as the attitude of the daughters of Milton to polygamy?

A) Accept and understand it completely.

B) Accept with reservations.

C) Defy without hesitation.

D) Disagree with understanding.

Task 4 Blank Filling

Directions: Watch the video clip again and fill in the following blanks.

He is a very good father to us. He is a very good father. I have to say that because he (1) ________________ us in every way he can. Yeah, to (2) ________________ that we live in a big family and all the stuff because whenever we meet something, all our needs are (3) ________________ by him and all at once he does satisfy some of the…yeah like all parents do. I really like it living in a big family. Yeah, I like it.

Task 5 Oral Practice

Directions: Look at the following topic carefully and then deliver a short (1–3 minutes) presentation on them.

Can you understand how a child of polygamy views polygamy?

Task 6 Back Translation

Directions: Please watch the clip attentively and then translate the following Chinese sentences into English.

1. 他们不会复制其父亲的生活方式，但是他们非常喜欢成为这个大家庭中的一员。

____

2. 虽然有多位母亲，但是他们的核心却是这位父亲。

____

Pass 9 Unlikely Marriage

(Difficulty: ★★★★)

背景知识

阿尔巴尼亚与塞尔维亚的积怨由来已久，主要的矛盾在于科索沃地区的争夺。科索沃独立不是一个孤立的事件，而是阿尔巴尼亚和塞尔维亚两大民族历史矛盾的沉淀和外部大国势力插手的结果。阿族和塞族对科索沃都有一种难以割舍的情结，前者把它视为自己的"摇篮"，而后者认定它是自己的"圣地"，如此之争至少有上千年的历史。但是，如果单靠阿族人自己，科索沃的地位恐怕很难有所改变。它最终能够宣布独立，起关键作用的还是西方国家。因此，科索沃独立的影响也超出了巴尔干地区。

2008年2月17日，科索沃正式宣布独立。表面上看，这是一个发生在特定时空中的孤立事件，可事实上并非如此。从科索沃问题到科索沃危机，再到科索沃战争，最后到科索沃独立，这一过程持续了近百年，而在这些背后起作用的阿尔巴尼亚人和塞尔维亚人之间的恩怨则更为久远。另外，由于地理位置和地缘政治都十分重要，巴尔干地区在历史上大多数时间里都是大国争夺的重点，阿族与塞族之间的矛盾和冲突就是这种争夺的后果之一。

（资料来源：http://blog.sina.com.cn/s/blog_636cf4a70102v50m.html。）

Vocabulary

perch	[pɜːtʃ] *vi.* 坐落在
giggle	[ˈgɪgl] *vi.* 咯咯地笑；傻笑
enclave	[ˈenkleɪv] *n.* （被他国领土包围的）飞地
sworn enemies	不共戴天的仇敌；死对头

Task 1 Word Hunting

Directions: Try your best to spot the following words and expressions while watching the video clip.

1. 像少女般傻笑

____

2. 更高的生活水平

____

3. 宣布独立

____

Task 2 True or False

Directions: Watch the video clip again and tell whether the following statements are true or false (T/F).

1. ( ) It's been unthinkable for Serbs and Albanians to become husband and wife.
2. ( ) The end of 1999 war in Kosovo means a better standard of living.
3. ( ) The Serbian enclaves in Kovosohave recognized that the territory has declared independence.

Task 3 Blank Filling

Directions: Watch the video clip again and fill in the following blanks.

Here in the north of the (1) __________ city of Mitrovica. The Serbs are living a totally (2) __________ life from the Kosovan Albanians. Belgrade still runs all the institutions here and people spend dinars instead of Euros used in the rest of Kosovo. Although not uncommon elsewhere in the former Yugoslavia, (3) __________ marriages have always been (4) __________ in Kosovo. And since the war they are practically unheard of. But new unlikely partnerships in the rural population here could now be starting to butt that (5) __________.

Task 4 Oral Practice

Directions: Look at the following topics carefully and then carry out a discussion with your partner.

How does the live version of Romeo and Juliet sound to you?

Task 5 Back Translation

Directions: Please watch the clip attentively and then translate the following Chinese sentences into English.

1. 他们是经媒人介绍认识的。

____

2. 为了寻找更好的前景，当地所有的女性都离开了。

____

Pass 10 Royal Wedding

(Difficulty: ★★★★★)

背景知识

英国威廉王子和凯特·米德尔顿 (Kate Middleton) 的婚礼于 2011 年 4 月 29 日举行，这是英国最隆重的喜事之一。英国《太阳报》率先披露获邀出席婚礼的宾客名单，多达近 1 900 人，包括全球多国王室成员。伴郎由威廉王子的弟弟哈里王子担任，伴娘由凯特的妹妹担任。

威尔士威廉王子殿下，全名为威廉·亚瑟·菲利普·路易斯·蒙巴顿—温莎，是英国王室的成员之一，英国王储威尔士亲王查尔斯和威尔士王妃戴安娜的长子，英国王位第二号继承人。凯特·米德尔顿 1982 年 1 月 9 日出生。2001 年 9 月，威廉和凯特在苏格兰圣安德鲁大学相识。

该场婚礼创下了吉尼斯世界纪录：电视观众最多的婚礼，网络搜索最热的婚礼，蛋糕最贵的婚礼，最盈利的婚礼。

（资料来源：http://baike.baidu.com/link?url=4HFmFWce6svcUAYV3LxdxhGnJYvh395 Eo9mvHNbn-OO6LziwgTnO96ggcK1DNujDtfZz8LpPiTyFghyffcCVrK。）

Vocabulary

matrimony	['mætrɪmənɪ]	*n.*	结婚，婚姻生活
troth	[trəʊθ]	*n.*	誓言
cherish	['tʃerɪʃ]	*vt.*	珍爱
covenant	['kʌvənənt]	*n.*	誓约
asunder	[ə'sʌndə(r)]	*adv.*	分开地；分离地
wedlock	['wedlɒk]	*n.*	婚姻；已婚状况

Task 1　Word Hunting

Directions: *Try your best to spot the following words and expressions while watching the video clip.*

1. 愿永远不被人分开。

____

2. 将对彼此忠诚。

____

3. 永远相爱。

____

4. 直至生命结束。

____

5. 无论好坏，无论贫穷还是富贵，无论疾病还是健康。

____

6. 我都会爱你、珍惜你，至死不渝。

____

Task 2 Blank Filling

Directions: Watch the video clip again and fill in the following blanks.

O Eternal God, (1)____________________, giver of all spiritual grace, the author of everlasting life: send thy blessing upon these thy servants, this man and this woman, whom we bless in thy name; that, living faithfully together, they may surely (2) ____________________ covenant betwixt them made, whereof this ring given and received is (3) ____________________; and may ever remain in perfect love and peace together, and live according to thy laws; through Jesus Christ our Lord. Amen.

Those whom God hath joined together let no man put asunder.

Forasmuch as William and Catherine have (4) ____________________, and have witnessed the same before God and this company, and thereto have given and pledged their troth either to other, and have declared the same by giving and receiving of a ring, and (5) ____________________; I pronounce that they be man and wife together, in the name of the Father, and of the Son, and of the Holy Ghost. Amen.

Task 3 Oral Practice

Directions: Look at the following topic carefully and then deliver a short (1–3 minutes) presentation on them.

What is the ideal marriage vow in your eyes?

Task 4 Back Translation

Directions: Please watch the clip attentively and then translate the following Chinese sentences into English.

1. 根据上帝神圣的旨意，你是否愿意与这位女子缔结婚姻关系、共同生活？

____

2. 有生之年，你是否会爱她、安慰她、尊重她、保护她，无论健康还是疾苦，是否愿意舍弃一切，永远对她忠诚？

____

____

3. 我将娶你为我的合法妻子，从今往后，无论好坏，无论贫穷还是富贵，无论疾病还是健康，我都会爱你、珍惜你，直到死亡将我们分开。在上帝面前，我向你发誓。

____

____

4. 上帝保佑这枚戒指，保佑赠予戒指的人和接受戒指的人将对彼此忠诚，永远相爱，直至生命结束。

____

____

5. 以圣父、圣子、圣灵之名，我将娶你，赐你荣耀，与你分享我的财富。阿门。

____

____

6. 愿上帝使之结合的两人，永远不被人分开。

____

Part 4　英语听说秘籍之连读（Liaison）

(Difficulty: ★★★★★)

"连读"是英语口语中较普遍的现象。"连续"的英文是 Word Connections，借用法语的词汇是 Liaison，读音为 [lɪ'eɪzn]。连读是语调中非常重要的一个组成要素，语调是让别人更能听懂、更好理解的重要途径之一。在英语的口头表达中，一个节奏群或意群中前一个单词的最后一个音节可以与后一个单词的第一个音节连读。

连读的条件：相邻的两词在意义上必须密切相关，同属一个意群。连读所构成的音节一般都不重读，只需顺其自然地一带而过，不可读得太重。（连读符号：～）

1. "辅音 + 元音"型连读：在同一个意群里，如果相邻两词中的前一个词是以辅音结尾，后一个词是以元音开头，这就要将辅音与元音拼起来连读。

I'm～an～English boy.

It～is～an～old book.

Let me have~a look~at~it.

Ms Black worked in~an~office last~yesterday.

I called~you half~an~hour~ago.

Put~it~on, please.

Not~at~all.

Please pick~it~up.

2.“r/re+ 元音”型连读：如果前一个词是以 -r 或者 -re 结尾，后一个词是以元音开头，这时的 r 或 re 不但要发 [r]，而且还要与后面的元音拼起来连读。

They're my father~and mother.

I looked for~it here~and there.

There~is a football under~it.

There~are some books on the desk.

Here~is a letter for you.

Here~are four~eggs.

But where~is my cup?

Where~are your brother~and sister?

但是，如果一个音节的前后都有字母 r，即使后面的词以元音开头，也不能连读。

The black clouds are coming nearer and nearer.（nearer 与 and 不可连读）

3. “辅音 + 半元音”型连读：英语语音中的 [j] 和 [w] 是半元音，如果前一个词是以辅音结尾，后一个词是以半元音特别是 [j] 开头，此时也要连读。

Thank~you.

Nice to meet~you.

Did~you get there late~again?

Would~you like~a cup~of tea?

Could~you help me, please?

“音的同化”—— 常把 [d]+[j] 读成 [dʒ]，did you 听上去成了 [dɪdʒu]，would you 成了 [wudʒu]，could you 成了 [kudʒu]。

4. “元音 + 元音”型：元音对元音的连续实际上是在元音之间插入半元音 [j] 或 [w]，从而使纯元音音节之间的过渡变得自然、流畅，读起来更加上口。半元音插入情况如下：前面的单词以敞口元音 [e]、[ɪ] 结尾，紧随其后的单词以元音 [ɪ]、[e]、[aɪ]、[ɔɪ] 等开头，这时，在两个单词之间出现半元音 [j] 作为过渡。前面的单词以闭口元音 [ʊ]、[əʊ] 结尾，紧随其后的单词以元音 [ʊ]、[əʊ]、[aʊ] 开头，这时，在两个单词之间出现半元音 [w] 作为过渡。为了把两个相邻的词连在一起，人们往往在以 [ə][a] 结尾的词后面加上 [r] 音，以便和后一个词的首元音连接，这种添加的 [r] 称为“外加音”[r]。

I~am Chinese.

He~is very friendly to me.

She wants to study~English.

How~and why did you come here?

She can't carry~it.

It'll take you three~hours to walk there.

The question is too~easy for him to answer.

5. 当短语或从句之间按照意群进行停顿时，意群与意群之间即使有两个相邻的辅音与元音出现，也不可连读。

Is~it a~hat or a cat?（hat 与 or 之间不可以连读）

There~is~a good book in my desk.（book 与 in 之间不可以连读）

Can you speak~English or French?（English 与 or 之间不可以连读）

Shall we meet at~eight or ten tomorrow morning?（meet 与 at，eight 与 or 之间不可以连读）

She opened the door and walked~in.（door 与 and 之间不可以连读）

Practice（句子练习）:

1. in a minute
2. fall in the river
3. tell us a story
4. take care of it
5. wait for a student
6. for an hour
7. I can't hear it.
8. It isn't our mistake.
9. Could you open the door for us?
10. Here is your bag.
11. You need to work at it.
12. Would you like a weekend in Las Vegas?
13. Well, I wasn't clear about my future.
14. I made enough for an army.
15. I'll make you two fried eggs.

Practice（段落练习）:

Greetings, citizens of earth. My people have developed technologies which allow us to throw off our physical forms and travel great distances in the blink of an eye. We are in dialogue with your leaders to help the human race survive its infancy for we believe in you. We are helping your scientists find cures for diseases which afflict your bodies and helping you to preserve your planet's most precious resources. Many among us wage peace and one day with our help war may be a thing of the past. Our army is a billion strong and growing. We are the people of the Internet and together we are shaping the future of human kind.

Superpower the BBC's Internet Season coming soon.

English Listening-and-Speaking Learning Planner

Monday	**Tuesday**	**Wednesday**	**Thursday**	**Friday**
Practicing Hour: ________ Tape Hour: ________ Commitment: ________	Practicing Hour: ________ Tape Hour: ________ Commitment: ________	Practicing Hour: ________ Tape Hour: ________ Commitment: ________	Practicing Hour: ________ Tape Hour: ________ Commitment: ________	Practicing Hour: ________ Tape Hour: ________ Commitment: ________

Saturday	**Sunday**	**General Performance for Week _____:**
Practicing Hour: ________ Tape Hour: ________ Commitment: ________	Practicing Hour: ________ Tape Hour: ________ Commitment: ________	(vocabulary, long sentence, background information, etc.) Self-rating ☆☆☆☆☆

Monday	**Tuesday**	**Wednesday**	**Thursday**	**Friday**
Practicing Hour: ________ Tape Hour: ________ Commitment: ________	Practicing Hour: ________ Tape Hour: ________ Commitment: ________	Practicing Hour: ________ Tape Hour: ________ Commitment: ________	Practicing Hour: ________ Tape Hour: ________ Commitment: ________	Practicing Hour: ________ Tape Hour: ________ Commitment: ________

Saturday	**Sunday**	**General Performance for Week _____:**
Practicing Hour: ________ Tape Hour: ________ Commitment: ________	Practicing Hour: ________ Tape Hour: ________ Commitment: ________	(vocabulary, long sentence, background information, etc.) Self-rating ☆☆☆☆☆

Appendix

经典爱情誓言

(1) Where there is great love, there are always miracles.
哪里有真爱存在，哪里就有奇迹。

(2) Love is like a butterfly. It goes where it pleases and it pleases where it goes.
爱情就像一只蝴蝶，它喜欢飞到哪里，就把欢乐带到哪里。

(3) If I had a single flower for every time I think about you, I could walk forever in my garden.
假如每次想起你我都会得到一朵鲜花，那么我将永远在花丛中徜徉。

(4) Within you I lose myself, without you I find myself wanting to be lost again.
有了你，我迷失了自我。失去你，我多么希望自己再度迷失。

(5) At the touch of love everyone becomes a poet.
每一个沐浴在爱河中的人都是诗人。

(6) Look into my eyes, you will see what you mean to me.
看看我的眼睛，你会发现你对我而言意味着什么。

(7) Distance makes the hearts grow fonder.
距离使两颗心靠得更近。

(8) I need him like I need the air to breathe.
我需要他，正如我需要呼吸空气。

(9) If equal affection cannot be, let the more loving be me.
如果没有相等的爱，那就让我多爱一些吧。

(10) Love is a vine that grows into our hearts.
爱是长在我们心里的藤蔓。

(11) If I know what love is, it is because of you.
因为你，我懂得了爱。

(12) Love is the greatest refreshment in life.
爱情是生活最好的提神剂。

(13) Love never dies.
爱情永不死亡。

(14) The darkness is no darkness with thee.
有了你，黑暗不再是黑暗。

(15) We cease loving ourselves if no one loves us.
如果没有人爱我们，我们也就不会再爱自己了。

(16) There is no remedy for love but to love more.
治疗爱的创伤唯有加倍地去爱。

(17) When love is not madness, it is not love.
如果爱不疯狂，就不是爱了。

(18) A heart that loves is always young.
有爱的心永远年轻。

(19) Love is blind.
爱情是盲目的。

(20) Love is like the moon, when it does not increase, it decreases.
爱情就像月亮，不增则减。

(21) The soul cannot live without love.
灵魂不能没有爱而存在。

(22) Brief is life, but love is long.
生命虽短，爱却绵长。

(23) Who travels for love finds a thousand miles not longer than one.
在爱人眼里，一千里的旅程不过一里。

(24) Love keeps the cold out better than a cloak.
爱比大衣更能驱走寒冷。

(25) Take away love, and our earth is a tomb.
没有了爱，地球便成了坟墓。

(26) My heart is with you.
我的爱与你同在。

(27) I miss you so much already and I haven't even left yet!
尽管还不曾离开，我已对你朝思暮想！

(28) I'll think of you every step of the way.
我会想你，在漫漫长路的每一步。

(29) Wherever you go, whatever you do, I will be right here waiting for you.
无论你身在何处，无论你为何忙碌，我都会在此守候。

(30) Passionate love is a quenchless thirst.
热烈的爱情是不可抑制的渴望。

(31) The most precious possession that ever comes to a man in this world is a woman's heart.
在这个世界上，男人最珍贵的财产就是一个女人的心。

(32) Every day without you is like a book without pages.
没有你的日子就像一本没有书页的书。

(33) Love is hard to get into, but harder to get out of.
爱很难投入，但一旦投入，便更难走出。

(34) Love is a light that never dims.
爱是一盏永不昏暗的明灯。

(35) May your love soar on the wings of a dove in flight.
愿你的爱乘着飞翔的白鸽，展翅高飞。

(36) She who has never loved, has never lived.
人活着总要爱一回。

(37) Life is the flower for which love is the honey.
生命如花，爱情是蜜。

(38) No words are necessary between two loving hearts.
两颗相爱的心之间不需要言语。

(39) Precious things are very few in this world. That is the reason there is just one you.
这世上珍贵的东西总是罕有，所以这世上只有一个你。

(40) You make my heart smile.
我的心因你而欢笑。

(41) The road to a lover's house is never long.
通往爱人家里的路总不会漫长。

(42) Why do the good girls, always want the bad boys?
为何好女孩总喜欢坏男孩?

(43) Being with you is like walking on a very clear morning.
和你在一起就像在一个清爽的早晨漫步。

(44) It is never too late to fall in love.
爱永远不会嫌晚。

(45) To the world you may be just one person. To the person you may be the world.
对于世界，你可能只是一个人，但对于某个人，你却是整个世界。

(46) Where there is love, there are always wishes.
哪里有爱，哪里就有希望。

(47) You don't love a woman because she is beautiful, but she is beautiful because you love her.
你不会因为美丽去爱一个女人，但她却会因为你的爱而变得美丽。

(48) Love is something eternal; the aspect may change, but not the essence.
爱是永恒的，外表可能改变，但本质永远不变。

(49) Love is not a matter of counting the days. It's making the days count.
爱情不是数着日子过去，它让每个日子都变得有意义。

(50) With the wonder of your love, the sun above always shines.
拥有你美丽的爱情，太阳就永远明媚。

(51) Love is a fabric that nature wove and fantasy embroidered.
爱情是一方织巾，用自然编织，用幻想点缀。

(52) First love is unforgettable all one's life.
初恋是永生难忘的。

(53) In the very smallest cot there is room enough for a loving pair.
哪怕是最小的茅舍，对一对恋人来说都有足够的空间。

(54) Love without end hath no end.
情绵绵，爱无边。

(55) Love's tongue is in the eyes.
爱情的话语全在双眼之中。

(56) In love folly is always sweet.
恋爱中，干傻事总是让人感到十分美妙。

(57) There is no hiding from lover's eyes.
什么也瞒不过恋人的眼睛。

(58) The only present love demands is love.
爱所祈求的唯一礼物就是爱。

(59) The heart that once truly loves never forgets.
真挚恋爱过的心永不忘却。

(60) Love warms more than a thousand fires.
爱情的炽热胜过千万团火。

(61) Your smiling at me is my daily dose of magic.
你嫣然的微笑是我每日享受到的魅力。

(62) Your kiss still burns on my lips, everyday of mine is so beautiful.
你的吻还在我的唇上发烫，从此我的日子变得如此美丽。

(63) Love understands love; it needs no talk.
相爱的心息息相通，无须用言语倾诉。

(64) Love me little and love me long.
不求情意绵绵，但求天长地久。

(65) One word frees us of all the weight and pain in life.That word is love.
有一个词可以让我们摆脱生活中所有的负担和痛苦，那就是“爱情”。

(66) When the words “I love you” were said by you for the first time, my world blossoms.
第一次听到你对我说“我爱你”，我的世界一瞬间鲜花绽开。

(67) Tell me you are mine. I’ll be yours through all the years, till the end of time.
请告诉我你是我的。岁岁年年，我都属于你，永远永远。

(68) Love is a fire which burns unseen.
爱情是无形燃烧的火焰。

(69) I feel happy at times we have had angry words but these have been kissed away.
我们生气争执时，爱的双唇把它们吻得无影无踪，我的心也顿觉甜蜜。

(70) You cannot appreciate happiness unless you have known sadness too.
不知道什么是忧伤，就不会真正感激幸福。

Chapter 4

Advertisements

Part 1 Famous Quotes

Good advertising does not just circulate information. It penetrates the public mind with desires and belief.

—Leo Burnett

好广告不只在传达信息，它能以信心和希望穿透大众心灵。

——李奥·贝纳

Great advertising writing, either in print or TV, is always deceptively and disarmingly simple. It has the common touch without being or sounding patronizing.

—Leo Burnett

伟大的创意或平面广告，总是出其不意地单纯，触动人心而不凿斧痕。

——李奥·贝纳

Ideas alone enable a man to survive and flourish.

—Leo Burnett

创意给人生命和生趣。

——李奥·贝纳

Part 2 Background Knowledge

(1) A Brief Introduction of Advertising

Vocabulary

ideological	[ˌaɪdɪə'lɒdʒɪkl]	*adj.*	思想的；意识形态的
sponsor	['spɒnsə(r)]	*n.*	赞助者；主办者；保证人
brand	[brænd]	*n.*	商标；烙印；牌子
innovative	[ˌɪnə'veɪtɪv]	*adj.*	创新的；革新的
campaign	[kæm'peɪn]	*n.*	战役，活动，运动
conglomerate	[kən'glɒməreɪt]	*n.*	密集物，混合体

Advertising is a form of marketing communication used to persuade an audience to take or continue some action, usually with respect to a commercial offering, or political or ideological support.

Advertising messages are usually paid for by sponsors and viewed via various old media, including mass media such as newspapers, magazines, television advertisements, radio advertisements, outdoor advertisements or direct mails; or new media such as blogs, websites or text messages.

Commercial ads often seek to generate increased consumption of their products or services through "branding", which involves associating a product name or image with certain qualities in the minds of consumers. Non-commercial advertisers who spend money to advertise items other than a consumer product or service include political parties, interest groups, religious organizations and governmental agencies. Non-profit organizations may rely on free modes of persuasion, such as a public service announcement (PSA).

Modern advertising was created with the innovative techniques introduced with tobacco advertising in the 1920s, most significantly with the campaigns of Edward Bernays, who is often considered the founder of modern, Madison Avenue advertising.

Internationally, the largest ("big four") advertising conglomerates are Interpublic, Omnicom, Publicis, and WPP.

Task 1 Partner Discussion

Directions: Please brainstorm as many advertising quotes as possible, and discuss with your partner the reasons why they are impressive.

Tip: You may jot down your ideas while brainstorming. Make a list and find the common reason for their attractiveness. Then, you may dig deeper about each advertisement for its unique novelty. In the process of discussion, new ideas may come up, and you may seize and explore them.

Task 2 Speaking Practice

Directions: Choose a relevant topic and present comments.

1. A really good creative person is more interested in earnestness than in glibness and takes more satisfaction out of converting people than in "wowing" them.
2. Make it simple. Make it memorable. Make it inviting to look at. Make it fun to read.
3. A real idea has a power of its own and a life of its own.

(2) Evolution of Advertising

Vocabulary

ware	[weə]	*n.*	制品，货物，器具
magnitude	['mægnɪtjuːd]	*n.*	大小，重要性
publicity	[pʌb'lɪsətɪ]	*n.*	公开，宣传，人尽皆知
engrave	[ɪn'greɪv]	*v.*	刻上，铭记，雕刻
parchment	[pɑːtʃmənt]	*n.*	羊皮纸
papyrus	[pə'paɪrəs]	*n.*	纸莎草纸
placard	['plækɑːd]	*n.*	公告，海报，布告
almanac	['ɔːlmənæk]	*n.*	历书；年鉴
swaddle	['swɑdl]	*v.*	用布包住

The only method of advertising known to the ancients was the word of mouth. The merchant who had wares to offer brought them to the gate of a city and there cried aloud, making the worth of his goods known to those who were entering the city, and who might be induced to turn aside and purchase them. We are not more amused by the simplicity of the ancients than we are amazed at the magnitude of the modern systems of advertising.

As soon as printed symbols were invented the advertising man made use of them to give publicity to his merchandise. We find advertisements engraved on walls and tombs, written on parchment and papyrus, and printed by the first printing presses. Although these various forms of advertising were employed, but little thought and care seem to have been expended upon them. Painted signs, street-car placards, booklets, calendars, almanacs, handbills, magazine and newspaper advertising have now become forms of advertising so well established that we look upon them as a necessity, and are surprised to learn that most of them are modern innovations.

The first advertisement printed in English appeared in the Imperial Intelligence in March, 1648. Advertising in magazines was not begun until comparatively recent times. For instance, the first advertisement appeared in *Harper's Magazine* in 1864. In this magazine more space has been devoted to advertising during the past year than the sum total of space for the twenty-four years from 1864 to 1887, inclusive. Indeed, advertising may be said to have been in its swaddling clothes until about the year 1887. The most rapid development has taken place during the last fifteen years. The change has been so great that the leading advertisers say that in comparison with today there was in existence fifteen years ago no advertising worthy of the name.

The gain in the quantity of advertising can be seen by observing the increase in the number of pages devoted to advertisements in any of our publications. There has not only been an increase in the number of advertising pages in the individual publications, but the number of publications has increased enormously of recent years. The increase of population in the United States has been rapid during the last fifty years, but the increase in the total number of copies of the different publications has been many fold greater.

Task 1 Partner Discussion

Directions: Discuss with your partner about the phases of advertising development.

Task 2 Speaking Practice

Directions: Present comments on the following topic.

In which direction is the advertising industry going?

(3) Online Advertising

Vocabulary

advent	['ædvənt]	*n.*	出现；到来
boom	[buːm]	*n.*	景气，繁荣
guerrilla	[gə'rɪlə]	*n.*	游击队
encounter	[ɪn'kaʊntə]	*n.*	相会，遭遇，相遇
unpredictable	[ˌʌnprɪ'dɪktəbl]	*adj.*	不可预知的
embed	[ɪm'bed]	*v.*	使插入，使嵌入；使深留脑中
equity	['ekwɪtɪ]	*n.*	股权
registrar	[ˌredʒɪ'strɑː]	*n.*	记录者，登记官员，登记者

With the advent of the ad server, online advertising grew, contributing to the "dot-com" boom of the 1990s. Entire corporations operated solely on advertising revenue, offering everything from coupons to free Internet access. At the turn of the 21st century, some websites, including the search engine Google, changed online advertising by personalizing ads based on web browsing behavior. This has led to other similar efforts and an increase in interactive advertising.

Guerrilla marketing involves unusual approaches such as staged encounters in public places, giveaway of products such as cars that are covered with brand messages, and interactive advertising where the viewer can respond to become part of the advertising message. This type of advertising is unpredictable, which causes consumers to buy the product or idea. This reflects an increasing trend of interactive and "embedded" ads, such as via product placement, having consumers vote through text messages, and various campaigns utilizing social network services such as Facebook or Twitter.

The advertising business model has also been adapted in recent years. In media for equity, advertising is not sold, but provided to start-up companies in return for equity. If the company grows and is sold, the media companies receive cash for their shares.

Domain name registrants (usually those who register and renew domains as an investment) sometimes "park" their domains and allow advertising companies to place ads on their sites in return for per-click payments. These ads are typically driven by pay per click search engines like Google or Yahoo, but ads can sometimes be placed directly on targeted domain names through a domain lease or by making contact with the registrant of a domain name that describes a product. Domain name registrants are generally easy to identify through WHOIS records that are publicly available at registrar websites.

Task 1 Partner Discussion

Directions: Discuss with your partner about the following topic with some examples.

What are the features of online advertising?

Task 2 Speaking Practice

Directions: Present comments on the following topic.

If you are to design an advertisement, which aspects should be taken into consideration? Come up with an ad on whatever subject you may choose.

(4) The Psychology of Advertising

Vocabulary

sarcastic	['sɑːkæstɪk] *adj.*	讽刺的，挖苦的
prophecy	['prɒfɪsɪ] *n.*	预言
editorial	[ˌedɪ'tɔːrɪəl] *n.*	社论，评论
enlightened	[ɪn'laɪtnd] *adj.*	被启发的，文明的，进步的
inestimable	[ɪn'estɪməbl] *adj.*	无价的；无法估计的

The leaders of the advertising profession feel that their work has grown till it is beyond their control and comprehension. They have been successful, and hardly know how it has all come about. The men who have been the most successful are often the ones who feel most deeply their inability to meet new emergencies. They believe that there should be some underlying principles which could help them in analyzing what they have already accomplished, and assist them in their further efforts. As their entire object is to produce certain effects on the minds of possible customers, it is not strange that they have turned to psychology in search of such principles. If ever there was ground to expect sarcastic and pessimistic prophecies from the hardheaded business man, it was when it was proposed to establish advertising on a theoretical basis deduced from psychology.

In 1895 in one of the leading advertising journals appeared the following editorial: "Probably when we are a little more enlightened, the advertisement writer, like the teacher, will study psychology. For, however diverse their occupations may at first sight appear, the advertisement writer and the teacher have one great object in common—to influence the human mind. The teacher has a scientific foundation for his work in that direction, but the advertisement writer is really also a psychologist. Human nature is a great factor in advertising success; and he who writes advertisements without reference to it is apt to find that he has reckoned without his host."

In *Publicity*, for March, 1901, appeared a leading article on psychology and advertising. The following is a quotation from it:

"The time is not far away when the advertising writer will find out the inestimable benefits of a knowledge of psychology. The preparation of copy has usually followed the instincts rather than the analytical functions. An advertisement has been written to describe the articles which it was wished to place before the reader; a bit of cleverness, an attractive cut, or some other catchy device has been used, with the hope that the hit or miss ratio could be made as favorable as possible. But the future must be full of better methods than these to make advertising advance with the same rapidity as it has during the latter part of the last century. And this will come through a closer knowledge of the psychological composition of the mind. The so-called 'students of human nature' will then be called successful psychologists, and the successful advertisers will be likewise termed psychological advertisers. The mere mention of psychological terms, habit, self, conception, discrimination, association, memory, imagination and perception, reason, emotion, instinct and will, should create a flood of new thought that should appeal to every advanced consumer of advertising space."

Task 1 Partner Discussion

Directions: Discuss with your partner about the following topics.

1. Why do the leaders of the advertising profession turn to psychology?
2. What are the "inestimable benefits" that the knowledge of psychology give on advertising?

Task 2 Speaking Practice

Directions: Give a speech on the importance of the study of advertising psychology.

Part 3 Listening and Speaking Practice

Pass 1 Indian Ocean

(Difficulty: ★★★)

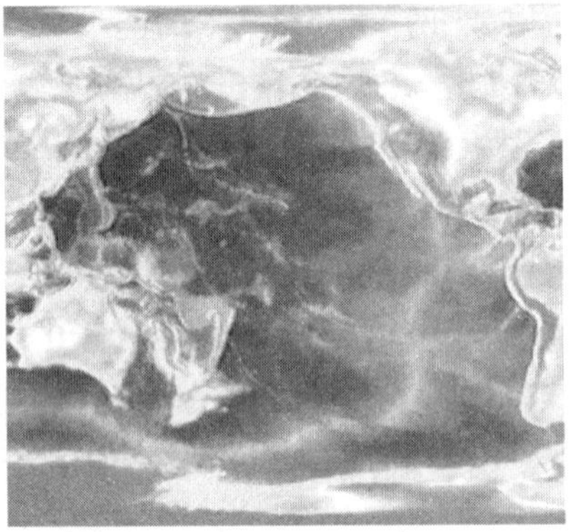

背景知识

印度洋 (Indian Ocean)，位于亚洲、非洲、大洋洲和南极洲之间，大部分在南半球。它的面积为 7 492 万平方千米，约占世界海洋总面积的 21.1%，是世界第三大洋；平均深度为 3 854 米，最大深度在阿米兰特海沟，达 9 074 米。

印度洋在古代被称为“厄立特里亚海”，最早见于古希腊地理学家希罗多德所著《历史》一书及其编绘的世界地图中。“厄立特里亚”（ERYTHREA）希腊文原意为红色，全名意为红海。

印度洋的地理位置非常重要，是沟通亚洲、非洲、欧洲和大洋洲的交通要道。向东通过马六甲海峡可以进入太平洋，向西绕过好望角可到达大西洋，向西北通过红海、苏伊士运河，可入地中海。

明朝时期的西洋是指今文莱以西的东南亚和印度洋沿岸地区。“郑和下西洋”“西洋镜”中的西洋就是此义。

（资料来源：http://wapbaike.baidu.com/view/29284.htm。）

Vocabulary

exotic	[ɪg'zɒtɪk]	*adj.*	异国的，外来的
pristine	['prɪstiːn]	*adj.*	原来的，原始的，古时的
marine	[mə'riːn]	*adj.*	海的；航海的；海产的
pirate	['paɪrət]	*n.*	海盗，盗印者

Task 1 General Understanding

Directions: Watch the video, and then sum up its main idea. You may do this either in Chinese or English.

Tip: Write out words that are clear to you, and take a guess of the gist by making sense of the words sequence.

Task 2 Further Understanding

Directions: Watch the video again and check its main idea. You may do this either in Chinese or English.

Tip: Ask yourself if your guess of the main idea is right. Have you caught any information which might change your idea?

Task 3 Blank Filling

Directions: Listen to the clip again and fill in the following blanks.

(1) ________________ sunsets.
It's an amazing place to visit.
Exotic (2) ____________,
Such a cute thing!
And pristine beaches are only half the story.
Threatening the entire marine (3) ____________.
This is the 21 century and you are going after the pirates.
Sixteen countries with a story to tell.
Such a special place!
Simon Reeve gets (4) ________________ the surface of the Indian Ocean, this weekend on BBC World News.

Task 4 Word Hunting

Directions: Please listen and find out the equivalent English expressions.

1. 异域风情 ________________________________
2. 生态系统 ________________________________
3. 原始的 ________________________________
4. 海洋的 ________________________________

Task 5 Shadow Speaking Practice

Directions: Listen to the ad a couple of times and repeat the words that you've just heard. Retell the ad on your own and then check your work with your partner.

Pass 2 South Africa

(Difficulty: ★★★)

背景知识

南非地处南半球，有“彩虹之国”的美誉，位于非洲大陆的最南端，陆地面积为 1 219 090 平方千米，其东、南、西三面被印度洋和大西洋环抱，其西南端的好望角航线历来是世界上最繁忙的海上通道之一，有“西方海上生命线”之称。南非是世界上唯一存在三个首都的国家。南非是非洲第二大经济体，人均生活水平在非洲名列前茅，工业体系是非洲最完善的，深井采矿技术位居世界前列，矿产是南非经济的主要来源。

罗本岛是南非“种族隔离”时代南非总统纳尔逊·曼德拉及其战友被囚禁达数十年之久的地方。这一富有历史意义的小岛已经成为了世界遗址，并被列为自然保护区。花园大道全长 600 千米，从开普敦到齐齐卡马大森林 (Tsitsikamma Forest)，沿途分布着各式各样的小镇、酿酒厂、农庄和渔村。南非拥有 3 000 千米长的海岸线，从夸祖鲁 – 纳塔尔省 (KwaZulu-Natal) 直到狂野海岸 (Wild Coast)，从东开普省 (Eastern Cape) 延伸到西海岸 (West Coast)。

（资料来源：http://www.360doc.com/content/15/1206/08/475573_518243853.shtml。）

Vocabulary

ancestor	['ænsestə]	*n.*	祖宗，祖先；先驱
shebeen	[ʃɪ'biːn]	*n.*	地下酒吧；低级的酒吧

Task 1 General Understanding

Directions: Watch the clip once and try to grasp its main idea. You may do this either in Chinese or English.

Task 2 Back Translation

Directions: Please translate the following Chinese sentences into English.

1. 因为你不仅仅是游览南非，你是遇见南非。

____

2. 你会夜晚散步，这一晚永生难忘，因为你会感到你是第一次看到了星辰。

____

3. 离开时的你不再是刚来时的你。

____

Task 3 Shadow Speaking Practice

Directions: Watch the ad a couple of times and repeat the words that you've just heard. Retell the ad on your own and then check your work with your partner.

Task 4 Self-dictation

Directions: Please write out the material on a piece of paper. You may pause word by word at the beginning; gradually pause phrase by phrase; and then sentence by sentence. You may pause anywhere you need during the dictation. Pay attention to the stress, rhythm, linkage, tone and sense unit.

Pass 3 Malaysia Truly Asia

(Difficulty: ★★★)

背景知识

马来西亚分为 13 个州，包括西马的柔佛、吉打、吉兰丹、马六甲、森美兰、彭亨、槟榔屿、霹雳、玻璃市、雪兰莪、丁加奴以及东马的沙巴、沙捞越。另有 3 个联邦直辖区：首都吉隆坡、纳闽和布特拉加亚。

早年的印度文明支配着马来西亚。从印度输入的印度教和佛教文化，主导了早期马来西亚的历史。公元初马来半岛有羯荼、狼牙修等古国。15 世纪初以马六甲为中心的满刺加王国统一了马来半岛的大部分。从 7—14 世纪，在苏门答腊的三佛齐文明达到高峰，其影响力延伸至苏门答腊、爪哇、马来半岛和婆罗洲的大部分地区。

马来人没有固定的姓，所以在称呼他们时并不以他们的姓作为称呼。马来人的名字可分为两个部分，第一个部分是他们的名字，中间隔着 “bin” 或 “binti”。第二个部分是他们父亲的名字。马来人的见面礼十分独特，他们在见面时会用双手握住对方的双手互相摩擦，然后将右手往心窝点一点。对不相熟的女士则不可随便伸手要求握手，男子应该向女子点头或稍行鞠躬礼，并且主动致以口头问候。

（资料来源：http://news.xinhuanet.com/ziliao/2002-04/15/content_358691.htm。）

Vocabulary

amongst	[ə'mʌŋst]	*prep.*	在……中间；在……之中
conquer	['kɒŋkə]	*v.*	征服；占领；战胜；得胜
soothe	[su:ð]	*v.*	使平静，使缓和或减轻，安慰

Task 1 Summarize and Compare

Directions: Summarize the main idea of the two clips once and compare them. Which one do you like better, and why? You may do this either in Chinese or English.

Task 2 Shadow Speaking Practice

Directions: Watch the first clip a couple of times and repeat the words that you've just heard. Retell the ad on your own and then check your work with your partner.

Task 3 Self-dictation

Directions: Please write out the first clip on a piece of paper. You may pause word by word at the beginning; gradually pause phrase by phrase; and then sentence by sentence. You may pause anywhere you need during the dictation. Pay attention to the Stress, rhythm, linkage, tone, if there are any.

____

____

____

Task 4 Blank Filling

Directions: Watch the second clip again and fill in the following blanks.

(1) ____________________________
begin in such an extraordinary way
(2) ____________________________
and be near enough to touch it
Or find yourself (3) ____________________________

And yet have so many friends
Where can you walk (4) ______________
And not feel small
Or become king and (5) ______________
All in a day
Where can you feel (6) ______________
and be (7) ______________
Malaysia Truly Asia

Task 5 Sing the Song

Directions: Listen to the song a couple of times and repeat the words that you've just heard. Mimic and sing the song for fun.

Pass 4 Qatar Foundation

(Difficulty: ★★★)

背景知识

卡塔尔基金会是一个私人的、非营利性的慈善组织。它的全称是“卡塔尔教育科学与社会发展基金会”，该组织是 1995 年在卡塔尔酋长的组织下成立的，着重于促进教育、科研和社区方面的发展。现在，在卡塔尔基金会下已有大学、学术研究院和多种培训计划，而且卡塔尔基金会下设的工业技术园区已拥有了超过 21 家科技公司的参与。卡塔尔基金会着重于发出提高生活品质的倡议，包括在社区、半岛电视台少儿频道以及亚洲多家媒体举办著名的多哈辩论等。该组织与合资公司密切配合，进行政策方面的探讨、科学领域的研究，以促进通信技术等方面的发展。所有这一切都是卡塔尔基金会为实现既定目标所作出的努力。

（资料来源：http://www.hssxg.com/shownews.asp?id=519。）

Vocabulary

potential	[pə'tenʃl]	*n.*	潜在性，可能性 *adj.* 有潜力的，潜在的，可能的
authority	[ɔː'θɒrətɪ]	*n.*	专家，权威，威信
innovative	[ˌɪnə'veɪtɪv]	*adj.*	创新的；革新的

Task 1 General Understanding

Directions: Watch the two clips once and try to grasp the main idea of each clip. You may do this either in Chinese or English.

Task 2 Shadow Speaking Practice

Directions: Watch the first clip a couple of times and repeat the words that you've just heard. Retell first on your own and then check your work with your friends.

Task 3 Visual Translation

Directions: Translate the whole passage of the first clip into Chinese. Please note that your translation should be in accordance with the original material in terms of genre and style.

Task 4 Blank Filling

Directions: Listen to the second clip again and fill in the following blanks.

Love cannot happen (1) ________________. When the man is higher than the woman, and older, and (2) ___________ like custom law, you cannot have a relationship between unequals. But (3) ________________ . It's more related to you as a whole. Mind, especially mind. Men are used to love the body of the woman. She is young. She (4) ________________. She is like that albeit doing (5) ________________. She is stupid, but she is beautiful. You know. They don't link the mind of the woman with her body. Men are afraid of (6) ________________.

Task 5 Dubbing Practice

Directions: Turn down the volume and try dubbing the second clip until you sound just like the speaker. Now you may record your dubbing for comparison or just for fun.

Task 6 Compare and Discuss

Directions: Compare these two clips and find their common aspects. What do you think is the purpose of Qatar Foundation?

Pass 5 Qatar Airways

(Difficulty: ★★★)

背景知识

Qatar Airways Company Q.C.S.C.is the state-owned flag carrier of Qatar. Headquartered in the Qatar Airways Tower in Doha, the airline operates a hub-and-spoke network, linking over 140 international destinations across Africa, Central Asia, Europe, Far East, South Asia, Middle East, North America, South America and Oceania from its base at Hamad International Airport, using a fleet of more than 150 aircraft.

Vocabulary

footprint	[fʊtprɪnt]	*n.*	脚印；足迹
cautious	['kɔːʃəs]	*adj.*	谨慎的；小心的
perception	[pə'sepʃn]	*n.*	知觉，领悟力，感觉
destination	[destɪ'neɪʃn]	*n.*	目的地

Task 1 General Understanding

Directions: Watch the two clips once and try to grasp the main idea of each clip. You may do this either in Chinese or English.

Task 2 Blank Filling

Directions: Watch the first clip again and fill in the following blanks.

A journey is not just A to B. It's also being (1) ________________, the taste of the air, the footprints (2) ________________. It's making new connections to a moment, a place.

A journey is cautious steps, a change in perception, and (3) ________________.

A journey is reaching the end and discovering you are only half way there.

Connecting over 110 destinations, stopover in Doha, with Qatar Airways, world's (4) ________________.

Task 3 Shadow Speaking Practice

Directions: Watch the first clip a couple of times and repeat the words that you've just heard. Retell first on your own and then check your work with your friends.

Task 4 Compare

Directions: Compare the two clips and report the differences. You may do this either in Chinese or English.

Task 5 Self-dictation

Directions: Please write out the second clip on a piece of paper. You may pause word by word at the beginning; gradually pause phrase by phrase; and then sentence by sentence. You may pause anywhere you need during the dictation. Pay attention to the stress, rhythm, linkage, tone, if there are any.

____

____

____

Task 6 Dubbing Practice

Directions: Turn down the volume and try dubbing each clip until you sound just like the speaker. Now you may record your dubbing for comparison or just for fun.

Pass 6: Palmer's

(Difficulty: ★★★)

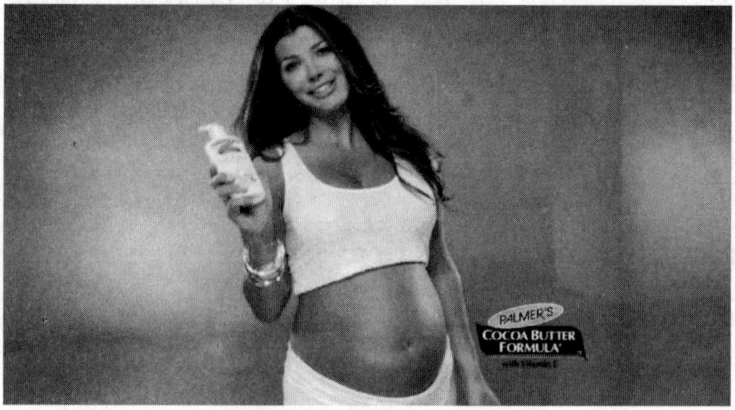

Vocabulary

formula	['fɔːmjələ] *n.* 配方
ingredient	[ɪn'griːdɪənt] *n.* 成分；因素
elasticity	[ˌɪlæ'stɪsətɪ] *n.* 弹力；弹性
massage	[mə'sɑːʒ] *n.* 化妆水
lotion	['ləʊʃn] *n.* 润肤乳

tummy	['tʌmɪ]	*n.*	胃，肚子
stretch mark	妊娠纹		

Task 1 General Understanding

Directions: Watch the clip once and try to grasp its main idea. You may do this either in Chinese or English.

Task 2 True or False

Directions: Watch the clip and tell whether the following statements are true or false (T/F).

1. ( ) Ali Landry uses Palmer's Cocoa butter Formula to fight speckles.
2. ( ) Palmer's contains an advanced blend of four ingredients.
3. ( ) Use Palmer's Massage Lotion during the day and Tummy Butter before bed.
4. ( ) In a recent independent study, skin elasticity improved in 87% women tested.

Task 3 Shadow Speaking Practice

Directions: Watch the ad a couple of times and repeat words that you've just heard. Retell first on your own and then check your work with your friends.

Task 4 Blank Filling

Directions: Listen to the clip again and fill in the following blanks.

As an actress I know how to fight (1) ___________. You use Palmer's Cocoa butter Formula. Palmer's® now contains (2) _____________, an (3) _____________ of five ingredients that help reduce the appearance of stretch marks.

In a recent independent study (4) _____________ improved in 97% women tested.

I use Palmer's Massage Lotion during the day and (5) _____________ before bed. And I love the results.

I'm Ali Landry. Palmer's® works. And I'm (6) _____________.

Palmer's Cocoa Butter Formula for stretch mark, perfect formula, (7) _____________.

Pass 7 Zero Trafficked Children

(Difficulty: ★★★)

背景知识

联合国儿童基金会 (United Nations Children's Fund—UNICEF) 于 1946 年 12 月 11 日成立，为联合国专门机构。其前身为联合国国际儿童紧急基金会，1953 年改为现名，简称儿童基金会，总部设在纽约。

该基金会的宗旨是帮助发展中国家儿童解决保健、福利和教育等问题。基金会下设领导机构执行局，成员由经社理事会按地区分配与主要捐款国和受援国代表性原则选举产生，任期三年，原有执委会 30 名，1983 年起扩大至 41 名，每年 5 月举行年会；秘书处负责处理日常事务，在各有关国家设有办事处，约有工作人员 5 000 名。现任执行主任是美国前农业部长安·维尼曼 (Ann M. Veneman)，2005 年任职。2010 年 3 月，美国总统奥巴马的前外交政策顾问安东尼·莱克被任命为执行主任。

该组织于 1965 年设立了莫里斯·佩特奖，以纪念联合国儿童基金会第一任执行主任莫里斯·佩特。

1979 年起，我国与该基金会发展合作关系；1980 年我国当选为执行局成员；1981 年在北京设有基金会办事处。

2012 年 4 月 5 日，中国演员陈坤正式出任联合国儿童基金会（UNICEF）中国大使。该基金会是首个任命名人为亲善大使的联合国机构。1954 年，美国喜剧明星丹尼·凯成为联合国儿童基金会首位亲善大使。今天，全球各地有超过 300 位名人和演艺界明星担任联合国儿童基金会国际级、地区级或国家级大使。

此前，联合国儿童基金会在中国任命的名人大使还包括杨澜和张曼玉。联合国儿童基金会的大使均为来自艺术、娱乐、体育或其他领域的杰出公众人物。他们热衷儿童公益事业，致力于提高公众对儿童问题的认知度，号召社会对儿童公益事业提供更为广泛的支持。

（资料来源：http://news.xinhuanet.com/ziliao/2003-01/27/content_709549.htm。）

Vocabulary

prostitution	[ˌprɒstɪ'tjuːʃən]	*n.*	卖淫
grueling	['gruːəlɪŋ]	*adj.*	累垮人的；令人受不了的
victim	['vɪktɪm]	*n.*	受害人，牺牲品，牺牲者
trafficking	['træfɪkɪŋ]	*n.*	非法交易
exploitative	[ɪk'splɒɪtətɪv]	*adj.*	剥削的，掠夺的
solitude	['sɒlɪtjuːd]	*n.*	孤独，孤寂，单独

Task 1 General Understanding

Directions: Watch the clip once and try to grasp its main idea. You may do this either in Chinese or English.

Task 2 Listening Comprehension

Directions: Listen again and choose the best answer from the choices marked A), B), C) and D).

1. What are the sold children forced to do?
   A) They are forced to work with high pay.
   B) They are forced to work and play.
   C) They are forced into prostitution or work with little or no pay.
   D) None of the above.
2. Angie Harmon believes the number of children suffering this way should be ________.
   A) reasonable few   B) zero
   C) numerous   D) none of the above
3. How many children are victims of forced labor and child trafficking all over the world?
   A) Five and a half million.   B) Five and a half thousand.
   C) Five and a half hundred.   D) None of the above.

Task 3 Self-dictation

Directions: Please write out the material on a piece of paper. You may pause word by word at the beginning; gradually pause phrase by phrase; and then sentence by sentence. You may pause anywhere you need during the dictation. Pay attention to the stress, rhythm, linkage, tone, if there are any.

____

____

____

Task 4 Shadow Speaking Practice

Directions: Listen to the ad a couple of times and repeat words that you've just heard. Retell first on your own and then check your work with your friends.

Task 5 Speaking Practice

Directions: Present an informative speech on the following topic.

In which ways can we combat child trafficking?

Pass 8 Environmental Protection Advertisement

(Difficulty: ★★★★)

背景知识

The United Nations Development Programme (UNDP) is the United Nations' global development network. Headquartered in New York City, the UNDP advocates for change and connects countries to knowledge, experience and resources to help people build a better life. It provides expert advice, training, and grant support to developing countries, with increasing emphasis on assistance to the least developed countries.

The UNDP focuses on poverty reduction, HIV/AIDS, democratic governance, energy and environment, social development, and crisis prevention and recovery. The UNDP also encourages the protection of human rights and the empowerment of women in all of its programmes. The UNDP Human Development Report Office also publishes an annual Human Development Report.

The UNDP is funded entirely by voluntary contributions from member nations. The organization operates in 177 countries, where it works with local governments to meet development challenges and develop local capacity. Additionally, the UNDP works internationally to help countries achieve the Millennium Development Goals. Currently, the UNDP is one of the main UN agencies involved in the development of the Post-2015 Development Agenda.

Vocabulary

bio-diversity	*n.* 生物多样性
reliable	[rɪ'laɪəbl] *adj.* 可靠的，可信赖的
pressing	['presɪŋ] *adj.* 紧迫的，迫切的
collaboration	[kəˌlæbə'reɪʃn] *n.* 合作；共同研究
nutritious	[nuː'trɪʃəs] *adj.* 有营养成分的
partner	['pɑːrtnə] *v.* 与……合伙

Task 1 General Understanding

Directions: Watch each of the two clips once and try to grasp their respective main idea. You may do this either in Chinese or English.

Task 2 True or False

Directions: Watch the two clips and tell whether the following statements are true or false (T/F).

1. ( ) Forests lost every minute are the size of 5 football fields.
2. ( ) The United Nations Development Program aims to protect forests.
3. ( ) Everyday there are 115,000 more people in the world than yesterday.
4. ( ) DuPont aims to arrive at more sustainable energy solution by partnering on a global scale.

Task 3 Compare

Directions: Compare the two clips and find their common and different aspects. Which one do you like better, and why?

Task 4 Shadow Speaking Practice

Directions: Listen to the first clip a couple of times and repeat words that you've just heard. Retell first on your own and then check your work with your friends.

Task 5 Self-dictation

Directions: Please write out the first clip on a piece of paper. You may pause word by word at the beginning; gradually pause phrase by phrase; and then sentence by sentence. You may pause anywhere you need during the dictation. Pay attention to the stress, rhythm, linkage, tone, if there are any.

____

____

____

Task 6 Blank Filling

Directions: Listen to the second clip twice and fill in the following blanks.

Today is unlike any other day because today there are (1) __________ in the world than yesterday, which means we face even bigger challenges than we did just last night. It means the need for (2) __________ is now more pressing, as is (3) __________ to find them. Working with one another is the only way we'll be able to provide more (4) ___________ to this ever-growing population. (5) ___________ is how we will arrive at more sustainable energy solutions for a planet that increasingly demands them. Coming together is how we will better protect the earth and the billions who call it home. DuPont is reaching out across (6) ___________ to find these answers. And we invite you to join us. Rest assured, we won't stop searching, exploring, collaborating until we all live healthier, better and safer lives. Welcome to the global collaborator, welcome to DuPont.

Pass 9 Russian Railways

(Difficulty: ★★★★)

背景知识

铁路运输是国际贸易运输中的主要运输方式之一。世界上的第一条铁路出现在 1825 年的英国，其后铁路建设迅速发展，到 19 世纪末，世界铁路总里程达 65 万千米，目前已有 140 多万千米。世界铁路分布很不平衡，其中欧洲、美洲各占世界铁路总长度的 1/3，而亚洲、非洲和大洋洲加在一起仅占 1/3 左右。

Vocabulary

reliable	[rɪ'laɪəbl]	*adj.*	可靠的，可信赖的
destination	[ˌdestɪ'neɪʃn]	*n.*	目的地
incorporate	[ɪn'kɔːrpəreɪt]	*v.*	合并；组成公司
Siberian	[saɪ'bɪərɪən]	*adj.*	西伯利亚的
St. Petersburg	圣彼得堡		
Helsinki	赫尔辛基		

Task 1 General Understanding

Directions: Watch to the clip once and try to grasp its main idea. You may do this either in Chinese or English.

Task 2 Shadow Speaking Practice

Directions: Watch the clip a couple of times and repeat the words that you've just heard sentence by sentence. Retell the passage first on your own and then check your work with your friends. Finally report the passage to your classmates.

Task 3 Blank Filling

Directions: Listen to the clip again and fill in the following blanks.

For 170 years Russian Railways has built (1) __________ between Europe, Asia and the most remote corners of Russia. Today Russian Railways is one of the largest (2) __________ in the world with (3) __________, operating the trans-Siberian railway, the longest in the world, linking Europe and Asia where 80% of Russian industrial potential is concentrated. Incorporating (4) __________, Russian Railways ensures careful and safe (5) __________. Further innovations will soon (6) __________ across the trans-Siberian railway in just 7 days. Developing (7) __________ including destinations between Moscow, St. Petersburg and Helsinki, tomorrow Russian Railways will bring Europe and Asia closer together faster than ever before. Russian Railways, linked to business, linked to life.

Pass 10 Advertisement Battle

(Difficulty: ★★★★★)

Vocabulary

surf	[sɜːf] *v.*	冲浪
ritual	['rɪtʃʊəl] *n.*	仪式，宗教仪式，典礼
icon	['aɪkɒn] *n.*	形象，图像；肖像，画像；偶像
overdo	[əʊvə(r)'duː] *v.*	做得过分，夸张，过度；过火
invincible	[ɪn'vɪnsəbl] *adj.*	不能征服的，无敌的
titan	['taɪtən] *n.*	巨人，大力士
poster child	榜样	
breakthrough	突破	
high-flying	高涨的，有雄心的	
branch into	拓展业务	

Task 1 General Understanding

Directions: Watch the clip once and try to grasp its main idea. You may do this either in Chinese or English.

Task 2 Q&A

Directions: Listen and answer the following questions.

1. What does Google and Yahoo! fight over? Who wins this war?
2. What do you learn about the founders of Google?
3. What other area(s) have Google and Yahoo! both branched into?

Task 3 Blank Filling

Directions: Listen to the clip again and fill in the following blanks.

Thank you. (1)__________ are if you've surfed the web you've used the search engines, Google and Yahoo!. But, here is something you might not know: behind every search is (2) __________ for (3) __________ and so far, Google is winning the war. More now from CNBC's Carl Quintanilla:

It's become a (4) __________: find something, anything you are interested in and Google it. Enough of the habit for millions of web users that (5) __________ are now getting hurt. This week, Yahoo!, one of the web's original (6) __________, said competition from Google is (7) __________ to make money. And experts like David Vice, co-author of a new book on Google, says the company is the biggest (8) __________ in media since the printing press.

Task 4 Back Translation

Directions: Please translate the following Chinese sentences into English.

1. Google 和 Yahoo! 的收入来源于你每次进行搜索时所看到的广告。据估计，截止到 2010 年，该行业的利润达 120 亿美元。

____

2. 但目前还没有哪家网站能赶超 Google 或其不断上涨的股票——近期每股价格已经达到 500 美元，这也把两个从斯坦福大学辍学的学生——Google 的创始人造就成了名流。

____

Part 4 英语听说秘籍之意群（Sense Group）与停顿（Pause）

(Difficulty: ★★★★★)

意群是指在意义和语法上密切相关的词群。意群是分析、理解英语语句的关键，一个意群便是一个信息单元，阅读时抓住意群则事半功倍；口头表达以意群为单位，则沟通顺畅；当然在一个较长的意群中，我们也可以做节奏上的停顿。

从阅读的意义上来讲，意群就是指我们平时阅读一篇文章时，视线每停留一次，进入我们视界范围的单词会有多个，而这些单词不带有任意性，单词与单词之间的逻辑意义紧密相连，我们可以暂且将这种意义紧密相连的多个单词视为一个意群。

在一个较长的句子中，如果按意群来读，意群之间稍加停顿，就可以让听者听清我们语流中的意群和句子，也可以喘一口气，然后接着再说，而且能体现出英语所特有的节奏和韵律，但是在一个意群中不可停顿。

停顿的方法：语言虽然是一个音一个音组成的，但不是一个音一个音或一个词一个词吐出来的，而是一组一组，一群一群相互密切联系的意群组合。意群可以由好几个单词组成，也可以只是一个单词。意群和意群之间可以有微弱的停顿（但不一定要停顿），为了在朗读或说话时把意群很好地联系在一起，就需要恰当的停顿、拖音或连读来一气呵成。至于意群之间停顿的频率问题，这就要看讲话或朗读的速度，讲得慢时停顿就多些，反之就少些。

示例：

里根总统第二任就职演说词：We must do what we know is right, and do it with all our might.（我们必须做我们认为是正确的事，而且要全力去做。）

本句绝不能读成 We/must/do/what/we/know/is right,/and do/it with all/our might. 长句中有短暂的停顿，借以调和呼吸，这是自然的现象，但停顿的地方必须恰到好处。停顿通常在有标点符号的地方，词组或意群之间。短语、从句等意群成一个单位，它们之间可以短暂停顿。例如：We must do/what we know is right,/and do it/with all our might.

例句1：The primary method previously used by paleontologists to estimate climatic changes that occurred during Pleistocene glacial cycles was the determination of 180/160 ratios in calcareous fossils.

例句2：In the Weary Blues, Hughes chose to modify the traditions that decreed that African American literature must promote racial acceptance and integration, and that, in order to do so, it must reflect an understanding and mastery of Western European literary techniques and styles.

例句3：The petition asked that during June, July, and August the working hours be changed from 8 to 5 with an hour off for lunch to 7 to 3:30 with a half-hour for lunch.

练习：朗读并用斜杠标出句子中的意群

1. There are so many Chinese dialects that two people from different provinces or even from the same province cannot understand each other.
2. As I wandered through the waking land, I heard from copse and farm and meadow the timid callings of the little new-born things, wondering to find them alive.
3. All of us have read thrilling stories in which the hero had only a limited and specified time to live. Sometimes it was as long as a year, sometimes as short as 24 hours. But always we were interested in discovering just how the doomed hero chose to spend

his last days or his last hours. I speak, of course, of free men who have a choice, not condemned criminals whose sphere of activities is strictly delimited.

4. They live in that large house on the other side of the bridge.
5. In the morning the boy goes to school early. Sometimes he was late, because his mother was in poor health.
6. It is very important for us to take part in manual labour from time to time.
7. Do you remember all those years when scientists argued that smoking would kill us but the doubters insisted that we didn't know for sure?
8. However, whether it comes from the common ancestor that the species had 35 million years ago, is, as yet, an unanswered question.
9. What is harder to establish is whether the productivity revolution that businessmen assume they are presiding over is for real.
10. She sells sea shells by the sea shore. The shells she sells are surely seashells. So if she sells shells on the seashore, I'm sure she sells seashore shells.
11. I cannot bear to see a bear bear down upon a hare. When bare of hair he strips the hare, right there I cry, "Forbear!"
12. There once was a man who had a sister; his name was Mr. Fister. Mr. Fister's sister sold sea shells by the sea shore. Mr. Fister didn't sell sea shells; he sold silk sheets. Mr. Fister told his sister that he sold six silk sheets to six shrieks. The sister of Mr. Fister said I sold six shells to six shrieks too!
13. How much wood would a woodchuck chuck if a wood chuck could chuck wood? A woodchuck would chuck all the wood a woodchuck could chuck if a woodchuck could chuck wood. How many cookies could a good cook cook? If a good cook could cook cookies, a good cook could cook as much cookies as a good cook who could cook cookies.
14. A snow-white swan swam swiftly to catch a slowly-swimming snake in a lake.
15. Once two hunters went hunting in the forest. One of them suddenly fell down by accident. He showed the whites of his eyes and seemed to have ceased breathing. The other hunter soon took out his mobile phone to call the emergency center for help. The operator said calmly: "First, you should make sure that he is already dead." Then the operator heard a gunshot from the other end of the phone and next he heard the hunter asking: "What should I do next".

English Listening-and-Speaking Learning Planner

Monday	**Tuesday**	**Wednesday**	**Thursday**	**Friday**
Practicing Hour: ________ Tape Hour: ________ Commitment: ________	Practicing Hour: ________ Tape Hour: ________ Commitment: ________	Practicing Hour: ________ Tape Hour: ________ Commitment: ________	Practicing Hour: ________ Tape Hour: ________ Commitment: ________	Practicing Hour: ________ Tape Hour: ________ Commitment: ________
Saturday Practicing Hour: ________ Tape Hour: ________ Commitment: ________	**Sunday** Practicing Hour: ________ Tape Hour: ________ Commitment: ________	**General Performance for Week ____:** (vocabulary, long sentence, background information, etc.) Self-rating ☆☆☆☆☆		

Monday	**Tuesday**	**Wednesday**	**Thursday**	**Friday**
Practicing Hour: ________ Tape Hour: ________ Commitment: ________	Practicing Hour: ________ Tape Hour: ________ Commitment: ________	Practicing Hour: ________ Tape Hour: ________ Commitment: ________	Practicing Hour: ________ Tape Hour: ________ Commitment: ________	Practicing Hour: ________ Tape Hour: ________ Commitment: ________
Saturday Practicing Hour: ________ Tape Hour: ________ Commitment: ________	**Sunday** Practicing Hour: ________ Tape Hour: ________ Commitment: ________	**General Performance for Week ____:** (vocabulary, long sentence, background information, etc.) Self-rating ☆☆☆☆☆		

Chapter 5

Health

Part 1 Famous Quotes

I stand in awe of my body.

—Henry David Thoreau

我敬畏我的身体。

——亨利·大卫·索罗

If you want happiness for an hour — take a nap.
If you want happiness for a day — go fishing.
If you want happiness for a month — get married.
If you want happiness for a year — inherit a fortune.
If you want happiness for a lifetime — help someone else.

—Chinese proverb

如果你想要一小时的幸福，那就打个盹吧。
如果你想要一天的幸福，去钓鱼吧。
如果你想要一个月的幸福，去结婚吧。
如果你想要一年的幸福，继承财富吧。
如果你想要一辈子的幸福，帮助他人吧。

——中国谚语

The secret of health for both mind and body is not to mourn for the past, not to worry about the future, not to anticipate the future, but to live the present moment wisely and earnestly.

—Buddlism Language

身心健康的秘诀：不悲过去，非贪未来，心系当下，由此安详。

——佛语

Part 2 Background Knowledge

(1) Why Is Health Important?

(See: http://www.buzzle.com/articles/why-is-health-important.html.)

Health is not just about a healthy body but also about sound mental health. Good health refers to the condition where both our body and our mind are functioning properly. There are many causes behind poor health condition, for example, diseases, improper diet, injury, mental stress, lack of hygiene, unhealthy lifestyle, etc. Over the past few years, our lifestyle has changed a lot and we often ignore the importance of healthy living in one way or the other.

There are several benefits of a healthy life. Your body becomes free from various forms of disorders and thus, you live longer. You can live a life without suffering from any aches, pain, or discomfort. In every sphere of your life, you will be able to perform to the best of your ability. Doing excellent work helps you to be a valuable member of a healthy society. Besides, when you are physically fit, it gets reflected on your face. So, you look attractive and start feeling good about yourself! If you have a fit body, then you can lead a physically active life even after growing old. This is because the body can heal the regular wear and tear associated with aging faster. In short, health and wellness brings about a drastic improvement in the overall quality of your life.

As a college student, it's vital for you to stay healthy. You need enough energy to spend the entire days in school. You should be able to focus in the classroom and fully participate in the activities on the field. To stay healthy, you need proper nutrition which includes carbohydrates, proteins, calcium, minerals, etc, and you also need to exercise regularly. Stay away from unhealthy habits like smoking and heavy drinking. It is also essential to keep the mind healthy by nurturing the right kind of thoughts and proper stress management.

Task Oral Practice

Directions: Look at the following topics carefully and then choose one topic and deliver a short (1–3 minutes) presentation.

1. As a college student, how can you live a healthy life?
2. Can you list some bad habits of college students that may do harm to their health?

3. What are some of the consequences of drugs, alcohol or tobacco to one's health?

Tip: We suggest that you start with a list of ideas. You may not use all of them; still you will find one or two great ideas. Sit down with a pen and a piece of paper. Make a list, what are some things you know about? Upon your list, you may pick your topic. Then, you can make an idea web in which you should put your ideas in order.

(2) Why Is Exercise Important?

(See: http://www.healthdiscovery.net/articles/exercise_important.htm.)

Vocabulary

flabby	['flæbɪ]	*adj.*	肌肉松垂的，肥胖的
crave	[kreɪv]	*vt.& vi.*	渴望，热望；恳求，恳请；要求，需要
diabetes	[ˌdaɪə'bi:ti:s]	*n.*	糖尿病；多尿症
stamina	['stæmənə]	*n.*	体力，耐力，持久力
ligament	['lɪgəmənt]	*n.*	韧带
cardio	['kɑ:dɪoʊ]	*n.*	有氧运动

Have you ever heard the expression "use it or lose it"? It's true! If you don't use your body, you will surely lose it. Your muscles will become flabby and weak. Your heart and lungs won't function efficiently. And your joints will be stiff and easily injured. Inactivity is as much of a health risk as smoking!

Helps Prevent Diseases

Our bodies were meant to move—they actually crave exercise. Regular exercise is necessary for physical fitness and good health. It reduces the risk of heart disease, cancer, high blood pressure, diabetes and other diseases. It can improve your appearance and delay the aging process.

Improves Stamina

When you exercise, your body uses energy to keep going. Aerobic exercise involves continuous and rhythmic physical motion, such as walking and bicycling. It improves your stamina by training your body to become more efficient and use less energy for the same amount of work. As your conditioning level improves, your heart rate and breathing rate return to resting levels much sooner from strenuous activity.

Strengthens

Exercising with weights and other forms of resistance training develops your muscles, bones and ligaments for increased strength and endurance. Your posture can be improved, and your muscles become more firm and toned. You not only feel better, but you look better, too!

Enhances Flexibility

Stretching exercises are also important for good posture. They keep your body limber so that you can bend, reach and twist. Improving your flexibility through exercise reduces the chance of injury and improves balance and coordination. If you have stiff, tense areas, such as the upper back or neck, performing specific stretches can help "loosen" those muscles, helping you feel more relaxed.

Controls Weight

Exercise is also a key to weight control because it burns calories. If you burn off more calories than you take in, you lose weight. It's as simple as that.

Improves Quality of Life

Once you begin to exercise regularly, you will discover many more reasons why exercise is so important to improving the quality of your life. Exercise reduces stress, lifts moods, and helps you sleep better. It can keep you looking and feeling younger throughout your entire life.

Task Word Hunting

Directions: Please find out the equivalent English expressions of the following words and expressions.

1. 僵硬 ____________________
2. 高血压 ____________________
3. 糖尿病 ____________________
4. 有氧运动 ____________________
5. 精力 ____________________
6. 耐力 ____________________
7. 协调水平 ____________________
8. 生活品质 ____________________
9. 提升情绪 ____________________
10. 柔韧性 ____________________

Part 3 Listening and Speaking Practice

Pass 1 Banning Smoking in Russia

(Difficulty: ★★★)

背景知识

2012 年底俄罗斯政府 (Russian government) 推出了一部严格的禁烟法案：2015 年起，俄罗斯任何公共场所 (public place) 禁止吸烟，包括餐馆和咖啡厅。

俄罗斯总理梅德韦杰夫 (Dmitry Medvedev) 始终坚持推动禁烟法案。他说：吸烟是一个大问题，会影响民众的生活质量，而过去我们对它过于忽略了，我们必须像世界其他地方一样走向文明。

禁烟令规定，政府办公室，教育、医疗、体育以及文化设施，公共交通以及居民区的公共场所首先禁止吸烟。从 2014 年 7 月开始，长途列车、飞机、酒店、市场以及商店等场所也禁止吸烟。2015 年，包括餐馆和咖啡厅等公共场所开始禁烟。此外，禁烟令还禁止烟草产品广告。

据有关统计数字显示，1/3 的俄罗斯人吸烟，烟民总数达 4 400 万人。俄罗斯卫生部长韦罗妮卡·斯克沃尔佐娃 (Veronika Skvortsova) 说，只要 10% 的烟民戒烟，就将为俄罗斯 2013 年预算额外增加 35 亿美元（约合人民币 219 亿元）可支配资金。

（资料来源：http://gb.cri.cn/27824/2012/10/192805s3893436.htm。）

Vocabulary

ounce	[aʊns]	*n.*	盎司
lobby	['lɒbɪ]	*vt.*	对……进行游说；陈情（试图努力影响某人采取有利行动）

legislation	[ˌledʒɪ'sleɪʃən]	*n.*	立法，制定法律
crack down on	打击		
video blog	视频博客		
be hooked on	对……上瘾		

Task 1 General Understanding

Directions: Listen to the news once and try to grasp its main idea. You may do this either in Chinese or English.

Task 2 Q&A

Directions: Listen to the news and answer the following questions.

1. According to Russian Prime Minister, what's the percentage of people who are addicted to smoking? And how many died of smoking-related causes every year?

____

____

2. What does the proposed bill claim to do?

____

3. What are some of the people's responses towards this campaign?

____

____

Task 3 Blank Filling

Directions: Listen to the news again and fill in missing words.

Russian (1) __________ Dmitry Medvedev is (2) __________ a campaign to (3) __________ smoking in Russia, the world's second biggest tobacco market after (4) __________.

In a message on his video blog, he warns that one in three Russians (5) __________ cigarettes and nearly 400,000 die each year from (6) __________ causes. The campaign includes a proposed bill to ban tobacco (7) __________, raise cigarette (8) __________ and (9) __________ ban smoking in public places.

However, Russians generally don't seem to be (10) __________ about the proposed law.

"I think people would be smoking no matter what. It's Russia."Vladimir, a resident of Moscow agrees. He says people will smoke despite the ban. But his friend Donia says some could possibly quit if cigarette prices go up to (11) __________ Rubles or about 10 US dollars a pack.

The bill is expected to be (12) __________ to parliament for (13) __________ in the coming days as big tobacco companies lobby to (14) __________ any new anti-smoking (15) __________.

Task 4 Shadow Speaking Practice

Directions: Listen to the news again and repeat after the speaker. Pay attention to your speed, pronunciation and intonation.

Task 5 Oral Practice

Directions: Look at the following topics carefully and deliver a short (1–3 minutes) presentation.

1. Why do people smoke?
2. Should smoking be banned in public places in China, too?

Pass 2 Radio Calisthenics

(Difficulty: ★★★)

背景知识

广播体操起始于美国。在 20 世纪 20 年代，美国大都会生活保险公司 (MetLife) 在美国的几个大城市推广了 15 分钟的广播体操。随后，在美国访问的日本邮政保险公司将其引进日本。在 20 世纪三四十年代，广播体操被广泛用来提高日本海内外士兵的身体素质，1951 年广播体操来到中国。时至今日，一些学校依旧将广播体操作为一项运动，一些公司也推广广播体操用以提振士气。

Vocabulary

calisthenics	[ˌkælɪsˈθenɪks]	*n.* 柔软体操，运动
work break exercise		工间操，课间操
occupational disease		职业病
the Beijing Federation of Trade Unions		北京总工会

Task 1 General Understanding

Directions: Listen to the news item once and try to grasp its main idea. You may do this either in Chinese or English.

Task 2 True or False

Directions: Listen to the news again and tell whether the following statements are true or false (T/F).

1. ( ) According to the news, work break exercise came to Beijing in October.
2. ( ) To prevent occupational diseases, companies have all adopted the same form of work break exercises.
3. ( ) After the exercises, many employees feel more relaxed and energetic.
4. ( ) The resumption of work break exercises is meant to remind people of the old good times.
5. ( ) Work break exercises will be abandoned in the near future.

Task 3 Back Translation

Directions: Please watch the video attentively and then translate the following Chinese sentences into English.

1. 经北京总工会的提议，工间操于八月初回归北京。

____

____

2. 在这个职业病知识深入人心的时代，很多公司创建了不同形式的体操来适应不同的工作环境和员工需求。

____

____

3. 工作了一天，我的腰和脖子都是酸的。

____

____

4. 特别是在新中国成立之初，它在提高人们的身体健康方面发挥了重要作用。

____

____

5. 现在很多公司组织员工在休息时间做广播体操，员工们利用这一机会让自己的血液活动起来。

____

____

6. 做了广播体操后，我觉得关节更加灵活，精力更充沛，工作效率也更高了。

____

____

Task 4 Blank Filling

Directions: Listen to the news again and fill in the following blanks.

As the Beijing Federation of Trade Unions (1) ________, work break exercise came back to Beijing in early August. In this (2) ________ of welcoming knowledge of occupational disease, many companies are creating different forms of exercise to (3) ________ their work conditions and (4) ________.

My work makes me always sit at the desk and face the computer. After a whole day's work my waist and neck are sore. Yoga calisthenics works many (5) ________ and by doing it during the (6) ________ I feel relaxed.

Fifty years ago, radio calisthenics were first introduced in China to develop mass (7) ________. All work units organized their staff to do it during work breaks every day. It played an important role in improving people's health, especially during the early period of the founding of the People's Republic of China.

Now many companies (8) ________ their staff to do radio calisthenics as work break exercise. The employees welcome this opportunity to get the blood flowing.

For our salespersons, who have been standing all day, the work break exercise is good for the health. After finishing about a radio calisthenics, I feel my joint loose enough. I have more energy and work more efficiently.

Radio calisthenics are simple, (9) ________ and good for the health. Its return brings back many (10) ________ to local people.

Chest out, and jumps ...

I did this since I was in school.

Task 5 Shadow Speaking Practice

Directions: Listen to the video again and repeat after the speaker. Pay attention to your speed, pronunciation and intonation.

Pass 3 Women and Alcohol

(Difficulty: ★★★)

背景知识

过量饮酒会使人的大脑不清醒，会做出一些失去理智的事情。但从另一个方面来讲，对于女性而言，喝酒还是有一些好处的，每天一小杯酒能起到养生的作用。适当喝点酒，还能起到减肥、美容的效果，但是，酒好却不能贪杯。

Wine: 有时专指酒精含量较低的葡萄酒和果酒。

Spirit: 指酒精度高的酒，常指烈性酒，一般用复数形式；指“酒精”时，用单数形式。

Alcohol: 指酒精，常指“含酒精的饮料”；指“各种酒类”时，包括果酒和烈性酒在内。

Liquor：指酒、酒类。英国人认为 liquor 指各种含酒精的饮品，与 alcohol 同义；美国人把高度烈酒称作 (hard) liquor；在美式法律英语中，liquor 泛指各种酒。

alcohol 与 wine 的区别：后者适用于生活气息比较浓厚的场合，比 alcohol 更贴近生活，更富人情味。

liquor 与 wine 的差别：前者用蒸馏法制成，后者用发酵法酿制。

Vocabulary

hangover	['hæŋəʊvə(r)]	*n.*	宿醉
concentrated	['kɑːnsntreɪtɪd]	*adj.*	浓缩的
infection	[ɪn'fekʃən]	*n.*	感染
ounce	[aʊns]	*n.*	盎司
liquor	['lɪkə]	*n.*	烈性酒，含酒精的饮料
pregnancy	['pregnənsɪ]	*n.*	怀孕
nono	['nəʊˌnəʊ]	*n.*	禁忌，禁例
deformity	[dɪ'fɔːmətɪ]	*n.*	畸形
cognitive	['kɑːgnətɪv]	*adj.*	认知的，认识的，有感知的
newborn	['nuːbɔːrn]	*n.*	婴儿
predisposed	[priːdɪs'pəʊzd]	*adj.*	有某种健康状态的，有……倾向的
cardiac	['kɑːdɪæk]	*adj.*	心脏的

Task 1 General Understanding

Directions: Listen to the news once and try to grasp its main idea. You may do this either in Chinese or English.

Task 2 Q&A

Directions: Listen to the news again and answer the following questions.

1. What is the meaning of "at a level playing field" according to the context?

   ____

2. Why does alcohol become more concentrated in women's bodies?

   ____

3. When alcohol becomes concentrated in women's bodies, what can it damage?

   ____

4. If women have two drinks a day, what may it lead to?

   ____

5. What is considered one drink in terms of beer, wine and hard liquor?

   ____

6. According to the government, what is considered heavy drink?

   ____

7. Why is it a real nono to drink during pregnancy?

   ____

8. If pregnant women drink alcohol, what are the different influences on daughters and sons?

   ____

9. Is there any benefit that alcohol has?

   ____

10. In order to get the benefit, how many drinks should be taken a week?

    ____

11. Can women have the same benefit as men do?

    ____

Task 3 Back Translation

Directions: Please watch the video attentively and then translate the following Chinese sentences into English.

1. 男人和女人的喝酒水平不一样。

____

2. 研究人士称女性比男性的脂细胞多而水分少，因此在女性体内酒精的浓度更高。

____

3. 对女性来说，一天喝两杯酒可能引发很多疾病。

____

4. 根据政府部门的说法，女性只要每天喝酒超过一杯就是酗酒。

____

5. 对于那些易患乳腺癌的女性来说，喝酒对心脏并没有好处。

____

Task 4 Shadow Speaking Practice

Directions: Listen to the news again and repeat after the speaker. Pay attention to your speed, pronunciation and intonation.

Pass 4 Meditation Benefits

(Difficulty: ★★★)

Vocabulary

meditation	[ˌmedɪ'teɪʃən]	*n.*	沉思，冥想
meditate	['medɪteɪt]	*v.*	沉思，冥想
stressed	[strest]	*adj.*	紧张的，有压力的
focused	['fəʊkəst]	*adj.*	注意力集中的
clarity	['klærɪtɪ]	*n.*	清晰（度）
psychiatrist	[saɪ'kaɪətrɪst]	*n.*	精神科医生
trick	[trɪk]	*n.*	窍门
revelatory	['revələtɔːrɪ]	*adj.*	启示的

背景知识

“冥想”这个词来源于梵文的 DHYANA，在古代人们把这个词翻译成“禅”。冥想课程就是禅的课程。冥想、禅是一种感知状态。

“冥想”字面上的解释：冥，就是泯灭；想，就是你的思维。“冥想”就是去除妄想执着，得原本的如来智慧德相，以达到此身即佛身的真实境地。《金刚经》（*Diamond Sutra*）上说：凡所有相，皆是虚妄。所以通过修行以恢复我们本来如佛一样的智慧、神通、性德，就是冥想之一。冥想是从古代就有的，中国古代道家的养身气功以及佛家的功法都有。

冥想有助于注意力的训练。冥想时，人们静静地坐着，将注意力集中在自己的呼吸上。随着空气从鼻孔中出入，人们沉浸在自我感觉中。任凭思绪涌入脑海，又轻轻将其拂去，呼吸，拂去。研究发现，这样训练冥想三个月，大脑分配注意的能力将得到大大提高。

（资料来源：http://www.baike.com/wiki/%E5%86%A5%E6%83%B3%E8%AE%AD%E7%BB%83。）

Task 1　General Understanding

Directions: Listen to the news item once and try to grasp its main idea. You may do this either in Chinese or in English.

Task 2　Q&A

Directions: Listen to the news again and answer the following questions.

1. What are people's attitudes towards meditation?

____

2. How is Kevin Houston feeling even though it's only his second class on how to meditate?

____

3. What do researchers find about meditation?

____

4. According to psychiatrist Charles Raison, what is one of the most difficult tricks to practice meditation?

____

Task 3 Blank Filling

Directions: Listen to the news again and fill in the following blanks.

Close your eyes and bring your attention (1) ________.

This is Kevin Houston's second lesson on how to meditate and already the 46-year-old says he's feeling less (2) ________ and more (3) ________.

Meditation helps you just, I think, that's, to have some (4) ________ of mind, to have a little bit more, for me, a little bit more (5) ________.

What Kevin and his classmates might not realize is that researchers have shown even simple meditation (6) ________ can (7) ________ the entire body.

Relaxing your body, actually will turn down your (8) ________. It turns down your (9) ________________.

(10) ______________ Charles Raison says there are many different ways to (11) ________ meditation, but keeping your mind from (12) ________ is one of the most difficult (13) ________.

The experience of meditating, at least through my experience, is extremely (14) ________ and can often be kind of (15) ________ about your internal state.

For that reason, he recommends taking a class and practicing.

Over a period of time, you're able to focus and to look within for the (16) ________ and the (17) ________, no matter how stressful the moment is.

A lesson that goes beyond the class!

Task 4 Shadow Speaking Practice

Directions: Listen to the news again and repeat after the speaker. Pay attention to your speed, pronunciation and intonation.

Pass 5 Post Vacation Syndrome (PVS)

(Difficulty: ★★★★)

背景知识

现代社会的职场人士平时工作忙碌，压力大，都盼着到双休日或法定假期，特别是“五一”黄金周或国庆长假时可以好好休息，好好享受生活，得以调整身心。然而，一连几天的长假结束，许多人都可能会有以下一两种感受：假期结束前的一两晚，想到节日过完马上就要上班，突然感到心神不定，或是失眠、胡思乱想，无法入睡。节后两三天里总是感到厌倦，提不起精神，工作效率低，出现抑郁、失落、烦躁不安等不良情绪。这就是所谓“假日综合征”(Post Vacation Syndrome) 的典型表现。

Vocabulary

lounge	[laʊndʒ]	*vi.*	懒洋洋地躺或卧
cranky	['kræŋkɪ]	*adj*	脾气暴躁的
reputable	['repjətəbəl]	*adj.*	声誉好的
spike	[spaɪk]	*n.*	激增
anticipate	[æn'tɪsɪpeɪt]	*v.*	预期，期望
dip	[dɪp]	*n.*	下降

melatonin	[ˌmeləˈtəʊnɪn] *n.*	褪黑激素
sluggish	[ˈslʌɡɪʃ] *adj.*	缓慢的
lethargic	[ləˈθɑːdʒɪk] *adj.*	嗜睡的，无生气的
anti-depressant	[ˌæntɪdɪˈpresənt] *n.*	抗抑郁剂
dune	[duːn] *n.*	沙丘
pound	[paʊnd] *v.*	连续重击
run down	疲惫的	
boogie boarding	（美国俚语）滑板运动 (skateboarding)	
schedule in	把……列入计划表	
the Cleveland Clinic	克利夫兰心理诊所	

Task 1 General Understanding

Directions: Listen to the news item once and try to grasp its main idea. You may do this either in Chinese or English.

Task 2 Blank Filling

Directions: Listen again and fill in the following blanks.

It wasn't that long ago when you enjoyed the (1) _______, (2) _______, lazy days (3) _______ in (4) _______ rivers. But when you get back home from all these enjoyments, you may be attacked by a kind of syndrome, which is called (5) ____________________.

PVS isn't found in any (6) ________ medical (7) ________, but its gaining attention among (8) ________. They say they see a (9) ________ in people in need of help every year. People (10) ________ almost immediately right after the (11) ________.

Task 3 Back Translation

Directions: Please watch the video attentively and then translate the following Chinese sentences into English.

1. 如果你觉得疲劳，脾气暴躁，心情抑郁，你可能得了某种疾病：假期综合征。

____

____

2. 气温开始下降，太阳也开始早早下山。

____

3. 缺乏阳光会让我们觉得懒散，甚至嗜睡。

____

Task 4 Oral Practice

Directions: Look at the following topic carefully and deliver a short (1–3 minutes) presentation.

What is Post Vacation Syndrome? How can you deal with it?

Pass 6 Fighting Weight in Japan

(Difficulty: ★★★★)

Vocabulary

sumo	['suːməʊ]	*n.*	相扑
waistline	['weɪstlaɪn]	*n.*	腰围，腰线
bulge	[bʌldʒ]	*v.*	膨胀；凸出
enlist	[en'lɪst]	*vt.*	征募；赢得……的支持或合作
guru	['gʊruː]	*n.*	领袖；专家；古鲁（指印度教等宗教的宗师或领袖）

metaboly	[me'tæbəlɪ] *n.*	物质交替，新陈代谢
obese	[əʊ'biːs] *adj.*	极为肥胖的，肥大的
sedentary	['sedntərɪ] *adj.*	坐着的；（指人）不爱活动的
snap	[snæp] *vt.*	拍照；拍……的快照
reek	[rɪk] *vt.*	散发；用烟熏；发出……的气息
havoc	['hævək] *n.*	大破坏，浩劫；蹂躏，摧残
take one's toll		造成损失；造成伤亡，伤害某人；敲响丧钟
speed walking		快走
hit the gym		去健身

背景知识

日本被誉为世界长寿第一国，一向以低肥胖率和高长寿率著称。然而，日本厚生劳动省于 2012 年公布的一项国民健康调查数据却显示，该国 20 岁以上人群中肥胖者（BMI ≥ 25）已接近三成，其中男性肥胖率达 30.4%，女性肥胖者也占到了 21.1%。未来这一趋势还可能加剧。鉴于日本胖人队伍的不断扩编，日本肥胖学会甚至在考虑降低腰围标准，从而将更多人纳入健康检查的行列。

（资料来源：http://paper.people.com.cn/jksb/html/2012-02/27/content_1012521.htm。）

Task 1 General Understanding

Directions: Listen to the news item once and try to grasp its main idea. You may do this either in Chinese or in English.

Task 2 Word Hunting

Directions: Try your best to spot the equivalent English expressions of the following words and expressions while watching the news.

1. 相扑选手 ____________________
2. 健身教练 ____________________
3. 代谢综合征 ____________________
4. 寻求……的帮助 ____________________

5. 生活水准 ____________________
6. 卫生部官员 ____________________
7. 快走 ____________________
8. 健身俱乐部 ____________________
9. 拍照 ____________________
10. 医保体系 ____________________
11. 和体重作战 ____________________

Task 3 True or False

Directions: Listen to the news again and tell whether the following statements are true or false (T/F).

1. ( ) Japan is not known for its obese people.
2. ( ) Very few Japanese are fighting with weight.
3. ( ) Most Japanese are on a diet of fish and shrimps.
4. ( ) In Japan, only 13% of the people are considered obese.
5. ( ) The lifestyles of the Japanese become more sedentary today.
6. ( ) The number of fitness clubs have risen over 25% over from the last year.

Task 4 Blank Filling

Directions: Listen to the news again and fill in the following blanks.

(1) ________ is not known usually for big (2) ________, but many, they are trying to fight the battle of the (3) ________ before it becomes a problem. As Eunice Yoon reports, some of them (4) ________ the help of a well-known US (5) ________.

American's fitness guru Billy Blanks is helping millions of Japanese rust, (6) ________ and (7) ________ their way into (8) ________. These people are (9) ________ catching what's known here as metabolic syndrome, while (10) ________ the world would call getting fat.

Pass 7 Vietnam Obesity

(Difficulty: ★★★★)

Task 1 Word Matching

Direction: Match the words of Column A to their explanations in Column B.

A	B
eradicate	to destroy completely, as if down to the roots
malnutrition	a person who inhabits a particular place
dweller	a state of poor nutrition
carbohydrate	an essential structural component of living cells and source of energy

Task 2 True or False

Directions: Listen to the clip and tell whether the following statements are true or false (T/F).

1. ( ) In the past, Vietnam was a nation mainly associated with malnutrition.
2. ( ) The number of overweight people is decreasing steadily among the rich in recent years.
3. ( ) According to surveys by Vietnam Nutrition Institute, weight and obesity problems didn't happen in the country prior to 1995.
4. ( ) There're more obese women than men.
5. ( ) In Vietnam, overweight and obese cases are more common in poor people and low-income families.

Task 3 Q&A

Directions: Listen to the news and answer the following questions.

1. At the beginning of the report, it is said that "a new pattern has been emerging in recent years". What is the new pattern?

____

____

2. What is the rate of obesity cases in Vietnam?

____

3. What can make people become obese?

____

____

4. What kind of people tend to get overweight and obese?

____

____

5. Experts say that obese situation will soon hit the poor. Why?

____

____

6. What should people do to maintain long-term good health?

____

____

Task 4 Blank Filling

Directions: Listen to the news again and fill in the following blanks.

In the past, Vietnam was the nation mainly associated more with malnutrition than with obesity. The former hasn't been eradicated but a new pattern has been (1) ________ in recent years. The number of overweight people is increasing (2) ________ among the rich and the poor. VTV news has more.

According to (3) ________ by Vietnam Nutrition Institute, weight and obesity problems didn't happen in the country prior to (4) ________. However, the rate of obesity cases nationwide is now around 20%, along with HIV (5) ________, (6) ________ and (7) ________, obesity is considered an (8) ________ disease of modern time. There're more obese women than men. Eating sweets and fatty foods are a bad habit which can easily make people become obese.

Overweight and obese cases are more common in the people who live comfortable lives. However, (9) ________ experts have warned that the situation will soon hit poor people and low-income families. The reason is fresh vegetables will be more expensive in the coming years. And (10) ________ prefer meat of fish in the daily meals. Well families can afford expensive food, but (11) ________ poor families will tend to buy cheap and carbohydrate rich food.

It's high time to begin (12) ________ on proper diets for people's health. Scientists have begun specific studies to (13) ________ obesity. To maintain long-term good health, people should keep a balanced diet and exercise regularly.

Pass 8 Sleep Studies

(Difficulty: ★★★★)

背景知识

睡眠不足会给人的身心带来许多伤害：思考能力会下降，警觉力与判断力会削弱，免疫功能会失调，会失去平衡等。近年来，专家认为充足的睡眠、均衡饮食和适当的运动是健康生活的三个鼎足。少睡了，就像欠了债，你得付出代价。以前的睡眠研究都集中在睡眠的长短对健康的影响，不少研究发现，一般人如果两三天没睡好，他们会在几天内补过来而恢复正常。但最近的研究则注意到，如果每天少睡 1 个或半个小时，那长期累积下来的"睡债"会对一个人的健康有很大影响。

（资料来源：http://wenku.baidu.com/link?url=1QOJTb3pEr3VLdrO6FCsq9YRpcVa5GMOqcVebJT 9o7aWmXVqQwhjYlPl_ucFddVmHAqdVOFRjgk7WV5CJYF-ieXw3EL4WxLLEjC8xyeS7hW。）

Vocabulary

chronically	['krɒnɪklɪ] *adv.* 慢性地，习惯性地，长期地
sleep-deprived	[sliːp dɪ'praɪvd] *adj.* 剥夺睡眠的
shortfall	['ʃɔːtfɔːl] *n.* 缺少；不足之数；亏空
lapse	[læps] *n.* 失误，过失
impaired	[ɪm'peəd] *adj.* 受损的；有（身体或智力）缺陷的
consequence	['kɒnsəkwens] *n.* 后果；影响
stroke	[strəʊk] *n.* 中风；卒中
chronobiology	[ˌkrɒnəʊbaɪ'ɒlədʒɪ] *n.* 时间生物学，生物钟学

Task 1 General Understanding

Directions: Listen to the news item once and try to grasp its main idea. You may do this either in Chinese or English.

Task 2 Word Hunting

Directions: Try your best to spot the equivalent English expressions of the following words and expressions while watching the news.

1. 迟早 ______________________
2. 和……算旧账 ______________________
3. 夜以继日 ______________________
4. 不足 ______________________
5. 受试者 ______________________
6. 记忆差错 ______________________
7. 熬夜 ______________________

Task 3 Blank Filling

Directions: Listen to the news again and fill in the following blanks.

Studies show that in the modern world the majority of people are not getting enough sleep and that (1) ________ of sleep is going to cause some serious problems. Researchers say that as a society, we are chronically (2) ________. Most of us need (3) ________ a week but are only getting on average (4) ________ during a week. This is called the (5) ________. Day after day, living on (6) ________ amounts of sleep, people become more and more (7) ________, more (8) __________ caffeine, have more difficulty (9) ________, at greater (10) ________ for falling asleep, more difficulty (11) ________. Experiments show for the vast majority of people, sleeping six hours a night for a week will result in (12) ________ and (13) ________, as severe as if you'd (14) ________ all night long. (15) ________ lack of sleep can have serious (16) ________ on our health.

The less you sleep, the more (17) ________ you are to die of all causes, or to have (18) ________ or a (19) ________ or to have (20) ________ or to have (21) ________.

Task 4 Back Translation

Directions: Please watch the news attentively and then translate the following Chinese sentences into English.

1. 研究表明我们睡眠不足。迟早，睡眠不足会让我们吞食苦果。

____

2. 我们生活在一个不分白天和黑夜的世界。

____

3. 睡眠不足引发的不适不会自动消失。事实上，它会变得越来越严重。研究人士称之为我们的“睡债”。

____

____

4. 实验表明对绝大多数人来说，如果一整周每晚只睡六小时，会导致记忆差错，使人嗜睡，后果和通宵熬夜同样严重。

____

____

Task 5 Shadow Speaking Practice

Directions: Listen to the news again and repeat after the speaker. Pay attention to your speed, pronunciation and intonation.

Task 6 Oral Practice

Directions: Look at the following topics carefully and deliver a short (1–3 minutes) presentation.

1. How many hours' sleep do you get every night?
2. Have you ever experienced insomnia?
3. What is it that keeps you awake at night?

Pass 9 5-Hour Energy Drinks

(Difficulty: ★★★★)

背景知识

在美国的超市、卖场、药店、高速公路休息站等购物场所，人们经常能看到一些红色、黄色的小瓶子，向人们承诺可以提神达5个小时。这就是所谓的“能量饮料”。近年来能量饮料大行其道，尤其是在美国中学生和大学生人群中颇受欢迎。传统饮料的需求都在下滑，能量饮料却成为饮料公司的收入增长来源。

能量饮料从2003年诞生以来，到2011年已发展成零售额达10亿美元的畅销产品。然而，美国的14岁少女阿内斯·福尼尔在2011年因喝一种高能运动饮料“怪物能量”(MONSTER ENERGY)而引起咖啡因中毒，最终死于心律失常。2011年12月，阿内斯·福尼尔在24小时内喝了两罐“怪物能量”饮料，最终身亡。美国食品和药物管理局(FDA)

2012年10月22日发布的调查报告显示，已接到5起死亡报告和1起诱发心脏病发作报告，可能与饮用"怪物能量"饮料有关。一般人饮用它后可能会有不良反应，因为这种罐装饮料中含有240毫克咖啡因，相当于14罐普通可口可乐的咖啡因含量！

FDA称，尽管目前还没有明确的证据表明"5小时能量"会直接导致死亡或者疾病，但是FDA正在继续对这些报告进行调查。4年来，他们已经接到92起报告，其中包括33起入院报告和13起死亡报告，他们将继续调查。

（资料来源：http://qnck.cyol.com/html/2012-09/05/nw.D110000qnck_20120905_1-23.htm。）

Vocabulary

caffeine	[kæ'fɪn, 'kæfɪn]	*n.*	咖啡因；茶精（兴奋剂）
taurine	['tɔːriːn]	*adj.*	牛磺酸
amino acid	[ə'miːnəʊ 'æsɪd]	*n.*	氨基酸
FDA	美国食品和药物管理局（Food and Drug Administration）		

Task 1 General Understanding

Directions: Listen to the news once and try to grasp its main idea. You may do this either in Chinese or English.

Task 2 Q&A

Directions: Listen to the news again and answer the following questions.

1. What did the founder of the energy drink company say about the 5-hour shots?

____

____

2. How much caffeine is really in 5-hour energy?

____

3. How do you understand the expert's claim "Energy drinks take this to an entirely different level"?

____

____

4. How much caffeine does it take to kill a healthy person?

____

Task 3 Blank Filling

Directions: Listen to the news again and fill in the following blanks.

We know that people will go very far in the search for more energy and a lot of that time it means (1) ________ the caffeine. But can too much caffeine too fast be (2) ________? Tonight the FDA is looking into reports of more than a dozen people whose deaths might (3) ________ the 5-hour energy drink. And ABC's senior national (4) ________ Jim Avila has more on these potential caffeine bombs.

These YouTube videos are a (5) ________ on what not to do with the energy drinks. This is clearly 5-hour energy drink (6) ________. Videos that angered the founder of the billion-dollar company that sells 1.5 million 2-ounce bottles of the stuff every day.

"Don't get crazy and don't take too much, and that would really be a damn thing to do. If you do damn stuff you're gonna end up in the hospital."

And Manoj Bhargava says that's the only way his little bottle of Joy is dangerous, abuse. As for today's (7) ________ news of 13 deaths in 33 hospital organizations, the last 4 years reported to the FDA all claiming to be linked to this product.

Bhargava says just not true.

"Is there any risk to a healthy person drinking your…?"

"Not at all, none."

How much caffeine is really in 5-hour energy? A 2-ounce bottle contains 207mg of caffeine, equivalent to 2 8-ounce cups of coffee, 2.5 Red Bulls, or nearly 6 Coco Colas. And many doctors say research shows that it doesn't tell thc whole story.

"Energy drinks take this to an entirely different level, because there are other (8) ________, other ingredients in these drinks that take the caffeine and make it even more (9) ________."

One of the ingredients in 5-hour energy is Taurine, which scientists call "a caffeine potentiating amino acid" or "coffee turbo-charged", kicking up the caffeine (10) ________.

You knew you are capable of drinking, you know, 4 cups of coffee over the morning. You probably would feel very different if you (11) ________ four energy drinks.

How much caffeine does it take to kill a healthy person? About 5,000mg, that's 50 cups of coffee or 25 shots of 5-hour, more than most can physically drink and many more than the two bottles a day 5-hour energy (12) ________ .

Task 4 Shadow Speaking Practice

Directions: Listen to the above two paragraphs again and repeat after the speaker. Pay attention to your speed, pronunciation and intonation.

Pass 10 Global Health

(Difficulty: ★★★★★)

背景知识

“*The Lancet*”（中文译名《柳叶刀》）杂志是目前世界医学界最权威的学术刊物之一，也是影响因子最高的 SCI 刊物之一，其在医学界的影响甚至超过了“*Nature*”和“*Science*”。《柳叶刀》杂志由汤姆·魏克莱 (Thomas Wakley) 创立于 1823 年，是世界上历史最悠久的医学期刊之一，现主要由爱思唯尔集团（位于阿姆斯特丹）发行出版，主要涉及糖尿病、肿瘤、传染病等医学领域的研究。

（资料来源：http://baike.baidu.com/link?url=fTb3ll0BwXMCGZAzOOAlab5U6JUiADdshZnFUfA_nyua2 iMvpEM2hFH3Z5WKuve5z7UjbBZKTdpAJCb-g7RVv_。）

Vocabulary

sloth	[sləʊθ]	*n.*	怠惰，懒惰
lancet	['lɑːnsɪt]	*n.*	小刀，柳叶刀

Pelotas	[pə'lɔːtəs]	*n.*	佩洛塔斯（巴西南部港市）
conspire	[kən'spaɪə]	*vi.*	共谋；协力 *vt.* 密谋策划
flexing	['fleksɪŋ]	*n.*	挠曲，屈曲；可挠性
sluggish	['slʌgɪʃ]	*adj.*	萧条的；迟钝的；行动迟缓的
paradoxically	[ˌpærə'dɒksɪkəlɪ]	*adv.*	自相矛盾地；似非而是地；反常地
eschew	[ɪs'tʃuː]	*vt.*	避免；避开；远避
pertain	[pə'teɪn]	*vi.*	属于；关于；适合
Croatia	[krəʊ'eɪʃjə]	*n.*	克罗地亚（南斯拉夫成员共和国名）
Finland	['fɪnlənd]	*n.*	芬兰（欧洲）
Iraq	[ɪ'rɑːk; ɪ'ræk]	*n.*	伊拉克（西南亚国家）
Luxembourg	['lʌksəmbəːg]	*n.*	卢森堡（卢森堡公国首都）
Malta	['mɔːltə]	*n.*	马耳他（欧洲岛国）
Swaziland	['swɑːzɪlænd]	*n.*	斯威士兰（非洲东南部国家）
Saudi Arabia	['sɔːdɪ; 'saʊdɪ] [ə'reɪbɪə]	*n.*	沙特阿拉伯
Bangladesh	[ˌbɑːŋglə'deʃ]	*n.*	孟加拉国（亚洲国家）
couch potato	成天躺着或坐在沙发上看电视的人；极为懒惰的人		
the Federal University of Pelotas, in Brazil	巴西佩洛塔斯联邦大学		

Task 1 General Understanding

Directions: Listen to the report once and try to grasp its main idea. You may do this either in Chinese or English.

Task 2 Q&A

Directions: Listen to the report again and answer the following questions.

1. What does the paper in the *Lancet* compare? What is a portrait it describes?

____

____

2. What is suggested by the study led by Pedro Hallal of the Federal University of Pelotas, in Brazil?

____

3. What has made the flexing of muscles more an option rather than a necessity?

____

____

4. How much physical activity is sufficient according to Dr. Hallal and his colleagues?

____

____

Task 3 Blank Filling

Directions: Listen to the report again and fill in missing words.

There are common (1) ________ in different places. (2) ________, people in rich countries are (3) ________ active than those in poor ones, and old people are less active than young ones. Less obviously, women (4) ________ to exercise less than men—(5) ________ are inactive, compared with 28% of men.

But there are (6) ________. The women of Croatia, Finland, Iraq and Luxembourg, for example, move more than their male (7) ________. Malta wins the race for the most (8) ________ country, with 72% of (9) ________ getting too little exercise. Swaziland and Saudi Arabia (10) ________ in close behind, with 69%. In Bangladesh, by contrast, just 5% of adults (11) ________ exercise enough.

Surprisingly, America does not live up to its sluggish (12) ________. Six Americans in ten are (13) ________ active by Dr. Hallal's definition, compared with fewer than four in ten (14) ________.

Task 4 Back Translation

Directions: Please listen to the report attentively and then translate the following Chinese sentences into English.

1. 运动量减少不是新发现。

____

2. 自工业革命以来，科技和经济发展共同创造了这样的一个世界：锻炼肌肉不再是一种必需，而是一种选择。

____

3. 人们缺乏运动的比例之高让人担忧。在东南亚国家不到 1/4 的人每天至少坐 4 个小时，而在欧洲这一比例是 64%。即使是邻国也会有所不同。只有 2% 的瑞士人走路上班，而德国有 23% 的人走路上班。

____

____

4. 矛盾的是，人类似乎慢慢习惯于从体育锻炼中受益，但只要有可能就尽量避免锻炼。

____

____

5. 现在，缺乏锻炼与吸烟对于寿命有着同样的影响。

____

____

Task 5 Shadow Speaking Practice

Directions: Listen to the report again and repeat after the speaker. Pay attention to your speed, pronunciation and intonation.

Part 4 英语听说秘籍之弱读 (Reduction) 与缩读 (Contraction)

一、认识弱读、缩读

对于大多数非英语为母语的学习者来说，弱读是一个很陌生的概念。中国人说英语时几乎对每个英语单词（除了 the 和 a）都强读。但是，在用英语表达时，如果全部都是强读，则整个句子必然没有节奏，没有婉转的感觉。在这里，我们主要介绍一些具体单词的弱读形式：

单词	弱读音标	操练
and	/n/	You n' me are pretty good friends.
can	/kən/	I can drive a car.
are	/r/	We're from Hunan.

was	/wəz/	How was your winter break?
them/him	/əm/	1. Kill 'em.（kill him 也弱读为 /'kiləm/） 2. God bless him.
her	/ər/	I'll tell 'er.（连读）
at	/ət/	At the same time.
to	/tə/ 或 /t/	I have ta go.
of	/əv/ /ə/	1. Do you want a cup of water? 2. It's kinda funny. (a kind of)
for	/fər/	I will be right here waiting for you.
you	/yə/	1. See ya. 2. Let me tell ya.

缩读

在英语中，"缩读"可以理解为"弱读 + 连读"。如果能够灵活运用弱读和缩读，那么你的英语口语表达可以更加地道。

标准形式	缩读形式	实用例句
because	'cause /kəz/	'Cause I don't give a damn.
don't know	dunno /də'nəʊ/	Sorry, I don't know.
give me	gimme /gɪmɪ/	Gimme five.
going to	gonna /'gɒnə/	That's I was gonna say.
go to	gotta /'gɒtə/	1. I gotta go. 2. You gotta move on with your life.
want to	wanna /'wɒnə/	1. I wanna be different. 2. I wanna change my life!
-ing	-in' /ɪn/（一般用于进行时）	1. What's goin' on? 2. What's happenin'?
out of	outta /'aʊtə/	Let's get outta here.
had/would	'd /d/	That'd be great.
have	've /v/	I've heard so much about you.

二、弱读和强读规则运用

强读式和弱读式：

在一个句子中，有些词说得又轻又快，而且较为含糊，有些词则说得又重又慢，而且较为清晰。那些说得响亮而清晰的词就是句子重音所在。实词（包括名词、实义动词、形容词、副词、数词疑问词等）一般都接受句子重音，为重读词，采用强读式；虚词（包括介词、代词、连词、冠词、助动词、情态动词等功能词）一般都不接受句子重音，为非重读词，采用弱读式。

一般规律：

（1）弱读式只出现在句子的非重读词中。例如：Pass me/mɪ/ the/ðə/ book. me、the 弱读。

（2）单词单独出现或在句首或句尾时，都采用强读式。例如：What are you listening to/tuː/?

（3）被特别强调的词，无论是实词还是虚词都采用强读式。例如：I am/æm/ Peter. 我就是皮特。

虚词弱读规律：

（1）长音变短音，例如：she/ʃiː/ 弱读 /ʃɪ/。

（2）元音前面的辅音被省略，例如：him/hɪm/ 弱读 /ɪm/。

（3）辅音前面的元音被省略，例如：am/æm/ 弱读 /m/。

（4）元音一般弱读为 /ə/，例如：can/kæn/ 弱读 /kən/。

（5）部分虚词有多种弱读式，例如：would/wʊd/ 弱读 /əd,d/。

三、实战练习

1. 请读出下面句子，注意弱读。

（1）You can say that again. 你说得没错。

（2）Give me a break. 别逗了。

（3）I'll say. 的确。

（4）Nothing doing! 没门！

（5）Call him off. 叫他收手吧。

2. 练习 and 的弱读。

（1）**Struggle n' strife** come before success. 成功之前必有一番挣扎和竞争。

（2）I have traveled through **time n' space** to find you. 我穿越了时空找到你。

（3）Without you, my life will be **blank n' white**. 没有你，我的生活将暗淡无光。

（你知道吗？我们每当碰到 and 时，一般都会读作 /ænd/，殊不知，在美语口语里面，and 通常只需弱读为 /ən/，甚至是一个简单的鼻音 /n/。当说话者需要强调时则会把 and 读作 /ænd/。如果能够掌握好这个发音规则，我们的口语将更加流畅，听力理解也更加畅听无阻。）

English Listening-and-Speaking Learning Planner

Monday Practicing Hour: ________ Tape Hour: ________ Commitment: ________	**Tuesday** Practicing Hour: ________ Tape Hour: ________ Commitment: ________	**Wednesday** Practicing Hour: ________ Tape Hour: ________ Commitment: ________	**Thursday** Practicing Hour: ________ Tape Hour: ________ Commitment: ________	**Friday** Practicing Hour: ________ Tape Hour: ________ Commitment: ________
Saturday Practicing Hour: ________ Tape Hour: ________ Commitment: ________	**Sunday** Practicing Hour: ________ Tape Hour: ________ Commitment: ________	**General Performance for Week ____:** (vocabulary, long sentence, background information, etc.) Self-rating ☆☆☆☆☆		
Monday Practicing Hour: ________ Tape Hour: ________ Commitment: ________	**Tuesday** Practicing Hour: ________ Tape Hour: ________ Commitment: ________	**Wednesday** Practicing Hour: ________ Tape Hour: ________ Commitment: ________	**Thursday** Practicing Hour: ________ Tape Hour: ________ Commitment: ________	**Friday** Practicing Hour: ________ Tape Hour: ________ Commitment: ________
Saturday Practicing Hour: ________ Tape Hour: ________ Commitment: ________	**Sunday** Practicing Hour: ________ Tape Hour: ________ Commitment: ________	**General Performance for Week ____:** (vocabulary, long sentence, background information, etc.) Self-rating ☆☆☆☆☆		

Chapter 6

Etiquettes

Part 1 Famous Quotes

Etiquette to society is what apparel is to the individual.

—William Hazlitt

礼仪之于社会犹如衣着之于个人。

——威廉·黑兹利特

An irritable man is like a hedgehog rolled up the wrong way, tormenting himself with his own prickles.

—Thomas Hood

易怒的人像一只反过来蜷缩的刺猬，用自己的刺折磨自己。

——托马斯·胡德

Part 2 Background Knowledge

(1) History of Etiquette

Vocabulary

slang term	俚语说法	
precept	['pri:sept] *n.*	格言；规则；训诫

leitmotif	['laɪtməʊtiːf] *n.*	主题；主旨
concede	[kən'siːd] *v.*	让步，退让
entrench	[ɪn'tren(t)ʃ] *v.*	确立，牢固
demarcation	[ˌdiːmɑː'keɪʃən] *n.*	划分；划界；限界
enculturation	[ɪnˌkʌltʃə'reɪʃən] *n.*	对某种文化的适应
routinization	[ruːˌtiːnaɪ'zeɪʃən] *n.*	程序化；常规化；惯例化
alienation	[ˌeɪljə'neɪʃən] *n.*	疏远；精神错乱
encompass	[ɪn'kʌmpəs] *v.*	包含

Etiquette (/'etɪket/ or /'etɪkɪt/) is a code of behavior that delineates expectations for social behavior according to contemporary conventional norms within a society, social class, or group. Etiquette has changed and evolved over the years.

In the 3rd millennium BC, Ptahhotep wrote *The Maxims of Ptahhotep*. The Maxims were conformist precepts extolling such civil virtues as truthfulness, self-control and kindness towards one's fellow beings. Learning by listening to everybody and knowing that human knowledge is never perfect is a leitmotif. Avoiding open conflict wherever possible should not be considered weakness. Stress is placed on the pursuit of justice, although it is conceded that it is a god's command that prevails in the end. Some of the maxims refer to one's behaviour when in the presence of the great, how to choose the right master and how to serve him. Others teach the correct way to lead through openness and kindness. Greed is the base of all evil and should be guarded against, while generosity towards family and friends is deemed praiseworthy.

(2) Types of Etiquette

Curtis' also specifically outlines three manner categories: hygiene, courtesy and cultural norms; each of which help to account for the multifaceted role manners play in society. These categories are based on the outcome rather than the motivation of manners behavior and individual manner behaviors may fit in to two or more categories.

Hygiene Manners—are any manners which affect disease transmission. They are likely to be taught at an early age, primarily through parental discipline, positive behavioral enforcement of continence with bodily fluids (such as toilet training), and the avoidance or removal of items that pose a disease risk for children. It is expected that, by adulthood, hygiene manners are so entrenched in one's behavior that they become second nature. Violations are likely to elicit disgust responses.

Courtesy Manners—demonstrate one's ability to put the interests of others before oneself; to display self-control and good intent for the purposes of being trusted in social interactions. Courtesy manners help to maximize the benefits of group living by regulating social interaction. Disease avoidance behavior can sometimes be compromised in the performance of courtesy manners. They may be taught in the same way as hygiene manners but are likely to also be learned through direct, indirect (i.e. observing the interactions of others) or imagined (i.e. through the executive functions of the brain) social interactions. The learning of courtesy manners may take place at an older age than hygiene manners, because individuals must have at least some means of communication and some awareness of self and social positioning. The violation of courtesy manners most commonly results in social disapproval from peers.

Cultural Norm Manners—typically demonstrate one's identity within a specific socio-cultural group. Adherence to cultural norm manners allows for the demarcation of socio-cultural identities and the creation of boundaries which inform who is to be trusted or who is to be deemed as "other". Cultural norm manners are learnt through the enculturation and routinization of "the familiar" and through exposure to "otherness" or those who are identified as foreign or different. Transgressions and non-adherence to cultural norm manners commonly result in alienation. Cultural norms, by their very nature, have a high level of between-group variability but are likely to be common to all those who identify with a given group identity.

Rules of etiquette encompass most aspects of social interaction in any society, though the term itself is not commonly used. A rule of etiquette may reflect an underlying ethical code, or it may reflect a person's fashion or status. Rules of etiquette are usually unwritten, but aspects of etiquette have been codified from time to time.

Part 3 Listening and Speaking Practice

Pass 1 Business Etiquette in China

(Difficulty: ★★★)

Vocabulary

etiquette	['etɪket]	*n.*	礼节，礼仪
bribery	['braɪbərɪ]	*n.*	贿赂
undertone	['ʌndətəʊn]	*n.*	含意，潜在的意思
reciprocate	[rɪ'sɪprəkeɪt]	*n.*	报答，回报
palatable	['pælətəbl]	*adj.*	好吃的，可口的
satay	[sɑː'teɪ]	*n.*	加香烤肉；沙嗲
bullfrog	['bulfrɒg]	*n.*	牛蛙
sea slug			海参

Task 1 General Understanding

Directions: Listen to the clip once and try to grasp its main idea. You may do this either in Chinese or English.

Task 2 Blank Filling

Directions: Listen to the clip again and fill in the following blanks.

Dressing: ______________________________

Exchange of business card: ______________________________

Gifts exchange: ______________________________

Dining for business relationship: ______________________________

For undesired food: ______________________________

Toast: ______________________________

Task 3 Shadow Speaking Practice

Directions: Watch the clip a couple of times and repeat the words that you've just heard sentence by sentence. Retell the news first on your own and then check your work with your friends. Finally report the news to your classmates. Please note the original stresses, intonation, tone etc.

Task 4 Dubbing Practice

Directions: Turn down the volume and try dubbing the clip until you sound just like the actors. Now you may record your dubbing for comparison or just for fun.

Task 5 Visual Translation

Directions: Translate the following sentences into Chinese. Please note that your translation should be in accord with the original material in terms of genre and style.

1. The food is served via large communal dishes, and in nearly every case, you will be supplied with communal chopsticks for transferring food from the main dishes to your own. You should use the communal chopsticks if they are supplied. If they are not or you are unsure, wait for someone to serve food to their own plate, and then copy what they do. On occasion, an eager Chinese host may place food into your bowl or on your plate. This is normal.

____

____

____

2. It is rude to not eat what you are given. If you are offered something you absolutely can't stomach, finish everything else, and leave the rest on your plate. Leaving a little food generally indicates that you are full.

____

____

____

3. Don't stab your chopsticks into your bowl of rice. As with any Buddhist culture, placing two chopsticks down in a bowl of rice is what happens at a funeral. By doing this, you indicate that you wish death upon those at the table.

____

____

____

4. Do not play with your chopsticks, point at objects with them, or drum them on the table—this is rude. Do not tap them on the side of your dish, either, as this is used in restaurants to indicate that the food is taking too long, and it will offend your host.

____

____

____

5. When setting down your chopsticks, place them horizontally on top of your plate, or place the ends on a chopstick rest. Do not set them on the table.

____

____

____

6. Hold the chopsticks in your right hand between the thumb and index finger, and when eating rice, place the small bowl in your left hand, holding it off the table.

____

____

____

7. Do not stab anything with your chopsticks, unless you are cutting vegetables or similar. If you are in a small, intimate setting with friends, then stabbing smaller so as to grab items is okay, but never do this at a formal dinner or around those who

adhere strictly to tradition.

____

____

____

8. When tapping glasses for a cheer, be sure that the edge of your drink is below that of a senior member, as you are not their equal. This will show respect.

____

____

____

9. When eating something with bones, it is normal to spit them out onto the table to the right of your plate.

____

____

____

10. Do not get offended if your fellow diners eat with their mouth open, or talk with their mouth full. This is normal in China. Enjoy, laugh, and have fun.

____

____

____

Pass 2 Presentation Manners

(Difficulty: ★★★★)

Vocabulary

brewery	['brʊərɪ]	*n.*	酿酒厂
stout	[staʊt]	*n.*	烈性黑啤酒
nightcap	['naɪtkæp]	*n.*	临睡前喝的酒
lager	['lɑːgə]	*n.*	贮藏啤酒
takeover	['teɪkˌəʊvə]	*n.*	接管
bid	[bɪd]	*v.*	出价投标
resist	[rɪ'zɪst]	*v.*	抵制
corporate image	公司形象		
production	[prə'dʌkʃən]	*n.*	产量

Task 1　Q&A

Directions: Listen to the first part of the clip once and answer the following questions.

1. Does she consider the audience?

____

2. Does she have clear objectives/purpose?

____

Task 2　Discussion

Directions: Watch the clip again and discuss with your partner to make a conclusive checklist on a polite presentation.

Task 3　Reorganization

Directions: One of the worst things about Joanna's presentation is its lack of organization. Look at the "classic" presentation structure and listen carefully and make brief notes on the content of Joanna's presentation, then reorganize it.

The classic presentation structure:

Introduction — outline — main parts — summary — conclusion

Task 4 Visual Translation

Directions: ***Translate the following sentences into English. Please note that your translation should be in accord with the original material in terms of genre and style.***

1. 这个话题我本想多花些时间来阐述，但恐怕我们没有足够的时间。可是我还是想对前景说一些看法。今年我们已经遇到了一些主要的问题，明年我们将会面临更严重的问题。这一点是肯定的，因为市场竞争越来越激烈。

2. 众所周知，酿酒厂在 1982 年被买回。自购回之日起，公司就做出了一些很大的改变，我确信在座的各位都知道这点。今天我演讲的主要内容将集中在部分的改变上以及这些改变对公司运作的影响。不久前，新的公司所有人宣布了公司成长的新策略。这一策略有两个明确目标——营业额和利润都要有很大程度的增长。这些目标又将导致一些新的变化，特别是在生产和市场领域上。

Pass 3 Eating for Good Luck

(Difficulty: ★★★)

Vocabulary

navigate	['næviɡeit]	*vt.*	带人参观
pistachio	[pɪ'stæʃɪəʊ]	*n.*	开心果
lotus	['ləʊtəs]	*n.*	莲花
conjee (=congee)	['kɒndʒiː]	*n.*	稀饭，粥
longevity	[lɒn'dʒevətɪ]	*n.*	长寿

Task 1 General Understanding

Directions: Listen to the first part of the clip once and try to grasp its main idea. You may do this either in Chinese or English.

Task 2 Blank Filling

Directions: Listen to the clip again and fill in the following blanks.

As you can (1) __________ with the biggest Chinese holiday of the year,

(2) ___________ play a great part of it. In China, food is never (3) ___________ food. It's always (4) ___________ with heavy (5) ___________ meanings especially at a holiday like this. And my guide's navigating me through. This is Belinda Wang here. What is it that Chinese people everyone eats (6) ___________?

Well this is what every Chinese family has for New Year. It's "go". And the name "go" means "bobo go sing" which means (7) ___________. Nuts and seeds are very important for New Year. Now we have this black melon seeds which is very nice. Try one. (8) ___________. So I will put one in the basket. What about these ones? These are really happy-happy-nuts because pistachios in Cantonese is happy-happy. So this (9) ___________ a happy year.

Peanuts stand for (10) ___________ So you'll have a long life in the new year.

Task 3 Shadow Speaking Practice

Directions: Watch the clip a couple of times and repeat the words that you've just heard sentence by sentence. Retell the news first on your own and then check your work with your friends. Finally report the news to your classmates. Please note the original stresses, intonation, tone, etc.

Task 4 Dubbing Practice

Directions: Turn down the volume and try dubbing the clip until you sound just like the actors. Now you may record your dubbing for comparison or just for fun.

Task 5 Visual Translation

Directions: Translate the following sentences into English. Please note that your translation should be in accord with the original material in terms of genre and style.

1. 在中国，食物永远不仅仅是食物，通常它被赋予了浓厚的象征意义，特别是在春节这样一个盛大的节日中。

____

____

2. 步步高升

____

3. 不断地挑瓜子和吃瓜子的动作就像不断地捡钱。

4. 开心果确保了开心的一年。

5. 花生代表了长寿。

6. 莲子代表了很多孩子，可用来做甜点和汤。

7. 万事如意

8. 恭喜发财

9. 强烈推荐

Pass 4 First Contact

(Difficulty: ★★★)

Vocabulary

promote	[prə'məʊt]	*v.*	促销
package	['pækɪdʒ]	*n.*	一揽子计划
launch	[lɑːntʃ]	*n.*	（促销）活动
literature	['lɪtərətʃə]	*n.*	（总称）印刷品（如广告，传单等）
bring over	带来		
get onto	开始做		
if you'll excuse me...	请原谅		
black	（这里指不加牛奶的）咖啡		

Task 1 Q&A

Directions: Answer the following questions with details.

1. Watch Version 1 with the sound down. What do you notice about the behavior of the three characters? What sort of welcome does Maria get?
2. Watch Version 1 with the sound down. What does Maria expect to happen? How do you think Peter handles this first contact with Maria?
3. Watch Version 2 with the sound down. What differences are there in the behavior of the three characters?
4. Watch Version 1 with the sound up. List the things Peter does more effectively. How do you think Maria will feel after this first contact with Peter and Paula?

Task 2 Blank Filling

Directions: Watch Version 2 of the clip again and fill in the following blanks.

Peter: Have we got enough time to promote it, that's the worry. And do we have price right? Anyway, (1) ______________________________. Come in! Hello, you must be Maria. I'm Peter O'Donnell. Welcome to Tectron UK.

Maria: Thank you. (2) ______________________________.

Peter: Let me introduce you to Paula Field. Paula is (3) ______________________________.

Paula: Nice to meet you, Maria.

Maria: (4) ____________________________.

Peter: I'm sure you know that Maria is going to be with us for a couple of months.

Paula: Yes. (5) ____________________________. (to Peter) If you'll excuse me, I should be getting back. See you later, Maria.

Maria: Yes, bye.

Peter: See you later, Paula. (to Maria) Have a seat. Coffee?

Maria: Thank you.

Peter: (6) ____________________________?

Maria: Fine, only a little bit late.

Peter: Milk and sugar?

Maria: Black, please.

Peter: Paula and I (7) ____________________________. Isn't the Spanish office (8) ____________________________ soon?

Maria: That's right. (9) ____________________________.

Peter: Ah. That could be very useful!

Task 3 Socializing Practice

Directions: Modify the dialogue below to make it more formal and less direct.

A: Welcome to A&T. I am Johan Petersson. I look after the factory here.

B: Nice to meet you. My name's Susan Parkes.

A: Nice to meet you, Susan. How was your trip?

B: Slow. I got caught in awful traffic.

A: Sorry to hear that. Anyway, have you checked in?

B: Yes.

A: Everything OK?

B: Fine.

A: So how do you find our weather?

B: It's hot. When I left home, it was only ten degrees.

Pass 5 Dining Etiquette

(Difficulty: ★★★)

Vocabulary

fancy	['fænsɪ]	*adj.*	昂贵的；精选的
messy	['mesɪ]	*adj.*	乱糟糟的
violation	[ˌvaɪə'leɪʃən]	*n.*	违背
napkin	['næpkɪn]	*n.*	餐巾
buffet	['bʌfɪt]	*n.*	自助餐
refrain	[rɪ'freɪn]	*v.*	克制
wad up	揉成一团（卷）		
fashion blunder	打扮不得体的行为举止		
laid out	布置		

Task 1 General Understanding

Directions: Listen to the first part of the clip once and try to grasp its main idea. You may do this either in Chinese or English.

Task 2 Shadow Speaking Practice

Directions: Watch the clip and repeat the three rules mentioned in the video.

Task 3 Task Video of Fun

Directions: Watch the following clip for fun and point out what had happened.

Pass 6 Everyone Around You Has a Story the World Needs to Hear (1) [0:00–4:24]

(Difficulty: ★★★★)

Vocabulary

tight-knit	['taɪtnɪt]	*adj.*	关系紧密的
crushed	[krʌʃt]	*adj.*	崩溃的
strained	[streɪnd]	*adj.*	紧张的，不安的
pique	[piːk]	*v.*	激起，激发
cubicle	['kjuːbɪkl]	*n.*	小卧室；小隔间
clarion	['klærɪən]	*n.*	号角
flophouse	['flɒphaʊs]	*n.*	廉价的低级住所或旅馆
drag queens			男扮女装的男子同性恋者

Task 1 General Understanding

Directions: Listen to the first part of the clip once and try to grasp its main idea. You may do this either in Chinese or English.

Task 2 Blank Filling

Directions: Listen to the clip again and fill in the following blanks.

In many ways, "I exist" became the (1) ___________ call for StoryCorps, this crazy idea that I had a dozen years ago. The thought was to take (2) ___________ work and turn it on its head. Traditionally, (3) ___________________ documentary has been about recording (4) ________________ to create a work of art or (5) ________________ or education that is seen or heard by a whole lot of people, but I wanted to try something where the interview itself was the (6) __________ of this work, and see if we could give many, many, many people the (7) __________ to be listened to in this way. So in Grand Central Terminal 11 years ago, (8) ________________. You come to this booth and you're met by a facilitator who brings you inside. You sit across from, say, your grandfather for close to an hour and you listen and you talk. Many people think of it as, (9) ________________? At the end of the session, you walk away with a copy of the interview and another copy goes to the American Folklife Center at the Library of Congress so that your great-great-great-grandkids (10) ______________________.

Task 3 Shadow Speaking Practice

Directions: Watch the clip a couple of times and repeat the words that you've just heard sentence by sentence. Retell the story first on your own then check your work with your friends. Finally report the story to your classmates. Please note the original stresses, intonation, tone etc.

Task 4 Visual Translation

Directions: Translate the following sentences into English. Please note that your translation should be in accord with the original material in terms of genre and style.

1. 22 岁的时候，在我全身心投入制作广播故事时，很庆幸，我发现了我毕生所爱。

____

____

2. 这真是一个不可思议的故事，它激起了我的兴趣。于是我决定拿起我的录音机，进一步探索。

____

____

3. 通过录制下一段对话，我意识到麦克风是如何让我前往不曾涉足的地方，与素未谋面的人对话。

____

____

4. 随后的 15 年中，我制作了很多录音，力求发掘那些被媒体忽视的人们的故事。一次又一次我见证着，简简单单的访谈对某些人来说却意义深远，尤其是那些被告知自己的故事无关紧要的人。

____

____

____

5. 通常来讲，广播纪实来自于访谈，进而以艺术、娱乐或教育的目的呈现出来，以视听的方式传播给每个人。

____

____

6. 人们怀揣崇高的敬意来对待这段经历，奇妙的谈话就在里面产生了。

____

____

Pass 7 Everyone Around You Has a Story the World Needs to Hear (2) [4:24–11:28]

(Difficulty: ★★★★)

Vocabulary

excerpt	['eksɜːpt]	*n.*	节选
obsession	[əb'seʃən]	*n.*	痴迷；困扰；[内科][心理]强迫观念
cockroach	['kɒkrəʊtʃ]	*n.*	蟑螂
venomous	['venəməs]	*adj.*	有毒的
colic	['kɒlɪk]	*n.*	疝气；疝痛；急腹痛
authentic	[ɔː'θentɪk]	*adj.*	真正的，真实的；可信的
spectrum	['spektrəm]	*n.*	范围
snaggletooth	['snæglتuːθ]	*n.*	暴牙
resilience	[rɪ'zɪlɪəns]	*n.*	恢复力；弹力；顺应力
Asperger's syndrome	['sɪndrəʊm]		艾斯伯格综合征
picked on			刁难；欺负

Task 1 Summary

Directions: Listen to the second part of the clip once and try to summary the stories mentioned in this part.

Task 2 Listening and Interpretation

Directions: Listen to the second part of the clip and translate the following sentences into Chinese. Please note that your translation should be in accord with the original material in terms of genre and style.

1. The important thing for you is that you have a few very good friends, and really that's what you need in life.

____

____

2. But also because you think differently from what they tell you in the parenting books, I really had to learn to think outside of the box with you, and it's made me much

more creative as a parent and as a person, and I'll always thank you for that.

____

____

3. A lot of people talk about crying when they hear StoryCorps stories, and it's not because they're sad. Most of them aren't. I think it's because you're hearing something authentic and pure at this moment.

____

____

4. So many of these are just everyday people talking about lives lived with kindness, courage, decency and dignity, and when you hear that kind of story, it can sometimes feel like you're walking on holy ground.

____

____

5. I've learned about the poetry and the wisdom and the grace that can be found in the words of people all around us when we simply take the time to listen.

____

____

6. I've learned about the almost unimaginable capacity for the human spirit to forgive. I've learned about resilience and I've learned about strength.

____

____

Pass 8 Everyone Around You Has a Story the World Needs to Hear (3) [11:28–20:10]

(Difficulty: ★★★★)

Vocabulary

penitentiary	[ˌpenɪ'tenʃərɪ]	*n.*	监狱；教养所
transition	[træn'sɪʃən]	*v.*	过渡；转变
cut off	排挤		
mortality	[mɔː'tæləti]	*n.*	死亡
hospice	['hɒspɪs]	*n.*	收容所；救济院
floored	[flɔːrd]	*adj.*	惊讶的
ingredient	[ɪn'griːdɪənt]	*n.*	原料；要素；组成部分
beta version	测试版		
towering	['taʊərɪŋ]	*adj.*	高耸的；卓越的
visceral	['vɪsərəl]	*adj.*	发自肺腑的；出于本能的
fleeting	['fliːtɪŋ]	*adj.*	飞逝的；转瞬间的
inconsequential	[ˌɪnkɒnsɪ'kwenʃ(ə)l]	*adj.*	微不足道的

Task 1 Summary

Directions: Listen to the last part of the clip once and try to summary the stories mentioned in this part.

Task 2 Blank Filling

Directions: Listen to the clip again and fill in the following blanks.

Every day, people come up to me and say, "I wish I had (1) __________ my father or my grandmother or my brother, but I (2) __________ too long." Now, no one has to wait anymore. At this moment, when so much of how we communicate is fleeting and (3) __________, join us in creating this (4) __________ archive of conversations that are (5) __________ and important. Help us (6) __________ this gift to our children, this testament to who we are as human beings. I hope you'll help us make this wish come true. Interview a family member, a friend or even a (7) __________ Together, we can (8) ____.
Maybe these conversations will (9) __________ us what's really important. And maybe, just maybe, it will (10) ____.
Thank you very much.

Task 3 Shadow Speaking Practice

Directions: Watch the clip a couple of times and repeat the words that you've just heard sentence by sentence. Retell the story first on your own and then check your work with your friends. Finally report the story to your classmates. Please note the original stresses, intonation, tone, etc.

Task 4 Oral Practice

Directions: Watch the clip a couple of times and make a conclusion about what you have learned from this speech and whether it changes you in some way or not.

Pass 9 Dinner

(Difficulty: ★★★)

Vocabulary

concerned	[kən'sə:nd]	*adj.*	关心的
decaffeinated	[dɪ'kæfɪəneɪtɪd]	*adj.*	去咖啡因的
disillusioned	[ˌdɪsɪ'lu:ʒənd]	*adj.*	幻想破灭的；不抱幻想的
a sweet tooth	吃甜食的嗜好		
be fed up with	对……感到厌烦		
apathetic	[ˌæpə'θetɪk]	*adj.*	冷漠的；无动于衷的

Task 1 Q&A

Directions: Answer the following questions with details.

1. Watch Version 1 from 16:00 to 16:30 (up to Jens's request for decaffeinated coffee) with the sound down. What do you notice about Maria's and Jens's behavior?
2. Watch the sequence again with the sound up. In the opening extract, what do Maria and Jens fail to do?
3. Now watch Version 1 from 16:31 to 17:03. How does Maria feel? What could she have done to enter the discussion?
4. Watch Version 2 from 17:10 to 17:45 (up to Daphne's departure to make coffee). What differences do you notice in the behavior of Maria and Jens?

5. Now watch Version 2 from 17:46 to 18:30. How do Peter and Jens make sure Maria is not left out?

Task 2 Blank Filling

Directions: Watch Version 2 of the clip again and fill in the following blanks.

Jens: The point is (1) ________________________.

Peter: I don't believe that. Surely they've got to be (2) ____________.

Jens: That was delicious.

Daphne: Thank you. I've glad you enjoyed it.

Maria: It was wonderful. The puddings in England are really good.

Daphne: Do you think so? I suppose (3) ________________________. Now, what about some coffee? Maria?

Maria: That would be nice. Thank you.

Daphne: And for you, Jens?

Jens: Yes, please. Do you have (4) ____________?

Daphne: I think we've got some somewhere. Peter?

Peter: Just normal for me. Can I (5) ____________?

Daphne: No, thanks, I can (6) ____________.

Peter: So, what were you saying about politicians, Jens?

Jens: I think a lot of young people aren't really interested in politics.

Peter: I don't think that's true. What do you think, Maria?

Maria: I think you're wrong, Jens. A lot of my friends in Spain (7) ____________ local politics.

Jens: Really?

Maria: Yes. OK, they may (8) ____________ politicians, but this doesn't mean they don't do something about it.

Jens: I think that's quite rare. A lot of young people (9) ____________.

Maria: I think that's (10) ____________. For me, it's a sign of a big problem when people don't think (11) ____________.

Daphne: I agree with Maria. Everybody is (12) ____________ these days. But at least we have a democracy in this household!

Peter: Ah!

Task 3 Socializing Practice

Directions: Group work for 4 participants: choose one of the following topics and give your comment and reaction. Try to succeed in generating more discussion and make sure that all members of the group are included.

1. Smoking should be banned in all public places.
2. Working hours should not exceed 35 hours per week.
3. Private cars will have to be banned in the next century.

Pass 10 Body Language

(Difficulty: ★★★)

Vocabulary

broadly	['brɔːdlɪ] *adv.*	大体上，总体上
alternative	[ɔːl'tɜːnətɪv] *adj.*	供选择的；选择性的
cost cut	削减成本	
draw up	起草，拟订	
put forward	提出，建议	

Task 1 Q&A

Direction: Use this checklist to discuss the importance of body language in presentations.

Checklist:

Eye contact

Facial expression

Hands

Movement

Posture

Task 2 Table Filling

Directions: Watch Version 1 and 2 of the video with no sound. As you watch, make notes on Dr. Linden's body language. Use this checklist to help you.

Checklist:		
	Version 1	Version 2
General appearance		
Stance and posture		
Hands position		
Hands gestures		
Eye contact		
Facial expression		
Movement		

Task 3 Emphasis Hunting

Direction: Watch Version 2 of the Video again, this time listen to the sound. As you watch, underline the expressions in these extracts which are strongly emphasized.

a. These cost cuts are going to cause considerable pain.

b. We need to draw up a plan of action. I have put some ideas on the board.

c. These are some of the measures we could consider. There are broadly three approaches.

d. First, we could accept the cuts and reduce staff drastically...Secondly, we could fight and hope to achieve some reduction in the level of the cuts. Or thirdly, and this is what I support, we could put forward an alternative proposal. Now, this would mean we have to organize...

Task 4 Oral Practice

Direction: Choose one of the topics and prepare a brief presentation. Try to be persuasive.

1. Women make better managers of people than men.
2. The world is changing so fast that long-term planning is no longer feasible.
3. Body language is at least as important as spoken language.

Part 4 英语听说秘籍之跟读练习（Shadow-Exercise）

影子练习 (shadow-exercise)，即跟读训练。这种方法就是用同一种语言几乎同步地跟读原语发言人的讲话，它可以训练听说同步技巧和注意力的分配。刚开始训练时可以和原语同步开始，待操练了一阵子后，可以迟于原语片刻至一句话的时间跟读。跟读时耳朵、嘴巴和大脑要一起派上用场，耳朵听、嘴巴说、脑子记。这是需要精神非常集中的一种练习，也是提高语速、提高理解速度、修改语音语调的最好方法。在高语速条件下，边跟读边完全理解语义是有很大难度的，但这种训练能为口译打下扎实的基础。各种新闻、谈话节目、研讨会、音乐体育节目、演讲等都是上好材料。

Norman (*Memory and Attention*, 1976) 在其著作中详尽地对比了两种影子练习方式，音位跟述 (Phonemic shadowing) 和片语跟述 (Phrase shadowing)。我们来逐一分析下每种练习方式。音位跟述即跟述者重复念出每个他所听到的声音，无须等待一个完整的意思单位的结束（甚至是一个单词的结束），所以跟述者与说话者保持同步；片语跟述意为跟述者在与说话者间隔一定时间后，跟述出说话者的意思。换句话说，在第二种练习方法中，跟述者要等待一个完整的片语或是意群后才可开始他们的跟述活动。我们在对比了两种跟述练习后，再把焦点集中在大脑的记忆能力上来。根据人类记忆心理学研究，区分人类短期记忆 (Short-Term Memory, TM) 与长期记忆 (Long-Term Memory, LTM) 的概念。短期记忆的含义是短时期内保存信息，通常在 5~20 秒，最长不超过 1 分钟，如获取一个听力答案（记录电话号码、姓名、地址等）。而长期记忆的概念简单地说就是把记忆保持几天到几年，如课堂上获取知识。

综上所述，影子练习对于考生的短期记忆以及记忆广度来说是非常理想的一种训练方式。

跟读训练可以分为几个层次，这与练习者的已有语言运用水平有很大的关联：

一、初始阶段进行看、听、读相结合的训练

对于听力还处于初级水平的学习者，直接采用跟读所听内容的方式往往会打击其自信心，收不到预期的效果。因此，学习者应该根据自己的学习程度选择难易适中的材料。所

谓难易适中是指集中精神能够听懂其中一部分内容，但要经过5~6次反复听才能把握其含义。对于这类材料，学习者可以先把书面材料放在一边，仅凭耳朵听，以把握内容为主要目的。经过几次之后，翻开材料浏览一遍，看一看自己的理解是否正确，接下来就是边看、边听、边读。此时此刻的读绝不能是走马观花，此时对于听力内容的语音、语调以及其他规则要有所领悟，同时留意自己听的时候感觉模糊不清的地方，进行重点模仿，并且脱离听力语音材料自主地反复练习。这时，学习者要有的放矢，一方面针对自身的问题进行重点训练，另一方面从整体上把握整个材料的发音方法的要领。如果在已经读得惟妙惟肖之后，再来听，会发觉听力材料变得简单易懂，即使更换其他材料，也能够更加适应英语的节奏了，这是英语思维能力训练的第一步。

二、同声跟读

这种跟读方法并不像前面那一种那么重视书面材料，对于任意一个听力材料，开始播放后就立刻跟读所听到的词汇和句子，学习者所说内容与听到的内容只有一两个词的时间间隔。也就是说，听到什么就说什么，这样一方面可以纠正语音、语调、连读、爆破等，另一方面，也是更重要的方面，它可以进一步锻炼学习者的英语思维能力，听到某个词的同时需要在大脑中及时地做出反应，然后说出来，这个过程已经不知不觉地锻炼了学生的注意力和记忆力。许多学生感到开始的时候虽然困难，但经过一段时间发现，即使听的时候并不能迅速反映出这个词的意和形，但根据语音读出来后会比停下来冥思苦想更容易理解并且印象深刻，再听到时一般都会听懂，这也就是跟读与听力相辅相成的关系。要真正地使词汇、语法、句型永久地保留在脑海中，最好的办法便是形成音、形、意的结合体，再没有比通过跟读训练更能有效地达到这一目的方法了；从另一方面来看，积累了大量的音形意兼备词汇句型之后，听力也就迎刃而解了。

三、延迟跟读

延迟跟读是对同声跟读难度的提升，同声跟读是在听到一个词之后马上跟读，主要是要抓住眼前的这一个或两个单词；而延迟跟读是在听力开始后几秒钟甚至更长的时间后才开始跟读。这就要求学习者必须有更强的记忆力。曾有人说“一个人有好的记忆力不一定有好的听力，但一个人有好的听力必定有好的记忆力。”的确，没有好的记忆力，即使听懂了，一转眼就不记得自己听到什么了，又怎么能对所听内容进行比较、分析、进而做出反应呢？延迟跟读可以迅速有效地对学生的记忆力进行训练。如果学习者可以在上一阶段取得良好的成绩，那么只要逐步地推延开始跟读的时间，就可以达到这项训练的目的，但这说起来容易，做起来并不容易，如果说同声跟读是对语音的把握，那么延迟跟读就是对听力内容内涵的把握，同声跟读抓住点，而延迟跟读必须掌握全局，这是一个质的飞跃。再进一步，学习者在能够比较好地进行延迟跟读后则可以投入到更加专业的听力训练当中去，也就是把整段听力材料听完，然后重述内容，学生的英语思维在此过程中得到完善和提高。

English Listening-and-Speaking Learning Planner

<table>
<tr>
<td>Monday
Practicing Hour:
____
Tape Hour:
____
Commitment:
________</td>
<td>Tuesday
Practicing Hour:
____
Tape Hour:
____
Commitment:
________</td>
<td>Wednesday
Practicing Hour:
____
Tape Hour:
____
Commitment:
________</td>
<td>Thursday
Practicing Hour:
____
Tape Hour:
____
Commitment:
________</td>
<td>Friday
Practicing Hour:
____
Tape Hour:
____
Commitment:
________</td>
</tr>
<tr>
<td>Saturday
Practicing Hour:
____
Tape Hour:
____
Commitment:
________</td>
<td>Sunday
Practicing Hour:
____
Tape Hour:
____
Commitment:
________</td>
<td colspan="3">General Performance for Week ____:
(vocabulary, long sentence, background information, etc.)

Self-rating ☆☆☆☆☆</td>
</tr>
<tr>
<td>Monday
Practicing Hour:
____
Tape Hour:
____
Commitment:
________</td>
<td>Tuesday
Practicing Hour:
____
Tape Hour:
____
Commitment:
________</td>
<td>Wednesday
Practicing Hour:
____
Tape Hour:
____
Commitment:
________</td>
<td>Thursday
Practicing Hour:
____
Tape Hour:
____
Commitment:
________</td>
<td>Friday
Practicing Hour:
____
Tape Hour:
____
Commitment:
________</td>
</tr>
<tr>
<td>Saturday
Practicing Hour:
____
Tape Hour:
____
Commitment:
________</td>
<td>Sunday
Practicing Hour:
____
Tape Hour:
____
Commitment:
________</td>
<td colspan="3">General Performance for Week ____:
(vocabulary, long sentence, background information, etc.)

Self-rating ☆☆☆☆☆</td>
</tr>
</table>

Chapter 7

Chinese Culture

Part 1 Famous Quotes

The Tao that can be told of is not the Absolute Tao; the Names that can be given are not Absolute Names.

—Lao Tzu

道可道，非常道；名可名，非常名。

——老子

He who does not hold the position shall not involve himself in its affairs.

—Confucius

不在其位，不谋其政。

——孔子

You are not a fish; how do you know what constitutes the enjoyment of fishes?

—Chuang Tzu

子非鱼，安知鱼之乐？

——庄子

Part 2 Background Knowledge

(1) Chinese Culture: Customs & Traditions of China

By Kim Ann Zimmermann,
Live Science Contributor

(Extracted from: http://www.livescience.com/28823-chinese-culture.html.)

China is an extremely large country, and the customs and traditions of its people vary by geography and ethnicity. More than one billion people live in China, representing 56 ethnic minority groups. The largest group is the Han Chinese, with about 900 million people. Other groups include the Tibetans, the Mongols, the Manchus, the Naxi, and the Hezhen.

Culture includes religion, food, style, language, marriage, music, morals and many other things that make up how a group acts and interacts. Currently, there are five official religions in China, Buddhism, Taoism, Islam, Catholicism and Protestantism. There are seven major groups of dialects of the Chinese language, which each have their own variations. Mandarin dialects are spoken by 71.5 percent of the population, followed by Wu (8.5 percent), Yue (also called Cantonese; 5 percent), Xiang (4.8 percent), Min (4.1 percent), Hakka (3.7 percent) and Gan (2.4 percent). The official national language of China is Pǔtōnghuà, a type of Mandarin spoken in the capital Beijing, according to the Order of the President of the People's Republic of China.

Like other aspects of Chinese life, cuisine is heavily influenced by geography and ethnic diversity. Among the main styles of Chinese cooking are Cantonese, which features stir-fried dishes, and Szechuan, which relies heavily on use of peanuts, sesame paste and ginger and is known for its spiciness.

The largest festival — also called the Spring Festival — marks the beginning of the Lunar New Year. It falls between mid-January and mid-February and is a time to honor ancestors. The holiday is marked with fireworks and parades featuring dancers dressed as dragons. Many people make pilgrimages to Confucius' birthplace in Shandong Province on his birthday, Sep. 28. The birthday of Guanyin, the goddess of mercy, is observed by visiting Taoist temples. It falls between late March and late April. Similar celebrations mark the birthday of Mazu, the goddess of the sea (also known as Tianhou), in May or June. The Moon Festival is celebrated in September or October with fireworks, paper lanterns and moon gazing.

Task 1 Word Hunting

Directions: Try your best to spot the equivalent English expressions of the following words and expressions while reading the article.

1. 汉族，藏族，蒙古族，满族，纳西族，赫哲族

   ____

2. 天主教，基督教，佛教，道教，伊斯兰教

   ____

3. 官话方言，吴方言，客家方言，粤方言，闽方言，赣方言，湘方言

   ____

4. 阴历新年，孔子，妈祖，中秋节

   ____

5. 少数民族

   ____

Task 2 Oral Practice

Directions: Look at the following topics carefully and then choose one topic and deliver a short (1–3 minutes) presentation.

1. Every Chinese should be required to learn Mandarin.
2. Chinese workers should be guaranteed a ten-day leave for the Spring Festival.
3. The traditional Chinese culture value should be reintroduced to modern China.

Tip: When you plan, you should start with a list of ideas. You may not use all of them; still you will find one or two great ideas. Sit down with a pen and a piece of paper. Make a list, what are some things you know about? Upon your list, you may pick your topic. Then, you can make an idea web in which you should put your ideas in order.

(2) Chinese Opera

(See: http://www.travelchinaguide.com/intro/arts/chinese-opera.htm.)

Vocabulary

antimasque	[ˌæntɪ'mɑːsk]	*n.*	滑稽节目
gallop	['gæləp]	*v.*	奔跑

mingle	['mɪŋgl] *v.*	结合
erhu	[ɜː'huː] *n.*	二胡
gong	[gɒŋ] *n.*	铜锣
lute	[luːt] *n.*	琵琶
Chinese Opera	中国戏剧	
Greece Tragic-comedy	希腊悲喜剧	
Indian Sanskrit Opera	印度梵剧	
World Oral and Intangible Heritages	世界口头和非物质遗产	

Chinese Opera together with Greece Tragic-comedy and Indian Sanskrit Opera are the three oldest dramatic art forms in the world. The first opera school was established in the Tang Dynasty with the poetic name Liyuan (Pear Garden). From then on, performers of Chinese Opera were referred to as "disciples of the Pear Garden". Since the Yuan Dynasty (1271–1368) it has been encouraged by court officials and emperors and has become a traditional art form. During the Qing Dynasty, it became fashionable among ordinary people. Performances were watched in tearooms, restaurants, and even around makeshift stages.

It evolved from folk songs, dances, talking, antimasque, and especially distinctive dialectical music. Gradually it combined music, art and literature into one performance on the stage. Accompanied by traditional musical instruments like the erhu, the gong, and the lute, actors present unique melodies as well as dialogues which are beautifully written and of high literary value. These dialogs also promoted the development of distinct literary styles, such as Zaju in the Yuan Dynasty.

There are different styles of facial make-up in Chinese opera, which is one of the highlights and requires distinctive techniques of painting. Exaggerated designs are painted on each performer's face to symbolize a character's personality, role, and fate. This technique may have originated from ancient religions and dance. Audiences who are familiar with opera can know the story by observing the facial painting as well as the costumes. Generally, a red face represents loyalty and bravery; a black face, valor; yellow and white faces, duplicity; and golden and silver faces, mystery.

Besides color, lines also function as symbols. For example, a figure can be painted either all white on his face, or just around the nose. The larger the white area painted, the more viperous the role.

Chinese acrobatics are marvelous. Players can make fire spray out of their mouths when they act as spirits, or can gallop while squatting to act as a dwarf. This reflects a saying among actors: "One minute's performance on the stage takes ten years' practice behind the scenes."

Over the past 800 years, Chinese Opera has evolved into many different regional varieties based on local traits and accents. Today, there are over 300 dazzling regional opera styles. Kun Opera, which originated around Jiangsu Province, is a typical ancient opera style and features gentleness and clearness. This enabled it to be ranked among the World Oral and Intangible Heritages. Qinqiang Opera from Shanxi, known for its loudness and wildness, and Yu Opera, Yue Opera, and Huangmei Opera are all very enjoyable. Beijing Opera, the best-known Chinese opera style, was formed from the mingling of these regional styles.

Task 1 Word Hunting

Directions: Please guess the meanings of the following English words and expressions in the context.

1. disciples of the Pear Garden, court officials, makeshift

____

2. valor, duplicity, mystery, viperous

____

3. acrobatics, spirits, squat, Kun opera, Qinqiang opera

____

4. Yu Opera, Yue Opera, Huangmei Opera, Beijing Opera

____

Task 2 Oral Practice

Directions: Look at the following topics carefully and then choose one and deliver a short (1–3 minutes) presentation.

1. Chinese parents should enlarge their children's exposure to Chinese Opera.
2. More Americans need to learn Mandarin because China is going to be an increasingly important country.

Part 3 Listening and Speaking Practice

Pass 1 Chinese Yuppies

(Difficulty: ★★★)

背景知识

Yuppie（雅皮士）也被称为“优皮士”，指西方国家中年轻、能干、有上进心的一类人，他们一般受过高等教育，具有较高的知识水平和技能。雅皮士风貌兴起于20世纪80年代。雅皮士的着装、消费行为及生活方式等带有较明显的群体特征，但他们并无明确的组织性。随着我国中产阶级的崛起，“华人雅皮士”(China's Yuppies)逐渐为媒体所用，指那些高端消费者。为此，国外媒体甚至还用一个新词“Chuppies”（由“Chinese Yuppies”组成）来形容中国新一代拥有良好教育背景、收入不菲的年轻人。

雅皮士们在事业上十分成功，踌躇满志，恃才傲物，过着奢侈豪华的生活。雅皮士与嬉皮士们(hippy)不同，嬉皮士指西方国家20世纪六七十年代反抗习俗和当时政治的年轻人。雅皮士们没有颓废情绪，不关心政治与社会问题，只关心赚钱，追求舒适的生活。

（资料来源：http://baike.baidu.com/link?url=RzJyo4cUjemr5qvr8ko_51XrQwztF6fiCWaUiyYoYhZUBoCCdVdYdxvQxfPwtPbH。）

Vocabulary

Yuppie	['jʌpɪ]	*n.*	雅皮士（属于中上阶层的年轻专业人士）
Dior	['diːɒ]	*n.*	迪奥

Cartier	[kɑːˈtiːə] *n.*	卡地亚
Armani suit	[ʌˈmɑːnɪ] [suːt]	阿玛尼套装
Dunhill briefcase	[ˈdʌnhɪlˈbriːfkeɪs]	登喜路公文包

Task 1 General Understanding

Directions: Watch the video clip, and then sum up its main idea. You may do this either in Chinese or English.

Tip: Please write out a complete sentence based on your note or your understanding. Is it logically meaningful?

____

____

Task 2 Further Understanding

Directions: Watch the video again and check its main idea. You may do this either in Chinese or English.

Tip: Please read your sentence now, and ask yourself that if it makes sense logically. If you have caught any information which might change your previous idea, please rewrite your sentence.

____

____

Task 3 True or False

Directions: Watch the video and decide whether the following statements are true or false (T/F).

1. ( ) Yuppie is a long existing phenomenon in China.
2. ( ) China is the biggest consumer of luxury goods.
3. ( ) It is Chinese young people aged from 40 to 60 who are living high.
4. ( ) In China, most buyers of luxury are well educated.
5. ( ) Chinese Yuppie's average annual income ranges from 600 to 6,000 US dollars.

Task 4 Word Hunting

Directions: Try your best to spot the equivalent English expressions of the following words and expressions while watching the video.

1. 大学毕业生 ________________
2. 雅皮士 ________________
3. 阿玛尼套装 ________________
4. 登喜路公文包 ________________
5. 奢侈品 ________________
6. 中产阶级 ________________
7. 迪奥 ________________
8. 卡地亚 ________________
9. 突增 ________________
10. 顾客 ________________

Task 5 Self-dictation

Directions: Listen and write out all the numbers mentioned in the video.

____

____

____

Task 6 Back Translation

Directions: Please watch the video attentively and then translate the following Chinese sentences into English.

1. 随着中国大学毕业生的理想不断膨胀，在中国出现了雅皮士这一新现象。

   ____

2. 中国正在迅速跻身于最大的奢侈品消费国行列。据统计数据显示，中国年轻人的消费水平很高。

   ____

3. 在奢侈品消费方面，中国与西方国家有很大不同。

   ____

Task 7 Shadow Speaking Practice

Directions: Listen to the news item a couple of times and repeat the words that you've just heard. Retell the news first on your own and then check your work with your friends. Finally report the news to your classmates.

Task 8 Oral Practice

Directions: Look at the following topics carefully, choose one and then deliver a short (1–3 minutes) presentation.

1. The Chinese Yuppie reflects the economic strength of China as a new superpower.
2. Chinese Yuppies are the new driving forces in global luxury goods.
3. One can't expect to reach his/ her financial goals without developing a plan for spending and saving.

Pass 2 Chinese Food

(Difficulty: ★★★)

背景知识

中国菜是指发源于中国的烹饪方式，欧美称之为“Chinese Food”，乃中国文化的组成部分。菜谱 (Recipe) 来源于中国各个地区和不同民族的菜肴。中国菜的不同特点可以根据色 (Color)、香 (Aroma)、味 (Flavor)、意 (Meaning)、形 (Shape) 进行分析，被称为“国菜五品”。按烹饪特点又可分为：选料 (Ingredient)、刀工 (Cutting Technique)、火候 (Cooking) 和调味 (Seasoning) 四个方面。但不论如何，“中国菜”只是一个统称，中国的幅员广大，各个地方差异极大，中国的代表菜系有鲁菜（Shandong Cuisine）、川菜 (Szechuan Cuisine)、粤菜 (Cantonese Cuisine)、淮扬菜（苏菜）(Jiangsu Cuisine) 等。

许多中国食品都具有象征意义。比如，鸡蛋 (egg) 象征着繁衍，面条 (noodles) 象征长寿。鱼 (fish) 的象征意义来自汉语中“鱼”的发音，和表示富有和充裕的“余”同音。橘子 (tangerine) 和 橙子 (orange) 分别象征着吉祥和财富。韭菜 (Chinese garlic chives) 象征着永恒，而锥形的冬笋 (cone-shaped winter bamboo shoots) 也象征财富。

（资料来源：http://www.kankanews.com/a/2013-07-05/0042043025.shtml。）

Vocabulary

takeaway	['teɪkəweɪ]	*n.*	外卖饭菜
appetizing	['æpɪtaɪzɪŋ]	*adj.*	美味可口的
sodium	['səʊdɪəm]	*n.*	钠
overload	[ˌəʊvə'ləʊd]	*n.*	超量，超负荷
smother	['smʌðə(r)]	*v.*	涂上厚厚的佐料
deep-fried	['diːp 'fraɪd]	*adj.*	油炸的
greasy	['griːsɪ]	*adj.*	油腻的，多脂的
health-conscious	[helθ'kɒnʃəs]	*adj.*	有健康意识的
better	['betə(r)]	*v.*	改善，改进
canola oil	[kə'nəʊlə] [ɒɪl]	*n.*	菜籽油
tip the scales	[tɪp] [skeɪlz]		称重
contribute to	[kən'trɪbjuːt]		是……的部分原因
General Tso's chicken	左宗棠鸡，将军鸡		

Task 1　General Understanding

Directions: Watch the video once, and then sum up its main idea. You may do this either in Chinese or English.

Task 2　Further Understanding

Directions: Watch the video again and determine which one of the following statements is its main idea based on your understanding.

1. (　) Chinese food is appetizing.
2. (　) Chinese food is unhealthy.

Task 3 Listening Comprehension

Directions: Watch the video again and choose the best answer from the choices marked A), B), C) and D).

1. Why should people be careful when comes to Chinese restaurants, according to a new study from the US consumer group?
   A) Because Chinese dishes contain little sodium.
   B) Because Chinese dishes are too fatty.
   C) Because Chinese dishes are very appetizing.
   D) Because Chinese dishes taste so good.
2. Which one is most healthy among the following food according to the reporter?
   A) General Tso's chicken. B) Lemon chicken.
   C) Salty vegetables. D) Fried rice dishes.
3. Which one of the following statements is NOT mentioned in the video?
   A) Some people can't resist the unhealthy food.
   B) Salty vegetables are the dishes so soaked in sauce and deep fried that they are the ones to keep off your plate.
   C) According to the food expert, we might recognize the unhealthy food by using our common sense.
   D) When we enjoy the good taste of fried food, we need a mixture of vegetables.

Task 4 Back Translation

Directions: Please watch the video attentively and then translate the following Chinese sentences into English.

1. 研究发现，广受欢迎的菜肴如将军鸡的钠含量是普通成人一天所需量的 140%，而且热量超出正常需要量的一半以上。

   ____

2. 典型的中国菜里的钠含量相当于人体一天所需要的摄入量，这还不包括汤和开胃菜。你可能在一顿饭里就摄入了两天所需要的钠。

   ____

3. 因此建议很简单，不要油，也不要盐。

   ____

Task 5 Self-dictation

Directions: Please write out the script on a piece of paper. You may pause word by word at the beginning; gradually pause phrase by phrase; and then sentence by sentence. You may pause anywhere you need during the dictation. Pay attention to the stress, rhythm, linkage, tone, if there are any.

____

____

____

Task 6 Shadow Speaking Practice

Directions: Watch the news item a couple of times and repeat the words that you've just heard. Retell the news first on your own and then check your work with your friends. Finally report the news to your classmates.

Task 7 Oral Practice

Directions: Look at the following topics carefully, choose one topic and then deliver a short (1–3 minutes) presentation.

1. Chinese restaurants should get westernized in western countries.
2. Chinese food is much healthier than western food.

Pass 3 Kungfu Nuns

(Difficulty: ★★★)

背景知识

中国武术 (Chinese Kungfu) 又叫 "Martial Art"，是中国传统文化的重要一环，主要内容包括搏击技巧、格斗手法、攻防策略和武器使用等技术。中国武德包括"行"和"心"两个方面：行为上要谦 (Humility)、诚 (Virtue)、礼 (Respect)、义 (Morality) 和信 (Trust)；心灵上要勇 (Courage)、忍 (Patience)、恒 (Endurance)、毅 (Perseverance) 和志 (Will)。

Vocabulary

discipline	['dɪsəplɪn] *n.* 训练
mission	['mɪʃn] *n.* 使命
dragon dance	舞龙
at stake	在紧要关头

Task 1 General Understanding

Directions: Watch the video and then sum up its main idea. You may do this either in Chinese or English.

Task 2 Listening Comprehension

Directions: Listen again and choose the best answer from the choices marked A), B), C) and D).

1. When practicing Kungfu, ________.
   A) the men are able to do better because they are physically taller
   B) the women are able to do better because they are smarter
   C) the men are always able to do better because they are psychological stronger
   D) there will be no difference between men and women owing to women's practice and efforts
2. Which of the following statements is mentioned in the video?
   A) When you move the dragon left and right, you have to move it to the right side along with your right leg first.

B) The Kungfu master is confident of the nun's success in the dragon dance.

C) The Kungfu master suggests the nuns to practice a lot more and understand each other much better.

D) The Kungfu master is not serious about the lesson according to the reporter.

Task 3 Back Translation

Directions: Please watch the video attentively and then translate the following Chinese sentences into English.

1. 与舞龙、绘画并列的功夫是不会被人们遗忘的。这位功夫大师正在给竹笆女尼上课。

____

2. 大师的其他课程包括功夫和舞龙的训练和技能，他又回顾了一些基本功。

____

3. 竹笆女尼很看重功夫师父的教导，因为这不仅仅关系到一次舞龙的成败与否的问题，让女性处于舞台的中心是竹笆的使命。

____

Task 4 Self-dictation

Directions: Please write out the script on a piece of paper. You may pause word by word at the beginning; gradually pause phrase by phrase; and then sentence by sentence. You may pause anywhere you need during the dictation. Pay attention to the stress, rhythm, linkage, tone, if there are any.

____

____

____

____

Task 5 Shadow Speaking Practice

Directions: Watch the news item a couple of times and repeat the words that you've just heard. Retell the news first on your own and then check your work with your friends. Finally report the news to your classmates.

Task 6 Oral Practice

Directions: Look at the following topics carefully, and choose one topic and then deliver a short (1–3 minutes) presentation.

1. The Chinese Kungfu (also known as Kungfu or the Martial Arts) should be the compulsory course for Chinese youth.
2. Generally speaking, male Kungfu fighters are genetically stronger than female Kung-fu fighters.

Pass 4 Chinese Artists

(Difficulty: ★★★★)

背景知识

中国画 (Chinese painting) 的两个重要技能是工笔 (meticulous painting) 和水墨 (ink and wash painting)。中国画的绘画六法是由南北朝时期的画家、理论家谢赫在他的《画品》中提出的。“六法”者何？一曰气韵生动 (spiritual resonance)，二曰骨法用笔 (strength in brush using)，三曰应物象形 (correspondence to the object)，四曰随类赋彩 (suitability to type)，五曰经营位置 (division and planning)，六曰传移摹写 (transmission by copying)。

在绘画上，中国画重神韵，西洋画重形似。两者比较起来，有以下不同：中国画盛用线条，西洋画线条不显著；西洋画很像实物，而中国画不像实物，一望而知其为画；中国画注重意境，而西洋画注重透视法；中国画不重背景，西洋画很重背景；中国画题材以自然为主，西洋画题材以人物为主。中国画在汉代以前，也以人物为主要题材。但到了唐代，山水画即独立。一直到今日，山水常为中国画的正格。自希腊时代起，西洋画一直以人物为主要题材。

（资料来源：http://baike.baidu.com/subview/9845/5176553.htm。）

Vocabulary

booming	['buːmɪŋ] *adj.* 兴旺发达的
behold	[bɪ'həʊld] *v.* 看；看见
classical	['klæsɪkl] *adj.* 古典的
impressionistic	[ˌɪmpreʃə'nɪstɪk] *adj.* 印象派的
abstract	['æbstrækt] *adj.* 抽象派的
Van Gogh	梵·高
Venus	维纳斯
knock down	杀价
rip off	剽窃
fine art	美术作品
snap up	抢购

Task 1 General Understanding

Directions: Watch the video and then sum up its main idea. You may do this either in Chinese or English.

Task 2 Listening Comprehension

Directions: Listen again and choose the best answer from the choices marked A), B), C) and D).

1. Which of the following statements is mentioned in the video?
   A) Dafeng art village should be sued for selling the fake Mona Lisa.
   B) You may buy any masterpiece you are interested in for 13 dollars by the talented painters at Dafeng.
   C) Oil painting is a very huge business in China.
   D) There are 16 percent of the world's oil paintings and 5,000 artists in Shenzhen.
2. Which of the following statements is true of the artists in Dafeng?
   A) They are happy to copy masterpieces.

B) They did not like to create their own paintings.

C) They loved painting and art when they were very young.

D) They choose this profession because of its inspirations and profits.

Task 3 Back Translation

Directions: Please watch the video attentively and then translate the following Chinese sentences into English.

1. 现在几乎所有的东西都是中国制造，这似乎已经不是什么秘密。制造业处于繁盛阶段，但是艺术的繁盛却别有不同。

____

2. 这里的艺术家什么都画，从古典派、印象派到抽象派，绘画主题也异彩纷呈。

____

3. 是培养一些与生俱来的天赋还是薄利多销一些能够打动邻居的东西，这是你自己的选择。

____

Task 4 Self-dictation

Directions: Please write out the script on a piece of paper. You may pause word by word at the beginning; gradually pause phrase by phrase; and then sentence by sentence. You may pause anywhere you need during the dictation. Pay attention to the stress, rhythm, linkage, tone, if there are any.

____

____

____

____

Task 5 Shadow Speaking Practice

Directions: Watch the news item a couple of times and repeat the words that you've just heard. Retell the news first on your own and then check your work with your friends. Finally report the news to your classmates.

Task 6 Oral Practice

Directions: Look at the following topics carefully and then choose one and deliver a short (1–3 minutes) presentation.

1. Those painters in Dafeng violate the copyright law by painting the replica of masterpieces.
2. What is your point of view on buying replica of masterpieces?
3. What is the difference between Chinese paintings and the western ones?

Pass 5: Peking Opera Training

(Difficulty: ★★★★)

背景知识

京剧脸谱 (Facial Makeup in Peiking Opera)，是一种具有汉族文化特色的特殊化妆方法，是指中国传统戏剧中男演员脸部的彩色化妆。京剧脸谱以“象征性”和“夸张性”著称。这种脸部化妆主要用于净（花脸）和丑（小丑），运用夸张和变形的图形来展示角色的性格特征。内行的观众从脸谱上就可以分辨出这个角色是英雄还是坏人，聪明还是愚蠢，受人爱戴还是令人厌恶。红色脸象征忠义、耿直、有血性，比如《三国戏》里的关羽。黑色脸代表严肃、不苟言笑，如《包公戏》里的包拯，还可象征威武有力、粗鲁豪爽。比如《三国戏》里的张飞，《水浒戏》里的李逵。白色脸代表奸诈多疑，比如《三国戏》里的曹操、《打严嵩》中的严嵩。蓝色脸代表性格刚直，桀骜不驯，比如《上天台》中的马武、《连环套》里的窦尔敦。紫色脸代表肃穆、稳重，富有正义感，比如《二进宫》中的徐延昭、《鱼肠剑》中的专诸。金色脸象征威武庄严，表现神仙一类的角色，比如《闹天宫》

里的如来佛、二郎神。绿色脸象征勇猛，莽撞。其他还有黄色脸、粉色脸、银色脸等。京剧脸谱的色彩十分讲究，看起来五颜六色的脸谱品来却巨细有因，绝非仅仅为了好看。不同含义的色彩绘制在不同的图案、轮廓里，人物就被性格化了。

（资料来源：http://baike.baidu.com/view/4931.htm。）

Vocabulary

chunk	[tʃʌŋk]	*n.*	相当大的部分
debut	['deɪbjuː]	*n.*	首次登台演出
impulse	['ɪmpʌls]	*n.*	冲动
frantically	['fræntɪklɪ]	*adv.*	疯狂地

Task 1 General Understanding

Directions: Watch the video and then sum up its main idea. You may do this either in Chinese or English.

Task 2 Listening Comprehension

Directions: Listen again and choose the best answer from the choices marked A), B), C) and D).

1. Which one of the following statements is true about opera training for those foreign students?
   A) All of the students had performed drama before.
   B) All of the students think the gestures and movements are too difficult.
   C) The opera training has improved the students' singing skills.
   D) The opera training is too strict for most of foreign students to accept.
2. Which one of the following statements is NOT mentioned by the American student?
   A) The Beijing Opera builds from the outside in traditionally.
   B) The opera in the US requires you to follow the impulse of the character inside.
   C) The audience is supposed to judge actors' characters by their making-up in Beijing Opera.
   D) There is no making-up requirement, when the actors and actress performed in the US.

Task 3 Back Translation

Directions: Please watch the video attentively and then translate the following Chinese sentences into English.

1. 来自世界各地的 24 位大学生利用暑期的大部分时间来到上海，学习中国独特的艺术形式——京剧表演和唱腔。

   ____

2. 这些外国学生的表演使我们印象深刻，因为他们仅仅用了四周的时间就掌握了京剧的精髓。

   ____

Task 4 Self-dictation

Directions: Please write out the script on a piece of paper. You may pause word by word at the beginning; gradually pause phrase by phrase; and then sentence by sentence. You may pause anywhere you need during the dictation. Pay attention to the stress, rhythm, linkage, tone, if there are any.

____

____

____

____

Task5 Shadow Speaking Practice

Directions: Watch the news item a couple of times and repeat the words that you've just heard. Retell the news first on your own and then check your work with your friends. Finally report the news to your classmates.

Task 6 Oral Practice

Directions: Look at the following topics carefully and then choose one topic and deliver a short (1–3 minutes) presentation.

1. Please introduce different types of facial making-up in Peking Opera.
2. How to make Peking Opera popular around the world?

Pass 6 Oral and Intangible Heritage

(Difficulty: ★★★★)

背景知识

《牡丹亭》(*The Peony Pavilion*) 全名《牡丹亭还魂记》，是明代汤显祖的代表作。明代话本小说《杜丽娘慕色还魂》为《牡丹亭》提供了基本情节。《牡丹亭》与《西厢记》(*The Romance of West Chamber*)、《窦娥冤》(*Snow in Summer*)、《长生殿》(*The Palace of Eternal Life*)（另一个说法是《西厢记》《牡丹亭》《长生殿》和《桃花扇》并称中国四大古典戏剧。《牡丹亭》的故事情节如下：贫寒书生柳梦梅梦见在一座花园的梅树下站立着一位佳人，说同他有姻缘，从此经常思念她。南安太守杜宝之女名丽娘，才貌端妍，从师陈最良读书。她因读《诗经·关雎》而伤春寻春，从花园回来后在昏昏睡梦中见一书生持半枝垂柳前来求爱，两人在牡丹亭畔幽会。杜丽娘从此愁闷消瘦，一病不起。她在弥留之际要求母亲把她葬在花园的梅树下，嘱咐丫鬟春香将其自画像藏在太湖石底。其父升任淮阳安抚使，委托陈最良葬女并修建"梅花庵观"。三年后，柳梦梅赴京应试，借宿梅花庵观中，在太湖石下拾得杜丽娘画像，发现杜丽娘就是他梦中见到的佳人。杜丽娘魂游后园，和柳梦梅再度幽会。柳梦梅掘墓开棺，杜丽娘起死回生，两人结为夫妻，前往临安。杜丽娘的老师陈最良看到杜丽娘的坟墓被发掘，就告发柳梦梅盗墓之罪。柳梦梅在临安应试后，受杜丽娘之托，送家信传报还魂喜讯，结果被杜宝囚禁。发榜后，柳梦梅由阶下囚变为状元，但杜宝拒不承认女儿的婚事，强迫她离异，纠纷闹到皇帝面前，皇帝感慨二人的旷世奇缘，于是杜丽娘和柳梦梅二人终成眷属。

（资料来源：http://epaper.lsnews.com.cn/czwb/html/2015-11/01/content_830911.htm。）

Vocabulary

puppet	['pʌpɪt] *n.* 木偶
recital	[rɪ'saɪtl] *n.* 独奏
proclaim	[prə'kleɪm] *v.* 公布
captivate	['kæptɪveɪt] *v.* 使着迷
oblivion	[ə'blɪvɪən] *n.* 遗忘
ratify	['rætɪfaɪ] *v.* 批准
convention	[kən'venʃn] *n.* 公约
Uigur	['wiːgʊə] *n.* 维吾尔人
Mukam	木卡姆
Long Song	[lɔːŋ][sɒŋ] 长调
The Peony Pavilion	['piːənɪ][pə'vɪlɪən] 《牡丹亭》
Inner Mongolia	['ɪnə(r)] [mɒŋ'gəʊlɪə] 内蒙古
oral and intangible heritage	['ɔːrəl] [ɪn'tændʒəbl] ['herɪtɪdʒ] 口头和非物质遗产
The United Nations Educational, Scientific and Cultural Organization (UNESCO)	联合国教科文组织

Task 1 General Understanding

Directions: Watch the video and then sum up its main idea. You may do this either in Chinese or English.

Task 2 Listening Comprehension

Directions: Listen again and choose the best answer from the choices marked A), B), C) and D).

1. Which one of the following statements is TRUE about the performance?
   A) Guqin is the oldest yet still performed style of Chinese Opera.
   B) Mukam was performed by the singing shepherds from Inner Mongolia.
   C) “Water from the Source” was composed some 1,000 years ago.
   D) Kunqu is an art form mixing song and dance.

2. Which one is NOT included in the list of the UNESCO convention for the safeguarding of the intangible cultural heritage?

   A) Guqin. B) Kunqu. C) Folk songs. D) Long song.

Task 3 Back Translation

Directions: Please watch the video attentively and then translate the following Chinese sentences into English.

1. 在联合国教科文组织于巴黎举办的庆典活动中，表演艺术团和来自新疆的农民一起表演了木卡姆，他们共同演绎了这些口头和非物质文化遗产的经典之作是怎样与人们的生活交融在一起的。

   ____

   ____

2. 中国表演艺术这一非物质遗产因地域和民族不同而风格迥异，异彩纷呈。

   ____

3. 中国政府已经执行联合国教科文组织大会公约规定，教育本民族保护并继承这些艺术形式。

   ____

Task 4 Self-dictation

Directions: Please write out the script on a piece of paper. You may pause word by word at the beginning; gradually pause phrase by phrase; and then sentence by sentence. You may pause anywhere you need during the dictation. Pay attention to the stress, rhythm, linkage, tone, if there are any.

____

____

____

____

Task 5 Shadow Speaking Practice

Directions: Watch the news item a couple of times and repeat words that you've just heard. Retell the news first on your own and then check your work with your friends. Finally report the news to your classmates.

Task 6 Oral Practice

Directions: Look at the following topics carefully, and then choose one and deliver a short (1–3 minutes) presentation.

1. Please briefly introduce the story in "The Peony Pavilion".
2. How to protect "the oral and intangible heritage"?
3. How to launch the application for the UNESCO's intangible cultural heritage list?

Pass 7 Dai's Water Splashing Festival

(Difficulty: ★★★★)

背景知识

泼水节 (Water Splashing Festival) 是傣族（Dai people）最隆重的节日，也是云南少数民族节日中影响面最大，参加人数最多的节日。傣族泼水节一般持续 3 至 7 天。节日期间，傣族男女老少都穿上节日盛装，挑着清水，先到佛寺浴佛，然后就开始互相泼水，互祝吉祥、幸福、健康。

（资料来源：http://www.360doc.com/content/16/0217/08/16967035_535178012.shtml。）

Vocabulary

gorge	[gɔːdʒ] *n.* 峡谷
Vietnam	[ˌvjet'næm] *n.* 越南
Laos	[laʊs] *n.* 老挝
Dai people	[daɪ]['piːpl] *n.* 傣族
the Water Splashing Festival	['wɔːtə(r)][sp'læʃɪŋ]['festɪvl] 泼水节

Task 1 General Understanding

Directions: Watch the video and then sum up its main idea. You may do this either in Chinese or English.

Task 2 Listening Comprehension

Directions: Listen again and choose the best answer from the choices marked A), B), C) and D)

1. Which of the following locations is NOT mentioned as Dai's living places?
   A) The southwest corner of China.
   B) The borders of tropical Vietnam and Laos.
   C) The mountain lands in the cold far north.
   D) The remote southeast corner of China.
2. Which of the following statements about the Dai's Water Splashing Festival is NOT true?
   A) The Dai people bring river water to the temple.
   B) This festival exists over 2,000 years.
   C) It is the most important festival of Dai.
   D) The Dai people have a biggest water fight each year.
3. Which of the following items is NOT important for Dai people?
   A) Water.　　B) Buddhism.
   C) Taoism.　　D) Home.

Task 3 Back Translation

Directions: Please watch the video attentively and then translate the following Chinese sentences into English.

1. 这里，隐秘的溪谷培育出罕见珍奇的生物和多姿多彩的民族文化。

____

2. 傣族人敬谢养育他们文化的河川与良地。

____

3. 由于城镇的逐渐扩大以及都市化程度的不断加深，傣族的生活形态正逐步改变，但是人们仍然会欢度泼水节。

____

Task 4 Self-dictation

Directions: Please write out the script on a piece of paper. You may pause word by word at the beginning; gradually pause phrase by phrase; and then sentence by sentence. You may pause anywhere you need during the dictation. Pay attention to the stress, rhythm, linkage, tone, if there are any.

____

____

____

____

Task 5 Shadow Speaking Practice

Directions: Watch the material a couple of times and repeat the words that you've just heard. Retell the news first on your own and then check your work with your friends. Finally report the news to your classmates.

Task 6 Oral Practice

Directions: Look at the following topic carefully, then deliver a short (1–3 minutes) presentation.

How do people celebrate the Water Splashing Festival?

Pass 8 Year of Tiger and Your Money

(Difficulty: ★★★★)

背景知识

春节是我国一个古老的节日，也是全年最重要的一个节日，如何庆贺这个节日，在千百年的历史发展中，形成了一些较为固定的风俗习惯，有许多还相传至今。

扫尘（House Cleaning）

"腊月二十四，掸尘扫房子"，据《吕氏春秋》记载，我国在尧舜时代就有春节扫尘的风俗。按民间的说法：因"尘"与"陈"谐音，新春扫尘有"除陈布新"的含义，其用意是要把一切穷运、晦气统统扫出门。这一习俗寄托着人们破旧立新的愿望和辞旧迎新的祈求。每逢春节来临，家家户户都要打扫环境，清洗各种器具，拆洗被褥窗帘，洒扫六闾庭院，掸拂尘垢蛛网，疏浚明渠暗沟。

贴春联（Spring Festival Couplets）

春联也叫门对、春贴、对联、对子、桃符等，它以工整、对偶、简洁、精巧的文字描绘时代背景，抒发美好愿望，是我国特有的文学形式。这一习俗起于宋代。春联的种类比较多，依其使用场所，可分为门心、框对、横披、春条、斗方等。"门心"贴于门板上端的中心部位；"框对"贴于左右两个门框上；"横披"贴于门楣的横木上；"春条"根据不同的内容，贴于相应的地方；"斗斤"也叫"门叶"，为正方菱形，多贴在家具、影壁上。

贴窗花和倒贴"福"字（Paper-cut pictures & Chinese character "Fu"）

在民间人们还喜欢在窗户上贴上各种剪纸即窗花。窗花不仅烘托了喜庆的节日气氛，而且集装饰性、欣赏性和实用性于一体。剪纸在我国是一种很普及的民间艺术，千百年来深受人们的喜爱，因它大多是贴在窗户上的，所以也被称为"窗花"。窗花以其特有的概括和夸张手法将吉事祥物、美好愿望表现得淋漓尽致，将节日装点得红火富丽。

在贴春联的同时，一些人家要在屋门上、墙壁上、门楣上贴上大大小小的"福"字。春节贴"福"字，是我国民间由来已久的风俗。"福"字指福气、福运，寄托了人们对幸福生活的向往，对美好未来的祝愿。为了更充分地体现这种向往和祝愿，有的人干脆将"福"字倒过来贴，表示"幸福已到""福气已到"。民间还有将"福"字精描细做成各种图案的，图案有寿星、寿桃、鲤鱼跳龙门、五谷丰登、龙凤呈祥等。

守岁

除夕守岁是最重要的年俗活动之一，守岁之俗由来已久。最早记载见于西晋周处的《风土志》：除夕之夜，各相与赠送，称为"馈岁"；酒食相邀，称为"别岁"；长幼聚饮，祝颂完备，称为“分岁”；大家终夜不眠，以待天明，称曰“守岁”。“一夜连双岁，五更分二天”，除夕之夜，全家团聚在一起，吃年夜饭，点起蜡烛或油灯，围坐炉旁闲聊，等着辞旧迎新的时刻，通宵守夜，象征着把一切邪瘟病疫照跑驱走，期待着新的一年吉祥如意。这种习俗后来逐渐盛行，到唐朝初期，唐太宗李世民写有“守岁”诗：寒辞去冬雪，暖带入春风。直到今天，人们还习惯在除夕之夜守岁迎新。古时守岁有两种含义：年长者守岁为“辞旧岁”，有珍爱光阴的意思；年轻人守岁，是为延长父母寿命。自汉代以来，新旧年交替的时刻一般为夜半时分。

拜年

新年的初一，人们都早早起来，穿上最漂亮的衣服，打扮得整整齐齐，出去走亲访友，相互拜年，恭祝来年大吉大利。春节拜年时，晚辈要先给长辈拜年，祝长辈长寿安康，长辈可将事先准备好的压岁钱分给晚辈，据说压岁钱可以压住邪祟，因为“岁”与“祟”谐音，晚辈得到压岁钱就可以平平安安度过一岁。压岁钱有两种：一种是以彩绳穿线编作龙形，置于床脚，此记载见于《燕京岁时记》；另一种是最常见的，即由家长用红纸包裹起来分给孩子的钱。压岁钱可在晚辈拜年后当众赏给，亦可在除夕夜孩子睡着时，由家长偷偷地放在孩子的枕头底下。现在长辈为晚辈分送压岁钱的习俗仍然盛行。（小贴士：请对照本书第一章的英文背景知识部分进行阅读）

（资料来源：http://www.china.com.cn/ch-jieri/chunjie/3.htm。）

Vocabulary

superstitious	[ˌsuːpəˈstɪʃəs]	*adj.*	迷信的；有迷信观念的
symbolism	[ˈsɪmbəlɪzəm]	*n.*	象征主义，象征手法
unpredictability	[ˌʌnprɪˌdɪktəˈbɪləti]	*n.*	不可预测性，不可预知性
charm	[tʃɑːm]	*n.*	小装饰品
treat	[triːt]	*n.*	款待；招待
lingerie	[ˈlænʒərɪ]	*n.*	女用贴身内衣裤
scoop up	[skuːp ʌp]		铲起；舀

Task 1 General Understanding

Directions: Watch the video and then sum up its main idea. You may do this either in Chinese or English.

Task 2 True or False

Directions: Watch the News and tell whether the following statements are true or false (T/F).

1. ( ) Chinese use sesame balls to worship ancestors, and bring good luck in the New Year.
2. ( ) Roasted melon seeds mean lots of money.
3. ( ) Rice cakes in the shape of fish mean gold and silver.
4. ( ) The color of yellow represents promotion in career.
5. ( ) The color of purple symbolizes good luck in the new year.

Task 3 Blank Filling

Directions: Watch the video again and fill in the following blanks.

The Chinese are very (1) __________ and that means they take (2) __________ seriously. It's the year of the tiger, representing (3) ________________. Locals come to this market to buy good luck charms. Customers at this snack store are (4) __________ all sorts of New Year's treats.

It's a tradition for all of us Chinese to get these sesame balls during Chinese New Year. We use them to (5) ________________ and we say if we have more sesame balls at home then (6) ________________. It's really to bring us more wealth in the new year.

Roasted melon seeds symbolize (7)________, so this means (8)________________. Rice cakes in the shape of fish are big sellers too. In Cantonese the word for fish sounds the same as the word for (9) ________.

Another item locals wanna buy for the New Year for good luck is (10) __________. Red symbolizes (11) ________________ and the Chinese want new clothes for the New Year (12) ________________.

I'm willing to spend on underwear because it's like my second skin. Margar Wang buys three lingerie sets every New Year, believing red will bring her good luck.

I've been doing this for a long time. It's a tradition in my family to buy new clothes. I would feel strange if I didn't do this every year.

Lunar New Year is the most (13) _____________ year for this (14) __________ store.(15) __________ percent of purchases are red. The next best sellers are yellow which represents the(16) __________ and purple which symbolizes (17) __________.

The sales from these colors and these products account for(18) __________ of our sales during January to February.

The banks are also very busy with customers ordering (19) __________ to give away as New Year's gifts to younger relatives or junior colleagues. It's considered good luck for the (20) ________________.

Then everyone waits to see if the tiger comes out roaring down a path of good fortune.

Task 4 Back Translation

Directions: Please watch the video attentively and then translate the following Chinese sentences into English.

1. 中国人很迷信，很看重具有象征意义的事物。今年是虎年，虎年代表着勇气和未来的不可预测。

____

2. 红色代表财富和成功，中国人在新年时会从头到脚、从内到外地穿新衣服。

____

3. 银行频繁地接到为客户办理订购崭新钞票的业务。这些崭新的钞票将作为新年礼物送给年龄小的亲戚或者级别低的同事。送钱和接到钱的人都会得到好运。

____

Task 5 Self-dictation

Directions: Please write out the script on a piece of paper. You may pause word by word at the beginning; gradually pause phrase by phrase; and then sentence by sentence. You may pause anywhere you need during the dictation. Pay attention to the stress, rhythm, linkage, tone, if there are any.

____

____

____

____

Task 6 Shadow Speaking Practice

Directions: Watch the material a couple of times and repeat the words that you've just heard. Retell the material first on your own and then check your work with your friends. Finally report it to your classmates.

Task7 Oral Practice

***Directions:** Look at the following topics carefully, choose one topic and then deliver a short (1–3 minutes) presentation.*

1. How do people celebrate Spring Festival?
2. How do people celebrate Christmas?

Pass 9 Tibetan Culture

(Difficulty: ★★★★★)

背景知识

藏族人大多信仰藏传佛教，所以他们的很多风俗也与佛教有关。藏族的礼仪多种多样，主要有以下几种：

献哈达，是藏族最普遍的一种礼节。婚丧节庆、拜会尊长、觐见佛像、音讯往来、送别远行等，都有献哈达的习惯。献哈达是对人表示纯洁、诚心、忠诚的意思。藏族地区没有丝绸，以前就有用野兽和动物皮、羊毛等作为礼品和奖品的习俗。后来人们将羊毛织成巾和绢，替代此习俗，哈达的雏形由此形成。哈达的主色为白色，佛教在藏区的盛行为哈达的颜色注入了新的生命，如将观世音（洁白）、文殊（纯黄）、金刚手（深蓝）三怙主的颜色作为哈达的主要颜色。后来地（黄）、水（白）、火（红）、风（黑）四种颜色也渐渐盛兴，但是黑色很少见，往往为深蓝色等其他颜色所替代。另外还有五彩哈达，是做彩箭用的，颜色为蓝、白、红、绿、黄。

磕头，也是西藏常见的礼节，一般是朝觐佛像、佛塔和活佛时磕头，也有对长者磕头的。

鞠躬，过去遇见长官、头人和受尊敬的人，要脱帽致礼。对于一般人或平辈，鞠躬只表示礼貌，帽子放在胸前，头略低，也有合掌与鞠躬并用的。

敬酒茶，在酒席上，主人端起酒杯先饮三口，然后一饮而尽，主人饮完头杯酒后，大家才能自由饮用。饮茶时，客人必须等主人把茶捧到面前才能伸手接过饮用，否则会被认为失礼。

（资料来源：http://mt.sohu.com/20150909/n420718852.shtml。）

Vocabulary

resound	[rɪ'zaʊnd]	*v.*	回荡
distinctive	[dɪ'stɪŋktɪv]	*adj.*	特殊的
unwieldy	[ʌn'wiːldɪ]	*adj.*	笨重的
substantial	[səb'stænʃl]	*adj.*	相当数目的
portion	['pɔːʃn]	*n.*	一部分
self-contained	[self kən'teɪnd]	*adj.*	独立的
isolated	['aɪsəleɪtɪd]	*adj.*	隔离的
monastery	['mɒnəstrɪ]	*n.*	寺院
enlightenment	[ɪn'laɪtnmənt]	*n.*	觉悟，智慧
literally	['lɪtərəlɪ]	*adv.*	确实地，真正地，不加夸张地
lama	['lɑːmə]	*n.*	喇嘛
doorstep	['dɔːstep]	*n.*	门阶

Task 1 General Understanding

Directions: Watch the video and then sum up its main idea. You may do this either in Chinese or English.

Task 2 Listening Comprehension

Directions: Listen again and choose the best answer from the choices marked A), B), C) and D).

1. Which of the following statements is NOT mentioned?
   A) The Tibetan horn's sound is unique.
   B) The Tibetan horn is designed by Lama.
   C) The nuns assemble every morning for practicing the Tibetan horn.
   D) The Tibetan horn is a very cumbersome instrument.
2. Which of the following statements about Tibetan's belief is FALSE?
   A) Tibetan believes in an endless cycle of rebirth in which the actions of this life will impact on the next.

B) The goal of Buddhism is to reach a state of speech freedom.

C) The reason Tibetan benefit all beings is that they might escape the cycle of life and death.

D) The Tibetan believes that every living creature has a soul.

3. Which of the following statements is NOT true about Lama?

A) Lama is an enlightened guide.

B) Lama is a spiritual teacher.

C) Lama has the right to decide people's birth or death.

D) Lama explains the concept of Buddhism.

Task 3 Back Translation

Directions: Please watch the video attentively and then translate the following Chinese sentences into English.

1. 尽管西藏日新月异地发展，但它的精神文化依旧根深蒂固。

____

2. 僧尼占社会人口比例的很大一部分，而且是封闭自足、离群索居的一群。

____

3. 西藏地处遥远，一千多年以来，人们一直奉行这种善待野生动物的信念，从他们的门槛之处就开始身体力行地实践着。

____

Task 4 Self-dictation

Directions: Please write out the script on a piece of paper. You may pause word by word at the beginning; gradually pause phrase by phrase; and then sentence by sentence. You may pause anywhere you need during the dictation. Pay attention to the stress, rhythm, linkage, tone, if there are any.

____

____

____

____

Task 5 Shadow Speaking Practice

Directions: Watch the material a couple of times and repeat the words that you've just heard. Retell the material first on your own and then check your work with your friends. Finally report it to your classmates.

Task 6 Oral Practice

Directions: Look at the following topics carefully and then choose one topic and deliver a short (1–3 minutes) presentation.

1. What do you know about Tibetan culture?
2. Do you believe that every living creature has a soul? Please explain.

Pass 10 Silk Road

(Difficulty: ★★★★★)

背景知识

丝绸之路 (Silk Road/Silk Route) 通常是指欧亚大陆北部的商路，与南方的茶马古道 (Ancient Tea-horse Road) 形成对比。西汉汉武帝时张骞从长安带队出使西域 (The Western Regions)，联合大月氏人，共同抗击匈奴，首次开拓丝绸之路，被称为“凿空之旅”。西汉末年，丝绸之路一度断绝，东汉时的班超又重新打通了隔绝 58 年的通往西域之路，罗马帝国也首次顺着丝绸之路来到当时东汉的首都洛阳。在通过这条漫漫长路进行贸易的货物中，中国的丝绸最具代表性，“丝绸之路”因此得名。历史上的一些著名人物，如出使西域的张骞，投笔从戎的班超，西天取经的玄奘，他们的一些故事都与这条路有关。

（资料来源：http://wenku.baidu.com/link?url=3QqAnsLH-y8alu95qoVY9qXXpTDa5XySllht5tEXNWeRdR_w-PE3nLpPVF35sZHktI_Tw5T1WpFk3hBM_v_rbtnA5aStJ5pzE-TXePcmhjO。）

Vocabulary

fortress	['fɔːtrəs]	*n.*	要塞，堡垒
meticulously	[mə'tɪkjələslɪ]	*adv.*	谨小慎微地，过分关心细节地

formidable	['fɔːmɪdəbl]	*adj.*	可怕的，令人敬畏的
outpost	['aʊtpəʊst]	*n.*	边远位置；界限，边境
utter	['ʌtə(r)]	*adj.*	完全的，彻底的
desolation	[ˌdesə'leɪʃn]	*n.*	荒芜
abrasive	[ə'breɪsɪv]	*adj.*	损伤性的
gluttony	['glʌtənɪ]	*n.*	暴饮，暴食
gland	[glænd]	*n.*	腺
cocoon	[kə'kuːn]	*n.*	茧
strand	[strænd]	*n.*	线，绳
unravel	[ʌn'rævl]	*v.*	解开，拆散
filament	['fɪləmənt]	*n.*	细丝，细线
dune	[djuːn]	*n.*	沙丘
millennia	[mɪ'lenɪə]	*n.*	millennium（一千年）的复数
mega-	['megə-]	*adj.*	许多
splay	[spleɪ]	*n.*	张开
sculpt	[skʌlpt]	*vt.*	雕刻
hazard	['hæzəd]	*n.*	危险
tramp	[træmp]	*n.*	沉重的脚步声
hum	[hʌm]	*n.*	嘈杂声
cavalcade	[ˌkævl'keɪd]	*n.*	骑者队列，马队
plight	[plaɪt]	*n.*	困境
traverse	[trə'vɜːs]	*v.*	穿过
Yardang	['jɑːdɑːŋ]	*n.*	风蚀土瘠，白龙堆

Task 1 General Understanding

Directions: Watch the video and then sum up its main idea. You may do this either in Chinese or English.

Task 2 Word Hunting

Directions: please try to guess the meanings of the following words and expressions while watching the video.

1. Chinese civilization ______________________

2. The Taklamakan ______________________
3. mulberry leaves ______________________
4. Hotan ______________________
5. wooden looms ______________________
6. Central Asia ______________________
7. Millennia ______________________
8. mega-dunes ______________________
9. Fury of God ______________________
10. Sea of Death ______________________
11. Silk Road ______________________

Task 3 Listening Comprehension

Directions: Listen again and choose the best answer from the choices marked A), B), C) and D).

1. Which of the following statements is TRUE about Jiayuguan?
   A) Jiayuguan was built in the Ming Dynasty over 160 years ago.
   B) It was said that less than 100,000 bricks were used in Jiayuguan.
   C) Jiayuguan is the weakest fortress of the man-made barrier—Chinese Great Wall.
   D) Jiayuguan Fortress was considered to be the output of Chinese civilization.
2. Which is NOT the proper description about the Taklamakan?
   A) It is the natural formidable barrier of Chinese civilization.
   B) It is a vast no-man's land of deserts.
   C) It lies in the Central Asia.
   D) Its size is about the same as that of Germany.

Task 4 Arrangement

Directions: Please arrange the following statements in a logical order.

1. Harvested cocoons are dropped into boiling water, which unravels the long filaments.
2. By this stage, 25% of their body mass is made up of silk glands.
3. Silk moths lay several hundred eggs.
4. In the process of turning into adult moths, they spin a cocoon from a single strand of silk which can be over 1,000 meters long.

5. These are then gathered and spun into raw silk thread.
6. The tiny caterpillars that emerge eat nothing but mulberry leaves.
7. After 50 days of gluttony they've grown 10,000 times heavier.

Task 5 Blank Filling

Directions: Watch the video again and fill in the following blanks.

Legend has it that around (1) ____________ years ago, a princess was walking in her garden when something unusual fell into her tea cup. (2) ____________ was extracted and it became more prized than (3) ____________ or (4) ____________. The thread was silk. For over 5,000 years, people built (5) ____________ on these delicate threads, which was why China became so powerful that it (6) ____________________. For the ancient Silk Road traders, the problem was how to get the valuable silk from (7) __________ through (8) __________ to (9) ______________. The name of Taklamakan has been translated as (10) ______________. It is a place of intense heat, abrasive wind-blown sand totally (11) ______________ to life, and is called by travelers (12) ______________ and (13) ______________. The desert routes those ancient traders took became the fabled (14) ______________.

Task 6 Back Translation

Directions: Please watch the video attentively and then translate the following Chinese sentences into English.

1. 早期的旅者沿着丝绸之路向西而行，其路途是难以想象的艰辛，他们要穿过很多可怕的地方。

   ____

2. 强风还会让沙漠中的旅者遭受其他危险。有时迷路的旅者会听到脚步声和嗡嗡声，好像在真正的行进路线的远处有一支正在前进的骑队。他们会以为这声音来自他们的同伴而跟着声音走，天亮后他们才发现自己受骗了。他们已经陷入恶劣的困境之中。

   ____

3. 但是，最严重的问题是缺乏水源，从卫星画面上可以了解为何此地如此干旱。中国的沙漠是地球上离大洋最远的地方。缺水造成了塔克拉玛干沙漠——全世界面积最大的流沙沙漠，大部分动物无法在这里生存。

   ____

Task 7 Self-dictation

Directions: Please write out the script on a piece of paper. You may pause word by word at the beginning; gradually pause phrase by phrase; and then sentence by sentence. You may pause anywhere you need during the dictation. Pay attention to the stress, rhythm, linkage, tone, if there are any.

____

____

____

____

Task 8 Shadow Speaking Practice

Directions: Watch the material a couple of times and repeat the words that you've just heard. Retell the material first on your own and then check your work with your friends. Finally report it to your classmates.

Task 9 Oral Practice

Directions: Look at the following topics carefully, choose one topic and then deliver a short (1–3 minutes) presentation.

1. Please talk about the function of Silk Road.
2. How do silkworms make silk?

Part 4 英语听说秘籍之中式口音（Accent）

有人把中国人说英语的方式归结为中式口音 (Chinese accent)。中国人日常交流时使用普通话。中国人说普通话时的发音方式与西方人说英语时的发音方式不同，这就决定了当中国人说英语时会夹杂普通话的发音特点。因此出现与西方人的英语发音特点不同的中式口音。

从单音来看，英语中的辅音群是很常见的，往往两个或三个以上辅音连在一起。但是，汉语中没有辅音群，汉语中的辅音往往和元音成对儿出现，因此中国学习者通常会在辅音之间加入元音，特别是 "er[ɜː(r)]" 音。例如，中国人在读 "crisps" 时，人们会在 "s-p-s" 之间加入元音，读成“cris-pe-s”。中国的英语学习者在说英语时的这种加音 (adding sounds) 现象会妨碍欧美人的理解。

从语流来看，中国人在用本民族语言汉语表达时强调字正腔圆，喜欢发音清楚、清晰。而英国人在发“t”和“d”时常常非常含糊，不易被我们的耳朵所捕捉到。如 account, 美国人会读成“[ə'kaʊn]”，这让中国学习者很难理解，造成沟通障碍。而对于欧美人来说，他们听中国人说话很吃力却是因为中国人把每个音都读得很重。同样，习惯把每个词都读得很重的中国人在处理连读 (word linkage) 问题时就显得不那么地道，因此也无法很好地辨别出欧美人的连读是哪些单词组合。

此外，汉语的字需要与声调搭配来表达不同的含义，而英语没有声调的要求。英语的节奏 (rhythm) 强调音节的强弱 (strong syllables and weak syllables)，这也会让中国学习者无所适从。

练习建议：

1. 中英文发音方式不同，因此，要模仿欧美人说英语的方式，就应该先做好准备，即摆对口型。英语有 44 个音素，其中 12 个单元音，8 个双元音以及 24 个辅音。发元音时，气流不受任何发音器官的阻碍，即口腔各部分没有相互接触。发好元音的关键是双唇开合的大小和舌位的高低。辅音则不同，不管是声带震动的清辅音还是不震动的浊辅音，气流都会受到发音器官的阻碍，因此摆对口型尤其重要。
2. 跟读、模仿地道的欧美人的说话方式，提高辨音能力；在练习连读的时候不要认为它们是一个个不同的单词，而是应该把它们看做是连接在一起的音。
3. 聆听英文歌曲，提高对节奏的感知度。
4. 扩大词汇量，提高英语口语表达的准确度。
5. 尽量发音清楚，接近标准口音，把你的意思表达清楚，让别人明白你的意思才是最重要的。

Additional Drills Walking Marriage

(Difficulty: ★★★★★)

背景知识

走婚 (Walking Marriage) 是云南和四川的少数民族摩梭人的习俗，摩梭人除了少数人为了增加家庭劳动人口而娶妻或招婿外，基本上没有婚姻制度。走婚是情投意合的男女通过男子到女子家走婚，维持感情与生养下一代的方式。由于母系社会中由女性当家，因此所生下的小孩归母家生养，生父会在满月时公开举办宴席，承认彼此的血缘关系。

（资料来源：http://baike.baidu.com/subview/54593/6577916.htm。）

Vocabulary

matriarchal	[ˌmeɪtrɪ'ɑːkl] *adj.* 母系的
initiative	[ɪ'nɪʃətɪv] *n.* 主动权
deft	[deft] *adj.* 灵巧的
footwork	['fʊtwɜːk] *n.* 步法
distinct	[dɪ'stɪŋkt] *adj.* 清楚的
whisk off	[hwɪsk ɒf] 飞快带走
butter up	['bʌtə] [ʌp] 奉承，甜言蜜语
Mosuo	*n.* 摩梭人
Lugu Lake	泸沽湖
flower chamber	['flaʊə(r)] ['tʃeɪmbə(r)] 花楼
mandarin orange	['mændərɪn]['ɒrɪndʒ] 橘

Task 1 General Understanding

Directions: Watch the video and then sum up its main idea. You may do this either in Chinese or English.

Task 2 Chinese Accent

Directions: Watch the video again, and focus on the Chinese Accent of Namu, did you find any ?

____

Task 3 True or False

Directions: Watch the video and decide whether the following statements are true or false (T/F).

1. ( ) It is the man who takes initiative in a relationship in walking marriage.
2. ( ) There are about 16,000 tourists who come to Lugu Lake for free sex per year.
3. ( ) Lugu Lake offers the beautiful views and fresh air to the tourists.

Task 4 Blank Filling

Directions: Watch the video again and fill in the following blanks.

Walking marriage means people (1) ____________________ and thus don't (2) ______________. There are neither (3) ______________ nor (4) ______________. The couples (5)________________ together. It's their (6) ______________ that take their fathers' responsibility. A woman wants to have someone or not, (7) ______________. She may open the (8) __________ for him if she wants to do it. If she doesn't want it, she closes it. Namu thinks walking marriage very healthy, because there is no (9)__________________.

Task 5 Back Translation

Directions: Please watch the video attentively and then translate the following Chinese sentences into English.

1. 娜姆行了佛家的"合十"礼，作秀式地亲了我一下。之后，飞快地带我去看她从小住过的房子。

   ____

2. 离开泸沽湖去更广阔的世界是她童年的梦想，但是她不想被遗忘。

   ____

3. 泸沽湖的清新空气有强大的力量，洗涤了，或者说轻轻擦拭了我的心灵。我觉得或许现在应该检查一下身体的其他部分。

   ____

Task 6 Oral Practice

Directions: Look at the following topics carefully and then choose one topic and deliver a short (1–3 minutes) presentation.

1. Please talk about the walking marriage around Lugu Lake.
2. How do people celebrate wedding ceremony in China?

English Listening-and-Speaking Learning Planner

Monday Practicing Hour: ________ Tape Hour: ________ Commitment: ________	**Tuesday** Practicing Hour: ________ Tape Hour: ________ Commitment: ________	**Wednesday** Practicing Hour: ________ Tape Hour: ________ Commitment: ________	**Thursday** Practicing Hour: ________ Tape Hour: ________ Commitment: ________	**Friday** Practicing Hour: ________ Tape Hour: ________ Commitment: ________
Saturday Practicing Hour: ________ Tape Hour: ________ Commitment: ________	**Sunday** Practicing Hour: ________ Tape Hour: ________ Commitment: ________	**General Performance for Week ____:** (vocabulary, long sentence, background information, etc.) Self-rating ☆☆☆☆☆		
Monday Practicing Hour: ________ Tape Hour: ________ Commitment: ________	**Tuesday** Practicing Hour: ________ Tape Hour: ________ Commitment: ________	**Wednesday** Practicing Hour: ________ Tape Hour: ________ Commitment: ________	**Thursday** Practicing Hour: ________ Tape Hour: ________ Commitment: ________	**Friday** Practicing Hour: ________ Tape Hour: ________ Commitment: ________
Saturday Practicing Hour: ________ Tape Hour: ________ Commitment: ________	**Sunday** Practicing Hour: ________ Tape Hour: ________ Commitment: ________	**General Performance for Week ____:** (vocabulary, long sentence, background information, etc.) Self-rating ☆☆☆☆☆		

Appendix

民间艺术	folk art
高雅艺术	refined art
戏剧艺术	theatrical art
电影艺术	cinematographic art
文化产业	culture industry
文化事业	cultural undertaking
文化交流	cross-cultural communication
文化冲突	culture shock
乡村文化	rural culture
民族文化	national culture
表演艺术	performing art
文化底蕴	cultural deposit
华夏祖先	the Chinese ancestors
同宗同源	of the same origin
中国文学	Chinese literature
中国武术	Chinese martial art/Kungfu
中国书法	Chinese calligraphy
哲学家	philosopher
四大发明	the four great inventions of ancient China
火药	gunpowder
造纸术	paper-making
印刷术	printing
指南针	the compass
四书	the Four Books
《大学》	*the Great Learning*
《中庸》	*the Doctrine of the Mean*
《论语》	*the Analects of Confucius*
《孟子》	*the Mencius*
孔子	Confucius
孟子	Mencius
老子	Lao Tzu (Laozi)

庄子	Chuang Tzu
墨子	Mo Tzu
孙子	Sun Tzu
中国画	traditional Chinese painting
水墨画	Chinese ink and wash painting
武术门派	styles or schools of martial art
习武健身	practice martial art for fitness
古代格斗术	ancient form of combat
武林高手	top martial artist
气功	Qigong
拳击	boxing
击剑	fencing
汉学家	sinologist
偏旁部首	radical
笔画	stroke
汉语的四声调	the four tones of Chinese characters
平声	level tone
上声	rising tone
仄声	falling-rising tone
去声	falling tone
《孙子兵法》	*The Art of War*
《西游记》	*Journey to the West; Pilgrimage to the West*
《三国演义》	*Romance of Three Kingdoms*
《红楼梦》	*Dreams of the Red Mansions*
《水浒传》	*Heroes of the Marshes*
《资治通鉴》	*History as a Mirror*
《春秋》	*The Spring and Autumn Annals*
《史记》	*Historical Records*
《诗经》	*The Book of Songs; The Book of Odes*
《书经》	*The Book of History*
《易经》	*The Book of Changes*
《礼记》	*The Book of Rites*
《三字经》	*Three-character Scripture/Three-word Chant*
八股文	eight-part essay/stereotyped writing

五言绝句	**five-character quatrain**
七言律诗	**seven-character octave**
篆书	**seal script / seal character**
隶书	**official script**
行书	**running script**
草书	**cursive script**
楷书	**regular script**
四合院	**quadrangle**
京剧	**Peking Opera**
独角戏	**monodrama**
杂技	**acrobatics**
相声	**witty dialogue comedy, standup comedy**
马戏	**circus show**
哑剧	**pantomime; mime**
踩高跷	**stilt walk**
说书	**story-telling**
木偶戏	**puppet show**
口技	**ventriloquism**
京剧票友	**amateur performer of Peking Opera**
篆刻	**seal cutting**
图章	**seal**
工艺	**workmanship/craftsmanship**
手工艺品	**handicraft**
泥人	**clay figure**
唐三彩	**trio-colored glazed pottery of the Tang Dynasty**
陶器	**pottery**
苏绣	**Suzhou embroidery**
文房四宝	**the four stationary treasures of the Chinese study (a writing brush, an ink stick, an ink stone and paper)**
才子佳人	**gifted scholars and beautiful ladies**
中华文明	**Chinese civilization**
文明摇篮	**cradle of civilization**
朝代	**dynasty**
佛教	**Buddhism**

儒教	Confucianism
道教	Taoism
形而上学	metaphysics
基督教	Christianity
新教	Protestant
天主教	Catholicism
洗礼	baptism
伊斯兰教	Islam
教堂	Church
寺庙	temple
修道院	abbey
礼拜堂	chapel
斋月	Ramadan; month of fast
喇嘛	Lama
宗教仪式	religious ritual
异教徒	infidel
宗教矛盾	religious contradictions
孔庙	Temple of Confucius
天主教堂	Cathedral
寓言	fable
神话	mythology
传说	legend
十二生肖	zodiac
公历	Gregorian calendar
阴历	lunar calendar
对联	antithetical couplet
天干	heavenly stem
地支	earthly branch
闰年	leap year
二十四节气	the twenty-four solar terms
本命年	one's year of birth in the circle of twelve years
传统节日	traditional holidays
春节	Spring Festival
元宵节	Lantern Festival

清明节	Pure Brightness Festival
端午节	Dragon-boat Festival
中秋节	Mid-Autumn Festival
重阳节	Double Ninth Day/the Aged Day
拜年	pay a new year visit
爆竹，鞭炮	firecracker
除夕	Eve of Chinese New Year
春联	spring couplets
辞旧迎新	bring out the old year and ring in the new
饺子	boiled dumpling
锅贴	pot sticker
庙会	temple fair
年画	traditional New Year pictures
年夜饭	the eve feast / family reunion dinner on Lunar New Year's Eve
年终大扫除	year end household cleaning
守岁	stay up late on the New Year's eve
压岁钱	new year gift money
舞龙	dragon dance
元宵	sweet sticky rice dumplings
花灯	festival lantern
灯谜	lantern riddle
狮子舞	lion dance
扫墓	perform sacrifices to one's ancestors or relatives
祭祖	offer sacrifices to the ancestors
踏青	go for an outing in spring
赛龙舟	dragon-boat race
粽子	Zongzi
亡灵	departed soul
月饼	mooncake
赏月	appreciate the glorious full moon
桂花	sweet osmanthus
赏菊	admire the beauty of chrysanthemum
登高	climb mountain

中药	TCM（traditional Chinese medicine）
秦始皇	the first emperor / emperor Qin
皇太后	empress dowager

图书在版编目（CIP）数据

文化万象：英语视听说. 基础篇/李海燕，余志红主编. —北京：中国人民大学出版社，2017.3
高级实用英语系列教材
ISBN 978-7-300-22624-8

Ⅰ. ①文… Ⅱ. ①李…②余… Ⅲ. ①英语-听说教学-教材 Ⅳ. ① H319.9

中国版本图书馆 CIP 数据核字（2016）第 046690 号

高级实用英语系列教材
文化万象：英语视听说（基础篇）
主　编　李海燕　余志红
副主编　杨　焯　褚　颖　曾　新
Wenhua Wanxiang: Yingyu Shitingshuo (Jichu Pian)

出版发行	中国人民大学出版社		
社　　址	北京中关村大街31号	**邮政编码**	100080
电　　话	010–62511242（总编室）		010–62511770（质管部）
	010–82501766（邮购部）		010–62514148（门市部）
	010–62515195（发行公司）		010–62515275（盗版举报）
网　　址	http:// www. crup. com. cn		
	http:// www. ttrnet. com（人大教研网）		
经　　销	新华书店		
印　　刷	北京昌联印刷有限公司		
规　　格	185 mm×240 mm　16开本	**版　　次**	**2016 年 4 月第 1 版**
印　　张	18.75	**印　　次**	**2017 年 8 月第 4 次印刷**
字　　数	404 000	**定　　价**	**39.00 元（附赠光盘）**

中国人民大学出版社外语出版分社读者信息反馈表

尊敬的读者：

感谢您购买和使用中国人民大学出版社外语出版分社的 ______________ 一书，我们希望通过这张小小的反馈卡来获得您更多的建议和意见，以改进我们的工作，加强我们双方的沟通和联系。我们期待着能为更多的读者提供更多的好书。

请您填妥下表后，寄回或传真回复我们，对您的支持我们不胜感激！

1. 您是从何种途径得知本书的：

   □书店　□网上　□报纸杂志　□朋友推荐

2. 您为什么决定购买本书：

   □工作需要　□学习参考　□对本书主题感兴趣　□随便翻翻

3. 您对本书内容的评价是：

   □很好　□好　□一般　□差　□很差

4. 您在阅读本书的过程中有没有发现明显的专业及编校错误，如果有，它们是：

   ____

   ____

   ____

5. 您对哪些专业的图书信息比较感兴趣：

   ____

   ____

   ____

6. 如果方便，请提供您的个人信息，以便于我们和您联系（您的个人资料我们将严格保密）：

您供职的单位：____

您教授的课程（教师填写）：____

您的通信地址：____

您的电子邮箱：____

请联系我们：黄婷　程子殊　于真妮　鞠方安

电话：010-62512737，62513265，62515037，62515576

传真：010-62514961

E-mail：huangt@crup.com.cn　chengzsh@crup.com.cn　yuzn@crup.com.cn

jufa@crup.com.cn

通信地址：北京市海淀区中关村大街甲 59 号文化大厦 15 层　邮编：100872

中国人民大学出版社外语出版分社